first loves

first
loves

a memoir

TED SOLOTAROFF

SEVEN STORIES PRESS

New York | Toronto | London | Melbourne

Seven Stories Press
140 Watts Street
New York, NY 10013
http://www.sevenstories.com

In Canada: Hushion House, 36 Northline Road, Toronto, Ontario M4B 3E2
In the U.K.: Turnaround Publisher Services Ltd., Unit 3,
Olympia Trading Estate, Coburg Road, Wood Green, London N22 6TZ
In Australia: Palgrave Macmillan, 627 Chapel Street, South Yarra VIC 3141

Library of Congress Cataloging-in-Publication Data
Solotaroff, Ted, 1928–
First loves : a memoir / Ted Solotaroff.
p. cm.
ISBN 1-58322-582-X (Cloth)
1. Solotaroff, Ted, 1928– 2. Solotaroff, Ted, 1928—Marriage.
3. Editors—United States—Biography. I. Title.
PN149.9.S66A3 2003
808'.027'092—dc21   2003005719

9 8 7 6 5 4 3 2 1

College professors may order examination copies of Seven Stories Press titles
free for a six-month trial period. To order, visit www.sevenstories.com/textbook,
or fax on school letterhead to (212) 226-1411.

Book design by Cindy LaBreacht

Printed in the U.S.A.

to Hyman Enzer

The young individual must learn to be most himself when he means most to others, the others being those who mean most to him.

—Erik Erikson

What writers of noble birth took from nature for nothing commoners purchase at the cost of their youth. Write a story, do, about a young man... write how this young man squeezes the slave out of himself, drop by drop, and how, on awakening one fine morning, he feels that the blood coursing through his veins is no longer that of a slave but that of a real human being.

—Anton Chekhov to A.V. Suvorin

acknowledgments

I'd like to thank a number of friends who read the manuscript and helped me to develop it: Max Apple, Aaron Asher, Lazare Bitoun, Robert Cohen, Judith Dunford, Stanley Moss, Alan Potofsky, Nessa Rapoport, John Reardon, Lynne Sharon Schwartz, and Irene Skolnick. My brother Bob Solotaroff and brother-in-law Hyman Enzer helped to retrieve and straighten out some of my memories. I'm grateful to Georges Borchardt for his candor and forbearance and to Dan Simon for his insistence that I remove the remaining scaffolding. The superb editing of Jill Schoolman has strengthened many of the chapters and improved virtually every page. And, once more, my wife, Virginia, has made it all possible.

Several passages have been adapted from my previous work. "Driving Bernard Malamud" appeared in the *New England Quarterly*.

contents

Grease of Destiny

⧗

I

My first image of Lynn is of her coming out of the ocean at the Lido Beach Hotel early in the summer of 1948. A small, shapely, sloe-eyed girl, she is wearing an ice blue bathing suit, cut provocatively for that still-modest time (we are more than a decade away from the bikini and the pill and the decline of erotic imagination). Beads of water cling to the slightly exposed sides of her pert breasts and sweet thighs as she ambles past me to her blanket. The gleaming olive skin, the sleek plait of long dark hair, the flash of her eyes: she is a walking advertisement for sunlight, the brightness that falls from the air in one of my favorite poems. Her expression is somewhere between sulky and bemused, as though someone had just said something annoying to her that she is thinking over. A glowing girl with a sexy-arty look and a brooding inner life. What more could I wish for? I turn back to *The Magic Mountain* and Hans Castorp, "life's faithful problem child," as Thomas Mann calls him, which I can relate to.

She was named Marilyn then. In the evening, in the staff dining room, where I dished out food, she would appear in her crisp white uniform, her hair coiled in two fetching rolls over her ears, which made a style out of the net the waitresses wore. Crinkling her crafty

Slavic eyes, she teased me for a breast of chicken, aware of my struggle to keep my eyes off hers.

Finally I asked her for a date. "I'll think about it," she said.

"I'm not proposing marriage, just a drink and some dancing at the canteen."

"What's good tonight?" she replied.

She let me dangle for another meal or two before saying that she was too tired to date right now.

"You're too tired to sit in the canteen and talk? You don't even have to dance."

"You must understand," she vamped, Greta Garbo–style. "I vant to be alone."

So she was dramatic too. "You look more Russian than Swedish," I said. "You look like Natasha in *War and Peace*."

"You never know," she said, and moved on with her tray.

Which left me nowhere and there I remained. I would try to banter with her when she came through the service line and I developed a kind of routine in which she was Natasha, the Russian princess, and I was Karatayev, Pierre's stalwart house serf, who would give her special helpings. Anything to keep her attention. She was so much my type and just the kind of classy girl I'd been dreaming about for the past two years of shipboard life and shore-leave binges. But then I heard that she was seeing one of the lifeguards and went back into my shell.

I was nearly twenty, two months out of the navy, and hadn't had much luck with girls whom I didn't pay. My self-image hadn't improved much from the ugliness that had dogged it through most of my adolescence because of a very large and very broken nose, abetted by jutting ears, unruly hair, and unusually swarthy skin. I won't go into the Gogol-like history of me and my nose except to say that I broke it again in boot camp, and during the second operation, six weeks before, a plastic surgeon had been called in who pinned back my ears while he was at it. So my present face was much improved, which I kept telling myself but only half-believed, for when I was in the presence of a girl like Marilyn or even a handsome guy like my partner Ira, the improvements tended to be whisked away in my mind, as though they were no more than a new shower curtain fronting an old grimy bathtub.

It didn't help that I was in a menial position. I had taken a job as "staff waiter" because it was all I could get after my face had healed. The Lido Beach Hotel was a big, swanky Jewish family resort that towered châteaulike over its vast Long Island domain of pools and cabanas, various courts, beaches, and golf course. The dining room and nightclub staff was so large that it was served cafeteria-style, and my partner and I weren't waiters but merely dished out food and kept the table pitchers filled with coffee or ice tea. Our lowly status didn't faze smooth, confident Ira, who was making steady progress in seducing waitresses when he wasn't using the beach to practice his bunker shots. But dressed in a kitchen outfit I hardly knew who I was or what I was doing there, since we were making hardly any tips.

In the afternoon, we would all be at the help's beach—the professional waiters and waitresses here, the college kids spread out there, and a dozen or so radical intellectuals and Greenwich Village types going off by themselves to read and commune and do modern dance exercises. Alone on my towel, I tried to stay interested in the stimulation of Hans Castorp, who, too, was on the fringe of the society at the opulent, sophisticated Berghof sanitarium.

Murray Gitlin, a member of the sophisticated group, was a junior at Michigan, where I was headed, and one afternoon he brought me into the magic circle down the beach. They were talking about putting on *Johnny Got His Gun*, an antiwar play by Dalton Trumbo, one of the Hollywood Ten, for Staff Night at the end of the season. It was about a basket case, just the play for all the war profiteers staying at the hotel. Then other plays and poems were proposed. Wanting to include me in, Murray asked if I had any suggestions.

All ten or twelve of those older, suave faces turned toward me. "I just got out of the service," I said. "I only know pro-war poems."

Murray put his arm around me and said with his rich baritone laugh, "I'm going to straighten Ted out."

Murray was a man of parts—a singer and dancer as well as an activist who was trying to organize the dining room staff to demand better pay and a day off a week. He lent me Edmund Wilson's *To the Finland Station*, and I put aside *The Magic Mountain*.

Until then my politics had been mostly World War II patriotism, braced by navy loyalty, joined to my faith in FDR and now Harry Truman, the tribunes of our great democracy. I was also strongly prolabor in this year of the hostile Taft-Hartley Act and was already planning a career as a labor lawyer and activist. This knightly liberal stance, taken partly in opposition to my father—a glass contractor who hated unions—had stubbornly withstood the efforts of my two Stalinist uncles to set me straight. But I was soon under the spell of Wilson's magisterial, literary-enriched history of European radicalism as well as being instructed by Murray and his friends' up-to-the-minute attacks on our dangerous Berlin policy, the HUAC and labor union witch hunts, the Democrats' compliance with racism, and so on. All that was solid in my mind about America melted into the air, as Marx and Engels had foretold, and in its place stood Capitalism and its Mafia-like reach into everything.

With enlightenment came exhilaration. I now had new truths about everything from the Marshall Plan (capitalist foreign policy) to segregation (class terrorism and manipulation), from Hollywood (sedation and mystification of the masses) to the *New York Times* (bourgeois liberalism). I had a new flashlight, the economic cui bono, to shine on all issues and positions. And I was just beginning. I now had great years ahead of reading everyone from Michelet to Lenin, whom Edmund Wilson was telling me about. But even more than a future, radicalism suddenly gave me a present and a new me to begin living it. Actually, it was the imaginative, sensitive, and self-doubting side of the old me that my mother loved and my father despised, that had kept me on the bench in basketball, among the outsiders in high school and on shipboard, and on my towel with my nose in other lives. All along, I now learned, I hadn't been out of step, I'd been "alienated," and needed only to find this new cohort to begin to live authentically.

This marvelous news came to me most tellingly from a girl named Doris. She wasn't a Marxist but a modern dancer, not beautiful like Marilyn but attractive in a lithe, fresh, down-to-earth way that grew on me. She was very clear, very straight, which helped to relax me amid all the talk of the labor theory of value and the New York and European culture scene: "Jim" Agee (a boyfriend of one of the waitresses) and someone named Camoo, the alienation effect and the *duende*, Ezra Pound's imprisonment and Balanchine's collaboration with Stravinsky—people and events that kept me on my tiptoes, trying to peer into the conversation. We all met around ten o'clock to rehearse *Johnny Got His Gun* and some other things, and then would drift down to the beach for more talk, jug wine, midnight swims, and, best of all, the songs I couldn't get enough of—from the Spanish Civil War and the Irish Rebellion, the picket lines and chain gangs.

There was no dating, since we were all together so much, but I would try to place myself near Doris because she was the one who seemed to understand me, who made me feel articulate instead of groping. She came from Vermont and had had to find her own way too. Though not much older than I was, she already lived in the East Village and studied with José Limón. As we were walking along the beach one day, she told me that I was a strange mixture of roughneck and sensitive, that the group couldn't quite figure me out. I said I couldn't either, that I was basically at loose ends wherever I was but felt more at home here than I had anywhere else.

"How old are you?"

"Almost twenty."

"Then you're right on schedule. You're still more in process than most of us. If you keep feeling at loose ends it means you've left who you were and are becoming who you're going to be. You just have to trust the process and go where it takes you."

We were walking along the smooth margin where the incoming waves hurried in like a long line of little masons, filling and leveling the tiny craters made by the suck of the outgoing ones. "The toiling masses of the sea," I said and pointed out what I meant.

"Where did *that* come from?"

"I don't know. Maybe I'm becoming a poet instead of a labor lawyer."

"You are *strange*," she said. Then, "Don't fret. Strange is good. When we like a new piece we say, 'That's really strange.'"

It was the "strange" that really got to me, to be told by someone like Doris that the strange side of me was the good side, that I was now following its direction—well, it was a revelation to go with the radical one, and the more time I spent with Doris, Murray, and the others, the more I realized that for the first time in my life, I was in my element.

≈

But the alienated me wasn't making any more money than the diffident me had, and since I would have no other income in college but the GI Bill stipend, I left to find a busboy or waiter job.

Just before I did, who should stride over to me but Marilyn, even more exotic with a full summer tan, to say in her low and suddenly interested voice that she'd heard I was going to Michigan. Did I have a ride? I said that I was taking the Wolverine, which ran directly to Ann Arbor. Why didn't she? She said she needed to save money. Besides, she was going to East Lansing.

"You're going to Michigan *State*?" She might as well have said she was going to the Michigan state penitentiary.

"I made a mistake in applying," she said with a frown and then a flash of those lustrous brown eyes that looked daggers, though more at herself than at me. "I'll transfer to Ann Arbor as soon as I can."

The composure that comes with loveliness had slipped, revealing an inexperienced kid who could somehow confuse the University of Michigan with a cow college.

"Where did you go to high school?" I asked,

"What are you asking me that for?" she snapped. "I don't need a ride to Erie, Pennsylvania, I need one to East Lansing."

"Erie, Pennsylvania. Ah, that explains it…" I began.

"Stop being so damned superior. If you hear of anyone driving to Michigan in the next two weeks…" She pulled her waitress's pad out of her pocket and scrawled her name and a phone number with a Trafalgar exchange. "It's in Manhattan," she said.

"No shit."

"No shit," she mimicked. "I didn't realize you were a Manhattan man," she said. "And so eloquent."

Now she was just playing me once again to do her a favor. I said I'd let her know if I heard of anything.

I put the slip in my wallet with close to zero interest. Along with being ignorant, she was arrogant and manipulative. I doubt that I would have called her if I'd heard of a ride.

Though maybe I would have. Remembering so vividly our wisps of conversation, I see that they carried the DNA, as it were, of the relationship to come. Anyway, desire being the grease of destiny, that night I copied the name of Marilyn Ringler and the Trafalgar phone number into my brand-new address book, where any pretty girl was welcome.

2

Because of my mother's dependency and my father's overbearingness, because of the family glass business where I'd served much of my adolescence, because of the navy where I'd served what remained, I had looked forward to the day I went away to college as a prisoner does his release date. Once and for all, I would be freed from other people's orders and needs, and on my way to the education I had been imagining and striving for since I was twelve. The experience at Lido Beach had made the prospect even more radiant. But as with most great expectations, the fantasy was one thing, the reality another.

Mom, my sister Sandy, brother Bobby, and I were living in Roselle Park, New Jersey, a Gentile community, where we still felt like refugees from the life we had known in Elizabeth. As part of my father's stealth operation to leave with as little expense to himself as possible, he had first moved us—from a pleasant house in the suburban section of the city to a gaunt, gloomy dwelling that wasn't on the wrong side of the tracks but right next to them. One of the popular songs of the era, "Blues in the Night," was like an anthem of our fallen condition, particularly on hot summer nights when the "lonely whistle blowin'" from the junction two blocks north would come through the open windows, followed by the loud rumble of the freight trains and sometimes the stench of the cattle cars that hung in the air.

The evening before the big day, my mother came into the bedroom I was sharing with Bobby. She stood uncertainly in the doorway, as she stood much of the time now, a woman whose dictatorial husband and his departure had left her not knowing where to put herself.

"I want you to have this," she said, handing me a book. It was a collection of Keats's poetry. I was reading only contemporary poets now but still... I put my arms around her. The book was her form of blessing, one that I needed, for I knew how much she wanted me to remain, to go to a college close by and be the much needed man of the house.

She sat down on the bed and clasped her hands, a habit she had developed to hide her fingers, which were disjointed by severe arthritis. Otherwise, she still looked younger than her forty-four hard years, her tentativeness and great legs adding to her girlish air. "So..." she sighed.

"So..." I sighed back.

"Tomorrow you'll be leaving again." She smiled, but it was an effort. "I should be used to that by now."

Exasperated and then sympathetic, I let the remark pass. I had been her confidant and consoler since I was five.

"Everyone's entitled to their own life," she said. "That's why I left Lakewood to marry Ben Solotaroff."

We both pondered that major mistake for a moment, as we had often done together.

"But that's life," she said, trying to be cheerful.

"I hope not necessarily," I said.

"And I do have the three of you. I knew he would give me handsome children," she said, falling back on her standard excuse for marrying him. Then she said, "You've waited a long time for tomorrow to come, haven't you. You've worked hard for it. You shouldn't let anything stand in the way of your education." It sounded rehearsed, but then, as though overtaken by her more mature self, she said, "Including me." She went on, her face and voice firming up. "Don't worry. I'll manage all right. The kids are getting old enough to help me. And I'll get a better bookkeeping job now that the veterans are all placed."

That was my mom, half patsy, half heroine. Despite her arthritis, she had worked two winters into the night in the barely heated office of the Standard Plate Glass Company so that I could play high school basketball.

"What do you think of Keats?" she asked.

"I haven't read him in a long time."

"I've been reading this book since I got it for you. There's something so sincere about him."

"Sincere? A poet has to be more than sincere, Mom."

"I know it's old-fashioned to say that but it's what I feel. It's what separates him from Byron and even Shelley. You can trust him. He doesn't strike poses. Also his magnificent emotional range. That's why he reminds me so much of Schubert. It's not just that they both died so young. The 'Ode to a Nightingale,' the darkness and the light, the sorrow that keeps stumbling on joy. It's just like the posthumous sonatas and quartets."

Her face was suddenly lit with pleasure. "The modulations are so wonderful. Do you remember the lines about Ruth? 'Through the sad heart of Ruth, when, sick for home, / She stood in tears amid the alien corn.' I've been saying those to myself. That's how I feel living in this dump in Roselle Park."

Only the last was familiar. Where was all of the rest coming from? She had never spoken this way about Keats's poetry before. Schubert, yes—the piano was her "raison d'être," as she often said, despite her arthritic hands. Despite. . .like everything else in her uncomplaining life, beginning with her husband and ending with me.

∾

After she left, I pondered the situation once more. When I'd been turned down at Columbia, I'd not tried to get into Rutgers or NYU, as I'd told myself to do. Nor had I even stayed home this summer and worked in Elizabeth, where I could probably have saved more money than I'd ended up making in the hotels. Instead I had left Mom (and the kids) to her sad, brave anarchy. But that the house was a mess (the three of them were presently refinishing some of the furniture) made me want to flee from it rather than stay and bring about some order. True, I had stepped in after my discharge and foiled Dad's plan to have his lawyer represent them both. But standing up to him was one thing, standing by her was another. Also Sandy who was a tense adolescent and Bobby an erratic eleven-year-old clearly needed a stabilizing presence. As the big brother, I had tried to shelter them in a household where anger was married to fear; Sandy had told me that the day I went into the navy was the saddest one of her life. Now I was going away again. They had adjusted to my absence, as they had to Dad's, but even so.

So that was what it came down to: being a *mensch*—as my uncle Gil, my boyhood hero, would say—or else doing what all my desires wanted me to do. Either/or. But not really. I was in process, as Doris had said. And I had done my time in this home and had to leave. But it wasn't easy, much less great or even clear. Acting on my new poetic license, I had thrown over the final bumper week of the season at my busboy job because I'd decided that I was in love with Doris and boldly hastened to be with her, only to find that she had taken up with someone else on the staff. So there was something in my nature as well as a good deal in life, known as reality, that being a radical wasn't necessarily the answer to.

3

My reasons for wanting to go to Michigan had evolved over the years—from its having my favorite football team, to its being in the American heartland that most of my favorite authors, from Mark Twain to Hemingway, wrote about; then for its reputation for intellectual quality and liberalism, and, in the past year, for its being twenty miles from Detroit. In the footlocker I lugged from the train station to the West Quad was a casebook on labor law written by the brother of a chief petty officer, who had given it to me. So far I had barely dipped into its gray prose, my career goal having been set in place by the accounts in *Time* and even more in *PM* (the left-wing newspaper of record in the 1940s) of the struggle of organized labor. My plan was to work summers in an auto plant, join the UAW, go to law school in three years, and thereby reach the barricades a year sooner. So did I inform my adviser during orientation week, when he asked why I wanted to take the introductory courses in political science and economics as my two electives.

His name was Irving Copilowitch. I had already checked him out: he was an associate professor of philosophy. But being a portly affable man in his thirties, he seemed another of the bland bourgeoisie, like my mother, aunts, and other uncles, who needed to be made aware of the intensity of my new convictions. When I'd finished displaying them, he chuckled, looked at me in a fatherly way, and said, "I was a member of the Trotskyite cell in the UAW not so long ago."

He could have said he was Trotsky himself, his death a ruse, and I would hardly have been more startled and impressed.

Meanwhile, he was looking over my application. "I see you like to read," he said. "Have you ever read any philosophy?"

More eager now to please than to convince, I said, "How about Bertrand Russell?"

It was his turn to look startled. "What have you read of Russell?"

"'A Free Man's Worship,'" I said,

He returned to his quizzical amusement. "Anyone else?" he asked.

"Well, some of Plat-to's *Republic*. We had this Armed Forces edition on my ship…"

"Plat-to, eh? Tell you what," he said. "I'm teaching a new course called Humanities I. I think you should take it and forget about political science and economics for at least a semester."

I was about to remind him of my career plan, but I didn't. He knew much better than I did what the labor movement needed.

~

Because the postwar campus was bulging at the seams, the men in Adams House lived three to a room. My roommates, Marv and Bernie, were older than I, veterans who had been in combat, both juniors, both from the rugged Upper Peninsula. Bernie was a journalist—jocular but shrewd. Marv was a digger with a hardheadedness handed down by two generations of Jews who had made a success of the general store in Iron River. Bernie and Marv talked mostly about politics, which in the intensely political fall of 1948 was what thinking students mostly talked about.

When I learned that Senator Glen Taylor, Henry Wallace's running mate, was campaigning in Ann Arbor, I made it my business to be there. The rally was held in a public park because the Regents had barred political speeches on campus and only at the last minute had the town council even allowed the use of loudspeaker equipment. Such opposition to our Progressive Party emphasized who we were and what we were doing: independent Americans striking through the barriers erected by the reactionary authorities to reach the American people and give them a choice between war and peace, between the profits of the few and the prosperity of the many.

That's how Senator Taylor framed the main issues of the race. He explained that the ominous Berlin crisis was mainly the result of a foreign policy that favored the interests of Big Business. This was why the Soviet Union, in its justifiable fear of a revived West Germany, had been driven to close off Berlin. The only presidential candidate who could break the standoff and defuse the threat of a truly cataclysmic war was Henry Wallace. Taylor reminded us that as early as 1946, Wallace had been pushed out of Truman's cabinet for his prophetic position that the tougher we got with Russia, the tougher Russia would get with us.

The speech took on the character and cogency of Senator Taylor himself: a lanky, forthright man who had been a welder and a country and western singer before he developed the constituency among the hillbillies and working stiffs of Idaho that sent him to the Senate. After Roosevelt and the New Deal died, he resumed his role of political maverick, carrying on a one-man filibuster against the postwar draft. "I don't want my sons dying on some Siberian steppe in any war I can do anything to prevent."

How we cheered at that. Glen Taylor may have been way behind in the polls but he wasn't losing. As suggested by his campaign entourage—even with his wife and children, it took up only two automobiles—he wasn't running for office so much as standing up for convictions that we common people who knew our own minds could rally around. At the end of his speech we sang "The Same Old Merry-Go-Round," the theme song of the Wallace campaign:

> The Elephant comes from the North
> The Donkey may come from the South
> But don't let them fool you,
> Divide and rule you,
> 'Cause they've got the same bit in their mouth.

When I returned to my room after the rally, Marv was studying at his desk in the khaki underwear he still wore. Short, square, and skeptical, he asked me what Taylor had said at the rally.

As I summed it up, Marv put down his economics textbook and gave me a look. "So the Berlin blockade is being caused by the Marshall Plan? Is that what you're saying?"

"Yes, by us sponsoring fascist revanchism," I said, employing one of the impressive phrases I had learned that summer.

"You don't know what you're talking about. Since when is helping an economy to revive supporting fascism? What do you expect these people to live on? Do you want to create the same conditions that bred a Hitler in the first place?"

Primed by the speech I had just heard, I said that the Marshall Plan was mostly devised to revive the cartels in West Germany and to keep the German industries that were supposed to be sent to the Soviet Union as reparations from being sent there. "The Charles Wilsons and the Krupps are climbing back into bed together under the covers of the Marshall Plan."

"That's just the Party line. The communists are doing everything they can to keep Western Europe as miserable as Eastern Europe. You think all those strikes that Thorez is calling in France are normal labor relations."

"I don't know about that," I said, which I didn't. "What I do know is that we're not sending plows and lathes to places like Greece. And what do you call Marshall wanting to rescind the diplomatic boycott of Spain if not aiding and abetting fascism and making the world safe for capitalism?"

Around then, Bernie made one of his pit stops. "We've got a real died-in-the-wool Red here," Marv told him.

"Let me ask you something," Bernie said in his affable way, after listening for a bit. "How would you like to see what happened a few months ago in Czechoslovakia happen in Italy and maybe France?"

I tried the thought on for size. It didn't fit. The French already had a democracy, a more democratic one than ours. Also, it was unthinkable that de Gaulle would jump or be pushed out of a window as Jan Masaryk had in Czechoslovakia. But somehow I hadn't let the noble Masaryk's death affect my idea of Russia's right to a buffer zone against Germany.

Meanwhile, Marvin was pressing on. "Do you want to see Greece become communist?"

"That's not the issue there," I said, back on more solid ground. "They're not communists. They're rebels trying to overthrow a corrupt and brutal regime. It's more like it was in Spain than Czechoslovakia."

"You don't know that the communist leaders purged and killed the anarchists in Spain who were the genuine revolutionaries there?"

"Just as they did in Russia," Marv joined in. "Or haven't you heard of the Moscow trials either?"

I'd heard of them, though vaguely. I had been a radical for only four months and mostly from conversations and reading *To the Finland Station* and *PM* and from what I was learning under the wide left wing of the *Michigan Daily*. Reeling from the one-two combinations my roommates had delivered, I realized that I had better read some recent history, that the truth wasn't all Glen Taylor and Woody Guthrie.

~

But for now there was my humanities course for which I was reading like mad and loving every hour of it. Whatever misgivings I'd had about getting off the fast track to law school had ended about three hours later when I took home the required texts for the course and lined them up on my bookshelf: crisp new Modern Library editions of *The Iliad*; *Three Greek Tragedies*; the histories by Herodotus, Thucydides, and Tacitus; Plato's *Republic*; *The Basic Writings of Aristotle*; *The Aeneid*; and Lucretius's *On the Nature of Things*. Except for *The Aeneid* and bits of *The Iliad* and *The Republic,* I hadn't read a word of them or even heard of some of their authors.

As I dipped into one and then another, a warm, deep stirring of anticipation came over me, a sensation not unlike falling in love. My higher, better self was being summoned as it had that summer in my struggle to keep up with Hans Castorp, and then Murray, Doris, and the others. I was about to come into my inheritance as the nephew of my aunt Fan and the pupil of Maude Austin, two high school English teachers who had guided me, and as the grandson of David Solotaroff, Zionist intellectual and scholar of the Koran, who died when I was four but whose ghostly example haunted me. These new books were their gift to me. Ignorant though I was, I was ready to receive it. I'd only needed Irving Copilowitch to bestow it.

Part of my gratitude came from the prestige of the classics as a kind of intellectual fundamentalism which the really well educated— i.e. those who knew Latin and Greek—turned to for guidance. But that aura soon faded in the common light the books took on in English. "An angry man—there is my story: the bitter rancor of Achilles, prince of the house of Peleus, which brought a thousand troubles upon the Achaian host." In the idiomatic prose of W. H. D. Rouse, Homer's harp became more like a fife, bugle, and drum. In high school I'd often had to grapple my way through *The Aeneid* phrase by phrase, but now I settled into Rouse's version of *The Iliad* as a rapt spectator at the dawn of Western literature: the darkness of a barbarous pirate culture giving way to a socialized warrior one, the poet and his muse standing halfway between awe and irony, myth and history, fatalism and autonomy.

So the inspiring Irving Copilowitch taught it: oppositions everywhere, human consciousness in its first brilliant display of self-questioning. I sat spellbound in his class, my mind stretched like a drum on which his ideas beat and resonated. By the time he and I finished *The Iliad* and went on to Herodotus, I wanted nothing more from college than to spend it listening to men like him and to scribble my thoughts in the margins of books like these. I still wanted to be a labor lawyer but, as he had pointed out, what was my hurry?

4

There was also college life, which I'd decided to try for a while. At an interdorm dance, I found a small, sweet-faced girl with a shy dignity who liked my patter, and soon we were dating. Greta Stein was the daughter of German Jewish refugees, which gave a certain gravity to the relationship, if only in my eyes. In her own, she was a happily conventional Michigan coed whose strong, foreseeing parents had trained her to look forward, not back. She wore Peter Pan collars, bobby socks, penny loafers, and a frequent smile.

The fastest way into a culture is a romantic attachment and Greta was a Jewish Miss Midwest. I hung on the way she pronounced *forest* and *water*, spoke eagerly of the "Frosh hop," knew the names of all the trees and plants in the Arboretum. Soon I was spending three evenings a week in the lounge of Stockwell, where decorous necking was permitted and, after we had become "serious," Sunday afternoons in the Arboretum where we went to grind against each other. Taking Greta to the homecoming dance, visiting her once again prosperous parents in Detroit, who showed me where her stability came from— I was "happy as a clam," as she would say.

There was also the easy, democratic fellowship of Adams House, its touch football team that I played on, the nightly study breaks when our circle of mostly brainy upperclassmen strolled over to the Union for the intense midwestern milkshakes you ate with a spoon. Best of all, on alternate Saturdays, were the home football games. By noon, a great maize-and-blue wave of expectation picked you up in its crest and carried you with the other hundred thousand celebrants to the great bowl of a stadium. Being freshmen, Greta and I sat in the end zone where the band assembled before the game and then, led by its unique prancing marshal, sent forth the rousing "Hail to the Victors" and, under our roar, quick stepped down the field like some huge, precise, joyous machine.

Then came the game itself, in which the heroes we had been reading about all week in the *Daily* performed like the national champions they had been the year before. I gave myself up entirely to the pageant, the contest, the intently peering or cheering communion. Michigan football, with its legendary Jewish quarterback, Benny Friedman, had initially led me to dream of coming here, and on Saturday afternoons the twelve-year-old me met up with the reader of *The Iliad* to root together for Chuck Ortman, the powerfully armed tailback; Al Wistert, the pillar of the offensive and defensive lines; "Killer" Kempthorn and Dan Dworsky, the havoc-making linebackers.

This was still the Bronze Age, so to speak, of college football, when men played both offense and defense and, substitutions being sharply limited, were on the field most of the game. Without face masks, they were as accessible to the eye and imagination as baseball players. Compared to the much more specialized, regimented, and complex game that was soon to come with the T-formation and unlimited substitution, single-wing college football of the late forties was more personal, more physical, and hence more classical in the Greek sense. It was what remained of the warrior society of Homer in which individual ability, stamina, and resourcefulness counted for more than strategy and team management.

The awesomeness of the players, the intensity of my feeling for them, came home to me one afternoon in November. I had gone out for the freshman basketball team and, to my surprise, was still there after the first two cuts. I had developed painful calluses on the balls of my feet, and one of the coaches sent me over to the training room to have them treated. It was the Friday before the Ohio State game that would decide the Big Ten championship, and when I entered the training area there they were—Ortman and Kempthorn, Wistert and Dworsky, along with the rest of the starting team and the few key substitutes—each sitting or lying in the buff on a training table with a white sheet around his middle, waiting for a rubdown. They were transfixing—sheer, heroic male beauty and force in their young prime, Achilles and Patroclus, Ajax and Ulysses, come again, at ease before battle. My eyes must have been as wide as a girl's, for one of the players rose from his elbows and gave me a What're-you-doing-here look.

I quickly turned away. I had been in plenty of locker rooms and envied this torso, those arms, that dick, but now, for the first time, the dart of ravishment had entered my heart. "This is what it must feel like to be queer," I thought.

The sentiment was to recur during the basketball season, as I watched the Hollywood-handsome Pete Elliot turn from quarterback to point guard. I attended the games as a civilian, having quit the freshman team before the final cut that would probably have landed on my neck anyway. Coming back exhausted to the dorm each afternoon, bearing the bruises of the picks and hacks and floor burns that serious basketball produced, I could barely focus on Thucydides, my latest discovery. Playing college basketball even at the freshman level had been one of my abiding fantasies, an accomplishment that would redeem my mediocre high school performance. But I was not that person anymore, I wanted to perform now with my mind.

∼

By Thanksgiving my relationship with Greta had begun to wear thin and a latent tendency in my character had emerged in full force. I had grown up in a household that produced a very skewed, to say the least, model of how men related to women. Of course I knew it was the wrong model but I still couldn't stop myself from playing Ben Solotaroff to Greta's Rose, with help from Greta's accommodating nature. At one point I caught myself being irritated by her noisily sipping through a straw the last of a soda and burst out with Dad's very words and tone, "I hate you to do that." The traits that had attracted me to her began to turn upside down and become faults that she should be doing something about—becoming better read, bolder, wittier—while the easiness and security of the relationship became bland and burdensome. Finally, she came back from a weekend at home to say that she needed "a breather."

I immediately became alarmed. "Did you see anyone in Detroit?"

"Just my parents. We had a long talk and they thought we shouldn't see each other for a while."

"I just think we should see a little less of each other. That we'd get more out of it."

"You think that?" she said hopefully.

"I missed you," I said, knowing I hadn't. I'd miss having a date on Saturday night, staying at Adams House with the grinds, the homely, the effeminate, hating the thought of being numbered among them until I could find someone else to date, which might not be soon. So I pushed Greta away with one hand and clung with the other, a situation that went on until the Christmas break. "You're kind of difficult," she'd say. And then, "But I know it's because you work so hard." Where had I heard that excuse before?

The political winds of 1948 continued to blow hard in Ann Arbor, pushing even its famous liberal president, Alexander Ruthven, from one side to the other. He gave a widely publicized speech in which he strongly defended the university as an institution of free inquiry and charged that many educational institutions today got permission about their policies from pressure groups. The last point came back to haunt him only a week later.

During the past four years, the university's Worker Education Service (WES) had been a national model in teaching blue-collar workers. Held in high schools and YMCAs, it offered an array of courses from social philosophy to collective bargaining and labor legislation to workshops in journalism and writing for radio and theater. The previous spring, WES had been charged by an official of General Motors with "imparting Marxist doctrines," and thereupon the entire program was suspended by the governor, Kim Sigler, who harrumphed that "nothing is further from the truth than that I am being pressed by one of the great institutions of the state to give up this program of workers' education."

A subsequent investigation of WES ended with the Regents' decision to maintain the program. But the day after its announcement, they fired the founding director of WES, placed the program under the university's extension service, and directed it to change its character from labor-oriented to general education. Walter Reuther and other labor leaders went on the attack, and the WES story was an even bigger one in the *Daily* than the struggle to oust the Communist faction from the American Veterans Committee, the liberal alternative to the American Legion and the Veterans of Foreign Wars. Also, its ramifications were much more significant, particularly to someone like myself who was envisioning a career as a spokesman of the working class. Yet, reading through the *Daily* fifty years later, I found that I vividly remembered the AVC story and the WES one hardly at all.

Which indicates that my attention was somewhere else, that my vocation as a labor lawyer was already consumed in the excitement of discovering the humanities and in trying to inform and think for myself politically. What reverberated most of all were a medley of well-written editorials and letters in the *Daily* about the choice between Wallace and Truman that bought back to mind the arguments I continued to have with my roommate Marv.

At one point he'd said to me, "You don't have a political position. You just want to feel bold and righteous. The truth is that if Dewey wins it won't make a damn bit of difference in your life. But it will in the lives of lots of people who don't have adequate housing or who can't organize their shop."

His arguments were becoming harder to deny. Moreover, as the intensity of Truman's campaign mounted in October, it was he rather than Wallace who came to be the main fighter against "the special interests." When Wallace said, "The common man is the forgotten man—the man who is as good as anybody else but who never had a break because of being born in the wrong locality and having little education, poor food, and no money," he was talking to another nation and age than the prospering America of 1948. As the campaign entered its final weeks, the image of him that stuck was of the almost Christlike figure speaking in the South amid a volley of eggs and tomatoes. But he also seemed no more relevant to the race than did Christ. Far into election night, I stayed up with Marv and Bernie, rooting hard for Harry Truman, the new spokesman for the common man.

5

My address book was still far from being the rake's progress that I had hoped for, and when I returned home for the Christmas vacation, the only name that leapt out was that of the fetching but aloof Marilyn Ringler.

Both qualities stayed my hand at the telephone. My relationship with Greta didn't appear to have qualified me for Marilyn's higher rung on the dating ladder. Finally, though, my impatience with myself became stronger than my memory of her attitude, and I made the call.

"I'm trying to reach Marilyn Ringler who worked last summer at the Lido Beach Hotel."

"That's me," she said, lightly. "Who are you?"

My heavily rehearsed line about Karatayev, the noble serf, suddenly seemed silly, leaving me to stumble around. "I was a staff waiter at the Lido Beach but then I left in the middle of the season and you gave me your address in case I heard of a ride…"

"You're Karatayev who knew all about applying to the right university."

Her surprising memory and mild sarcasm both helped to steady me. "No, just the right one in the state of Michigan. Did you ever get a ride to East Lansing?"

"No, I ended up taking a bus. Forever. Greyhound? They should call it Ox Lines."

"How do you like Michigan State?"

"Very pretty. All they need now is an interesting faculty and a good library. You were right about that."

There was a less edgy quality in her voice that made the huskiness that much more alluring. Her wit relaxed me enough to say smoothly, "I was hoping you might be free. This weekend. Say, Saturday night. I'm coming into New York to see this new Italian movie *Paisan*."

"Hmm… I'll have to let you know."

"Uh-huh," I said. "I think I've heard that song before."

"Different singer. I've been trying to get a decent job in the Catskills for the holidays. I'm just back from an indecent one that paid *garnish!* Know anyone at Grossingers?"

"No," I said. "I'm out here in New Jersey delivering Christmas mail."

"Maybe I should be doing that," she said. "Anyway, I ran into someone who suggested I try Longchamps, that they might take me on for the holiday rush at least. I'd love to see that movie with you. Have you seen *Open City*? No? You should. Could you call me in a day or two? I can never keep track of phone numbers. I'm glad to hear from you."

I put down the phone—elated, surprised, confused. The haughty kid from the Lido Beach had turned into a voluble, charming young woman.

She got the job at one of the classy restaurants in the Longchamps chain and turned out to be free Christmas night. So I found myself ringing the bell of a flat in a brownstone on West Ninety-fourth Street. The door was opened by a tall, stunning woman in a tailored suit, white silk blouse, and foulard, the first I'd ever seen on a woman. "I'm Lee," she said with a welcoming smile. "And you're the man from Michigan. But definitely not East Lansing. Come in, sit down, Marilyn is just getting out of the shower. My kid sister's a waitress at

Longchamps Thirty-fourth Street, where I used to take buyers. What do you think of that?"

She led me into a small, drab living room. An older and much plainer woman was sitting in a chair, looking through a photograph album, which seemed to make her unhappy. "This is our sister Esther," Lee said.

It was strange: the elegant Lee; the melancholy Esther, who looked like the room's decor. How, then, did Lee, who had Marilyn's features in a taller, *Vogue* version, fit in? More to the point, how did the girl I hardly knew fit in?

For the first few minutes we talked in the way people do who are waiting for the curtain to go up. Mostly I did the talking in response to the sisters' questions about why I had chosen Michigan, the courses I was taking, my plans to become a labor lawyer. Lee didn't think they were all that noble. She said many unions were crooked and she should know because her company had had to deal with the Teamsters Union.

"Not every union is run by the Jimmy Hoffas," I said. I began talking about the importance of unions in a democratic society. "Take the ILGWU and its role in…"

"You can take the ILG and shove it," said Lee, the smooth finish of her face seeming suddenly to crack. "A bunch of petty tyrants telling you to put in six more operators or they're pulling everybody out."

"Or an efficient sprinkling system so that you don't have another Triangle Shirtwaist fire."

I tried to keep it light, but Lee's affable charm had disappeared. This was clearly a woman who did not like to be disagreed with. "I didn't go to college and take a lot of history. You want to know why? Because this great ILG of yours put my father out of business."

"But Marilyn's putting herself through college," Esther said in a thin, uncertainly soothing voice.

"What does one have to do with the other," snapped Lee. The asperity of her words seemed to catch her up short. "Esther and I are products of the Depression," she said, resuming her manicured tone, which made her seem anything but. "Our college was the school of hard knocks."

Their voices were quite different. There was still a trace of Brooklyn or the Bronx in Esther's "college" and "Depression" and singsong rhythm. As we continued to talk, the differences between them became grounded in Jewish family typology: Esther the self-sacrificing daughter, the family drone; Lee the indulged, confident princess. What would Marilyn prove to be?

When she emerged from the bedroom, her loveliness pierced me all over again. She was wearing her hair in a French knot, the two strands bringing out the delicacy of her cheekbones. She had done something to her eyes that made them almost Oriental. The brows were well drawn scimitars. She gave me a friendly nod and her sisters nothing as she went directly to the coat closet.

"That's new," said Lee of her rich-looking red wool dress. "And not bad,"

"Klein's basement," said Marilyn as she leafed through coats and put on a stylish dark green corduroy with a hood.

"Cut it out, Marilyn," said Lee. And to me, "My kid sister, the kidder."

As she came back toward us Marilyn narrowed her shoulders and put her hands in the pockets of the coat and suddenly it was two sizes too big. "Klein's basement, too," she said. Then she withdrew her hands, raised her arms in the graceful curve of a Flamenco dancer, letting the lines of the coat resume their fit, and said, "McCrearys." Then she said to me," Let's go. I'm sorry to be late."

We went to a French restaurant in Midtown that a friend in Ann Arbor had mentioned. He hadn't mentioned the prices, which a quick estimate indicated would be about half what I would earn delivering mail in Roselle Park. Marilyn immediately read my expression. "Let's just order appetizers, so we'll have something left for the movie. Did my two sisters bore you spitless?"

"On the contrary," I said. "Your sister Lee has very strong ideas about unions, and we had a bit of an argument. I'm very pro-union," I said and went into my labor lawyer line.

"I know who Reuther is and what the political action committee does," she said, cutting me short. "I read *PM* when I'm in New York. I tried to get the dorm to order it. You'd have thought I was asking them to get the *Daily Worker* or maybe the *Jewish Forward*."

So she was also a radical. This surprising girl. It had been hard to talk on the subway, but once in the restaurant we barely stopped to eat. She told me that Lee was visiting from Boston, that she was married to a swell guy who had been a radical at Brooklyn College but now had a big job as the financial officer of a chain of supermarkets. "I think he hates it," she said. "He wanted to teach at a university until Lee put her foot down."

"Where did she get all that Fifth Avenue style?"

"On Seventh Avenue. She used to be an executive at a big dress manufacturer there."

"Maybe that's why she hates unions. She told me that unions had driven your father into bankruptcy."

"That's what she says, but who knows? He wasn't all that bright to begin with. His brothers were. He's a foreman now in a pants factory in Pennsylvania."

"That must be tough for him to take."

"No, what's tough for him to take is my mother. She'll never forgive him for losing the big apartment on Ocean Parkway and dragging her off to Erie, Pennsylvania."

"Oh, so that's why you went to high school there."

"Right," she said. "I was the only daughter lucky enough to go to Erie. Now let's change the subject? For example, what happened to your family in the Depression?"

"My father went bankrupt, too. But he's one agile son of a bitch and he was back in business three months later. But he still spends money like the Depression never ended—except on himself." I talked some about the situation at home, the meager settlement he was offering, knowing that Mom couldn't leave the wretched house unless she accepted it. "In some ways he's like a male version of your sister, only worse."

In the next hour we realized that we had a lot in common. We were both putting ourselves through college, I by enlisting just in time to get the GI Bill, Marilyn by coming to New York, where she quickly went from the typing pool to executive secretary. We were both products of a bad marriage between a selfish demander and a compliant giver. We were both headed for careers that would make a difference—she as a clinical psychologist, maybe working in Harlem. We had uncannily similar tastes: our favorite author was Dostoevsky, composer was Tchaikovsky, politician was Vito Marcantonio. Two young, middle-class Jewish rebels were meeting up.

6

I stayed on campus during the semester break in late January, hoping that Lynn, as I called her now, would answer my letter and invite me to East Lansing.

One freezing afternoon, I ran into my freshman composition teacher, an austere man who liked my writing but not my tendency to take a writing topic in a different direction, such as writing about e. e. cummings's "I Sing of Olaf" instead of arguing for or against the military draft. He was more friendly now, or maybe just relieved not to have me in his class anymore. He asked what I was doing between semesters, then suggested that I write a short story for the freshman Hopwood Awards.

I said that I'd never written a short story and wouldn't know what to write about.

"You'll find something," he said. His nose was red from the cold and he was eager to move on. "Just pretend it's one of my assignments and turn it into a story."

"You have to give me the assignment," I said.

"Oh, I don't know," he said from over his shoulder. "Something from your navy experience. Something significant you learned."

So, with time on my hands, I took out an anthology of short stories to see how to write one. Also, Lynn being on my mind, I thought about an episode in the movie we had seen together—the meeting of a drunken Negro soldier and a child pimp in Naples.

Its realism had bowled me over—each episode as natural and nuanced and open-ended as life itself. At the end of each one, we'd look at each other and share the thrill. After the one of the little boy and the soldier, I'd whispered, "I've never seen anything like this. Never." She'd smiled, taken my hand, and the relationship had begun.

So there was that, too—a muse to get me started. Then my mentor took over. The choice was well-nigh inevitable. What other writer would an American novice in 1949 go to, to write a war story set in Italy? So I sat there with my Modern Library Giant of *The First Forty-nine Stories* in my lap, checking to see how you punctuated dialogue but taking in much else as well. When I typed the first sentence, it came out, "Finally the bombs stopped falling and he opened his eyes and knew it had only been the dream again."

The "he" in the story was a seven-year-old pimp in Naples. I had known such a boy; he had helped me to lose my virginity on my first night of liberty in Italy when he took me and two of my shipmates to meet his three beautiful sisters, who turned out to be one much used woman living in a hovel and whose family got up and left so that she could take us on. What followed for me was less a sexual initiation than the continuation of a political one; the boy had taken us past children on the dock scavenging in the ship's garbage cans like a flock of gulls, and then through streets ravaged by poverty that was beyond anything I had ever seen, past people still living in the ruins of the bombing five years before. Until then I had believed that our enemies in World War II had gotten pretty much what they deserved, including the two atomic bombs. But here were all-but-starving children, the youngest of whom hadn't even been born when our bombs were falling. What evil had that hapless family done that forced them to turn over their home and daughter/sister/mother to three Americans? What had the precociously deceitful child pimp done except given us what we deserved for our three packs of cigarettes? This new awareness that seemed completed by a quick, sordid sexual initiation made the story.

But it wasn't the story I wrote. More influenced by *Paisan* than by my own experience, I turned the hardened and cunning little boy into the affecting urchin in the movie, sacrificing a cold truth for a warm poignancy. To heighten the pathos I made him a homeless orphan and gave him a younger brother to look after. It was an easy, almost natural fantasy. I had grown up amid the stresses and terrors of a marriage in which Dad had played the conquering U.S. army, Mom the ravaged and impoverished Italy, and I the provider for my kid sister and brother of a little shelter of reassurance amid the storms downstairs. Writing from sentimental vanity, I portrayed little Angelo dealing with the sordidness and peril of his life by making a fantasy of them—just as I had done with Sandy and Bobby—which at the end of the day overrides his common sense and betrays him, enabling the two brutal sailors he has conned to get hold of him.

Writing from what one thinks is fiction rather than from what one knows of life commonly occurs among beginning writers. It is the mistake that any serious writing teacher will immediately spot and prescribe for. But I was to remain blithely unaware of it. The story won second prize and I was off and running, away from my discernment, away from the experiences that led to it, away from their pain and complexity. The exhilaration of writing the story carried me into a writing course where I continued to follow my sentimental muse, to imitate one or another pumped-up style, and to be rewarded. For a time.

∼

After the new semester began, each day was centered around the afternoon mail, as though the letter I was waiting for were the announcement of my future. A week passed. Then a second weekend. Then another week, before a letter arrived from the Hopwood Room, telling me that my story had won. But it wasn't the letter I was obsessed with. When it came, I'd almost forgotten I had been waiting for it, too. What the award mainly signified was the pretext to phone Lynn.

We had gone out again, to a New Year's Eve party deep in Brooklyn that we couldn't find because one, it was snowing heavily; two, we lost our way; three, no one we asked knew where Myrtle Avenue was, though one passerby thought he did and misdirected us; and four, it didn't matter, we were having the time of our lives joshing, mimicking, hugging. The comic in each of us came out to play. What would our parents say if they found us wandering around like this? My father and her mother quickly took over.

"As I keep telling him, he don't know enough to come in out of the rain, much less the snow."

"She's going to come down with pneumonia. But first she'll travel all the way to Erie so that I have to take care of her, despite the fact that I may be losing my eyesight and also have a colitis condition which I should be under observation for."

"I could never tell him nothing."

"She lives to spite me."

"He'll never have a pot to piss in."

"I don't know what gets into her. You want to hear something? She once wanted to be a nun. Can you believe it? And not just any nun. A Catholic nun. You have no idea what I went through, Ben."

"I can imagine, Clara. He kept me up for years with his coughing every night. And you know why? Because his mother who's got a hole in her head let him go to a playground by himself when he was five years old and he promptly jumped up off a swing and broke his nose good so they couldn't do anything for it until he grew up."

"I can see you've had plenty of *tsuris*, Ben, with him."

"You don't know the half of it, Clara. He expected me to loan him the money for his nose operation after he walked out on me at my place of business. Well, he'll learn what it is to go without."

"I know exactly what you mean. She had to go and give up a job as the executive secretary to the president of a very big paper company and an office in the Empire State Building, instead of taking her courses at night."

"They get along well together," I said in my own voice. "They should have married each other."

"They would have deserved each other. She's a real ball breaker."

Finally we stumbled upon Myrtle Avenue. By now we were walking in the tire tracks in the street and peering at the brownstone buildings through the snow, looking for the number we needed. Lynn was wearing little galoshes over her heels and her ankles were as cold and wet as my feet, the snow deepening almost from block to block.

"Fyodor Benyavitch, I think we should have come in your sled."

"My apologies, Marya Jacobovna. I let my Matya celebrate the New Year with his large family. But I think I see the lights of the Trubetskoy mansion up ahead."

"Will there be dancing as well as cards?"

"Yes, both before and after the midnight supper."

At midnight we were still busy goofing, so when the horns and shouts suddenly broke out, it was natural to take this delightful, laughing girl in my arms and kiss her chastely. "Once more with feeling," she'd said, her eyes merry, her lips parting softly. That had done it. By the time we found the party, I was a goner.

Back in Ann Arbor, it had gotten worse. Everything that had worked so well the first semester to let me take my relationship with Greta in stride—my courses, the house basketball team, friendships I continued to make in the house and on campus, a brilliant older girl with whom I had a platonic but warm relationship—none of this sufficed to divert me. Not even my new passion for foreign films did. I

came away from one film haunted by its theme song, which continued to hover, just one thought away:

> Whenever we kiss
> I worry and wonder,
> You're close to me now
> But where is your heart?

We had only kissed twice, and each time I was so blissed out by
the soft sensuality of those parting lips and the inhalation of a light,
subtle scent that I didn't worry and wondered only where a musky,
reverberating kiss like that had been all my life. The worry came a
month later when finals were over and I still hadn't heard from her in
response to my drolly warm letter. What I now wondered and worried about was whether I should have inserted my tongue into the
space that could have been inviting me in. Had I gone down in her
book as a sensitive, jocular, awkward boy who was okay to date but
not to encourage, her silence being another way of saying that she was,
again, looking for or had someone like her summer lifeguard.

Instead of exulting about the Hopwood Award and courting congratulations, I spent the rest of the day trying to decide if I should call
her or write to her about the award or try to forget about her.

Around nine o'clock that evening, no longer able to stand myself,
I called Michigan State College and was put through to her room.

"Lynn, or rather Marilyn?" I asked the voice that came on the line.

"This is Dale. Just who are you looking for?"

"Marilyn Ringler. From New York. Or maybe Pennsylvania."

"She's called Mickey now. I'm her roommate. Who are you?"

"I'm a guy in Ann Arbor she went out with over Christmas."

"Oh, you must be Ted. The guy with the unerring sense of direction."

I could almost feel the sweat glands turn off in my palms, the lid
on my voice box fully open. "That's me. Long way Solotaroff. Luckily
it was snowing and beautiful."

"So I heard. Mickey is cutting stencils over in the psych department. What's your number?"

"That's okay, I'll call back. I'm flush. I just won a prize for a short story I've written."

After I'd hung up, I kicked myself all the way back to my room for the dumb boast. And just when I'd found out I might be getting somewhere. An upperclassman in Adams House had said to me, "You know, I didn't believe in the death wish until I met you." I hadn't been sure what that meant, so I'd asked my summer friend Murray Gitlin, who was a psych major, and he explained that the death wish was mostly unconscious, a self-destructiveness that usually came from Oedipal guilt.

Oedipus seemed pretty irrelevant to what the upperclassman was telling me until Murray said that if you had been really close to your mother and afraid of your father, you probably had a lot of self-destructive guilt. Which, of course, had been me in spades, as I told him. Murray gave me a long look back and asked in his solemn, sincere way, "Do you have homosexual desires?"

This worried me because of the incident in the training room. I probably would have been putty in one of those guys' hands if it had come to that. Murray then said, "Don't look so alarmed. It's not like leprosy."

But I was alarmed. "I like girls," I'd said. "I really do. I mean there's one right now I'm crazy about. You remember Marilyn Ringler, one of the waitresses at the Lido Beach last summer?"

I still wasn't clear about the death wish but I understood self-destructiveness from being the son of a father who could have built a big business if he hadn't antagonized everyone who worked for him. And I wasn't the most popular person in Adams House, because I had a tendency to say things that people didn't want to hear, that startled or infuriated them. I needed to impress or at least affect people, particularly in group or class situations, because I felt anonymous, diminished, unless I did.

Soon after I got back to my room, the phone rang. It was Lynn. So absent and now suddenly right there at the other end of the phone line. Startled, I struggled to remember why I had called her. "I won this prize. For a story in Italy about a kid. Like the one in *Paisan*. It's my first one."

"The story or the prize or the film?

"Huh?"

She laughed in her throaty way. "Did I wake you up?"

"No, I'm just surprised. I mean you hadn't answered my letter and I know every dollar counts with you…"

"Oh, I'm not much of a letter writer. I enjoyed yours though. I almost sent you a postcard. But what's the first—the prize, the story, the episode?"

"The story. I won second prize. Still, it's sort of like a home run the first time up."

"You don't sound all that thrilled."

"Oh, I'm thrilled all right but not about that." My mind cleared; my heart pumped with joy. She'd called me. What do you know?

"How're you doing?" I asked. "The last time I saw you, you had wet ankles."

"They dried. By the next day feeling returned. Since then I've been mostly running on them. I had to stay here during the break to make up an incomplete. I had a ride to New York, too."

"How many hours a week are you working?"

"About thirty."

Which reminded me. "Hey, this is costing a lot of money. Let me call you back from downstairs."

"That's okay. Easy come, easy go."

"I'd like to spend some of my prospective wealth on you. Can I visit this weekend?"

"Not this weekend. Maybe next. Let me talk to my social secretary." When she got back on, she said, "Come next Saturday. Let me know what bus you'll be on and I'll meet you. That way, Fyodor

Benyavich," she drawled liked a Russian Mae West, "I shall be sure to find you in this provincial town."

I put the phone down in wonderment, joy, gratitude. From the bilges to the quarterdeck in ten minutes. There was much to think about and all of it good—except for her being busy this weekend.

7

By the end of the first semester, I had used up the savings that had enabled me to stretch the monthly subsistence check from the GI Bill. Someone told me of an opening for an attendant at the V.A. mental hospital. It paid $1.80 an hour, almost twice the going rate for student work. Also, I was starting to think of myself as a fiction writer and hoped to find material there.

The facility was a small new building, adjacent to University Hospital. The patients were all ambulatory, except for one, and my job was mainly to "relate and observe" and then to write a note at the end of the shift about each patient's behavior. Since I worked the evening shift, I mostly related to them by playing Ping Pong, shooting pool, and talking to anyone who wanted to talk to me. Of the ten or twelve patients there at the time, all were at least five years older than I was and did not seem inclined to give me much to observe. Ernie Cullen, the other orderly whom I usually worked with, was older than anyone, a professional orderly who liked the job because "you don't have to handle shit, pus, and blood. Or stiffs." He looked like a former Michigan tackle with a beer problem. "I'm the bouncer on our shift," he said. "You see anyone about to go apeshit, you let me know pronto."

The one patient who needed assistance was a paraplegic named Bill Fenstemaker, who had just been placed on the ward for observation after a suicide attempt. He stayed in bed and had even fewer words for me than the others did. From time to time I would look into his room, but nothing changed there. He didn't read or listen to the radio or sleep. When I left at midnight, his lamp would still be on and he would staring into space, as though something were going on there that deeply interested him. He was not in a stupor; on the contrary, he had a sturdy, reliable, workmanlike air. If you hadn't known his situation, you might have thought from his sallow skin that he was convalescing from a recurrence of malaria and would be back at work at the body shop or construction site by the first of the month.

The first time he asked me for anything was to help him with an enema. I went to ask Cullen about it. He gave me his lurid smile and took me to the utility room, where he handed me a disposable enema and a bedpan. I said it might be better if he handled it and I watched to see how it was done. "There's nothing you need to watch," he said. "Just go in there and he'll tell you what to do."

As it turned out, there was nothing to do or even watch. Fenstemaker took the gear from me and said, "Why don't you come back in ten minutes." It was the first complete sentence he had said to me. When I returned, the bedpan was sitting on his bed table, the striped cover pulled tightly over it and tied off shipshape, as though it were a part that I had left with him that he had quickly repaired and wrapped for me. He had a little twinkle in his eye. He said, "There's nothing like a good shit in peace, is there?"

I took the bedpan away, marveling at his self-sufficiency, a feeling that lasted past the procedure that followed and took me back to his room. He was staring off again, but his face seemed more relaxed, brighter, as though he'd managed to take a shower as well. I asked if there was anything else I could get him. "Nah," he said, "you done good, letting me handle it myself."

"Isn't that what normally happens?"

Again the twinkle. "You weren't supposed to," he said. "I guess they're afraid that if I'm left alone I'll swallow the enema and then try to fracture my skull with the bedpan."

I took to dropping into Fenstemaker's room for a half hour or so after the other patients had gone to bed. He wasn't that much less taciturn than before. He didn't welcome me or send me away; it was as though he accepted my being there as he would a visit from a member of his family who brought him news. Though in this case, the news was usually about what I had studied in Humanities I. The Greeks interested him, particularly Socrates.

"We could have used a guy like that in the Pacific," he said. It was the first time he'd talked about the war.

"Actually, Socrates was supposed to have been a brave soldier,"

"I mean running the show. Someone who admitted he didn't know it all. Someone who asked questions instead of acting like he knew everything and everybody else knew nothing."

"You mean General MacArthur?"

"Who else? His vainglory got a lot of us killed or worse."

"Vainglory," I repeated, struck by this unexpected word as well as by "or worse." I wanted to see if he would go on, would say other significant things that I could put in my ward notes. We attendants were under strict orders not to talk to the patients about their problems, and if they tried to talk to us about them, to say that this was something they should take up with their doctor. But I felt beyond that with Bob, was too touched by him, was too curious—as well as eager to impress whoever read my notes.

"With the aid of God and a few marines, MacArthur returned to the Philippines," I said, quoting one of the few irreverencies I knew from the war.

But he didn't respond to that. Instead, he said, "Let's get back to Socrates. How did he end up, after making fools of everyone except this guy Plato?"

"The fools put him to death," I said. "They got into power and put him on trial for corrupting the youth and blasphemy and other bullshit charges and convicted him. But he made this great speech in a dialogue called 'The Apology'—"

"Let me get this straight. They put him to death just for talking? I thought you told me that Athens was the real cradle of democracy."

"I guess I meant self-government," I said lamely. "Actually, the authorities who gave him the death sentence called themselves democrats or something like that. It comes from the Greek word *demos,* which also means 'the mob.'" It was an unstringing thought. To me *democracy* had meant a concept like "of the people, by the people, and for the people," unsullied by anything like lynch mobs.

He thought about that or maybe didn't think about it—it was hard to know from his stony face if he was taking something in or had just gone back into his shell again. To keep the conversation going, I told him that Socrates didn't actually have to die, that he could have gone into exile as his friends were telling him to do, but that he choose to obey the law and drank the hemlock. As I spoke, I realized my mistake.

"You mean he committed suicide," Bob said. A look of satisfaction came over his face.

Could I tell him that Greeks and Romans committed suicide as a matter of course, that their terms for going on with their life or giving it up were much stricter than ours, that suicide could even be a kind of duty to yourself? But how could I tell him that, how could I put that in my notes? I was in too deep, a foolish kid once again. "He was an oddball," I said.

"No," Bob said. "He knew what he was doing."

∾

Fenstemaker continued to perplex me. I couldn't understand why someone as seemingly stoic as he was would want to kill himself and, even more, why he would insist on staying in bed when he could be wheeling himself around the ward and into the various therapy and recreational activities. I read his case history over again, but the social worker's account was almost as abstract and unrevealing as the medical one. He had grown up in Flint and had gone back there after he had been discharged from a VA hospital. An apprentice carpenter before the war, he had been able to support himself for the past four years by doing skilled lathe work at home. He still lived at home with his family, and though he kept to himself he had not "suffered loss of affect" and was not "overtly depressed." None of his family could tell what "triggering incident" had made him cut his wrists. If his brother hadn't come home early from work, he would have succeeded.

One evening I was handed a note from Dr. Mallon, the ward psychiatrist, who asked me to come to his office at five the next afternoon. A stocky, fair, prematurely balding man, he had the impassive look I associated with his profession and presumably the power I attributed to it as well. Freud was so much in the air that you seemed to know about him just from breathing, and I'd picked up the idea that a psychiatrist could read a person like a book, so telltale were our words and mannerisms to the initiated. The authority of a doctor combined with the special skills of a mind reader made Dr. Mallon formidable. Nor did he do anything to put me at my ease.

"I've asked you to come here, Mr. Solotaroff, because of your relationship with Bob Fenstemaker." He didn't indicate whether he thought it was a good or a bad one.

"It's not much of one," I said.

"Why do you say that?" His voice was as neutral as his gaze.

It was beginning already, I thought. But suddenly I didn't care. The one trait that could almost always trump my anxiety was my vanity. I had needed every bit of it in growing up under the demeaning thumb of my father. The struggle had also developed a calmness of opposition and an anger that energized it whenever I thought someone was lording it over me. "I said it because it's true."

"True?" he commented. He tapped his fingers and turned up the voltage of the eye contact.

"True to my experience," I countered. "I haven't gotten to first base with him."

"I think you have," he said. The rest of us have struck out so far."

The baseball imagery seemed to relax both of us, bring us out a little. "Why do you say that?" I asked more politely.

The irony in his expression almost pulled his face into a smile. "Because it's true," he said. Then he asked, "How old are you?"

"Twenty."

He nodded, as if that were about right. "And you're a lit major?"

"I'm just a freshman," I said.

He pulled over a rose-colored folder that I recognized from the ward, opened it to a page marked by a paper clip, and read, "'Mr. Fenstemaker doesn't ever seem depressed or distraught. He just seems adamant, like someone who is his own dictator, like Bartleby the scrivener in a story by Herman Melville.'"

He hadn't read the story and so I tried to explain the similarity between Bartleby's refusal to adjust and Fenstemaker's to get out of bed. If Dr. Mallon had Freud I had Melville, who knew all about what he called monomania. I also brought in Captain Ahab as another example of extreme single-mindedness to the point of suicide.

He was more interested in what Fenstemaker had remarked about MacArthur. "He said that he'd gotten a lot of men killed or worse?"

"Yes, those were his words."

"Was he… emotional about it?"

"Not really. He could have been talking about something else."

He nodded, then he thanked me for coming. As I got up to leave, I said, "What do you think will happen to him?"

"Mr. Fenstemaker will be starting shock therapy in a few days. We'll see how he does after that." He seemed as impersonal as when we began, so I was all the more startled when he said, "You're a caring person, Mr. Solotaroff, with a good deal of insight. You might want to think about going into psychology or even psychiatry."

"Thank you," I said. I was so startled I could think of nothing else to say. If I was so caring, I would still be in Roselle Park and going to college nearby.

As I walked back to the dorm I brooded about how uncaring Mallon appeared to be. A good man, a soldier who had made what was for him the supreme sacrifice, which had rendered his life no longer worth living, was apparently just a hard nut to crack to Dr. Mallon. Electroshock was done in the mornings, so I hadn't seen it up close yet, but two of the patients had gotten insulin shock, which put them into a coma for a day or more, and they emerged from it with what seemed like half their faculties. I didn't want to have anything to do with a profession that dealt with human complexity by turning a sui cidal will into a hypothesis and its victim into a vegetable. Psychiatrists, for all of their special radar into human personality, were not "involved in mankind" like John Donne was or Hemingway and Melville were. As for my unexpected qualification, I had grown up in a family that needed so much sympathy for my mother and understanding of my father that I felt I'd already paid those dues for a lifetime. The independent bohemian novelist's life, the one I'd glimpsed from barstools on my few forays into Greenwich Village, was where I now thought I was heading.

A week or so after his shock treatments began, Bob Fenstemaker was out on the ward in his wheelchair. He still wasn't one of the guys, but that seemed more a matter of temperament than depression. Nor did he have the stunned look you might associate with shock therapy. As I watched him playing pinochle one evening, a few days before his discharge, I said to Cullen, "You know, this electric shock stuff really works, doesn't it? Look at Fenstemaker there."

"Hang around," he said. "You'll probably see him back here in six months for another round. That's if he don't do himself in the next time."

8

I made three trips to East Lansing that winter and spring. None quite came up to my expectations. For one thing, Lynn was very busy. With her courses, part-time jobs, the circle of East Lansing radicals in which she moved, I turned out to be only one of the activities she was making time for. Though she still planned to transfer after the second semester, she had a lot going for her on campus and off, particularly, as I soon realized, a favored place in a radical group that connected the campus and the Negro community of East Lansing.

Unlike the left wing in Ann Arbor, which was almost all white, tightly organized, internationally focused, and either steely or stuffy, the radicals whom Lynn moved among were like an early interracial counterculture of students and professors, social workers, jazz musicians, actors, writers, young politicians, and intellectuals.

I was attracted, intimidated, resentful, jealous. My feelings were brought to a head by Lynn's friendship with one of the leading black figures in the group—a slim, well-favored fellow named Claude who had been a quarter-miler until he had given it up "to train for the real race" and who managed to be both smooth and serious. An occasional student in political science and history, he took courses when it suited his "reading," a word he used with the same gravity that I used now with "writing." Claude was a romantic figure on campus, a thinker intent on "staying with my people rather than climbing the ladder up and away from them," as he had told Lynn. I was with him only once, when the three of us went to a club after a Katherine Dunham dance recital on campus, and he treated me in the indifferent way that was standard in this circle, so I couldn't tell whether he saw me as a rival or just another Jewboy who thought he knew about Negro life from reading *Native Son*. My trips to East Lansing had led to my discovering James Baldwin but Claude hadn't read, or even seemed to know about, Baldwin's essay on Richard Wright, which I told him amounted to a declaration of independence for young Negro writers. He barely listened to me and then went on telling Lynn about "the Movement." His talk didn't reflect all that much "reading" to me.

Had I not been so jealous of him, I might remember him more justly. Lynn treated their relationship in the same aloof way she treated most matters that I might have some feelings about. She exuded the sense of being taken up by interests and relationships that left barely enough space for me. I often felt how Greta must have in the last month or two of our relationship.

But there was sometimes the feeling, as on New Year's Eve, of being in a new, right, charmed place. Her assignment one weekend was to listen to the structure of Beethoven's Pastoral Symphony. She took out a recording of it and we went to a listening room, an intimate closet where we were soon joined by the music to each other.

I'd grown up in a household where certain pieces by Chopin, Mozart, and Beethoven, along with Czerny exercises, were like Muzak. The piano was a sanctuary for my mother's spirit and the crux of my sister's identity. Sandy had perfect pitch and was both elevated by her gift and burdened by the weight of expectation that Mom attached to it. My adolescent ear had hardened against this high hullabaloo, and it was not until I got to college that the splendor of classical music freely broke through the occluding mists of domestic banality and sibling rivalry. But nothing like it did that afternoon.

I saw why the Greeks made the Muses lovely young women. Lynn, though in jeans, blouse, and sweater, might have been Euterpe herself, her face so vivid and pure in its spell of concentration. Those first flutes twittering through a valley of violins opened a vast green landscape of sunny phrases and murmuring chords. True, the Pastorale is musical painting but I didn't know that until Lynn led me through it. I heeded everything she said; my spirit was open on both sides, to her and to the music, and the experience became one of those moments in life when I realized I truly had a soul. This came to pass with the little four-line melody that comes out after the storm and floats through a series of exquisite variations. To which I ended up attaching these words:

> My love is transcendent
> I see it in the sky,
> A being forever
> For it can never die.

I was to hold on to this sentiment and its melody, through thick and thin, for years to come.

Something of my ecstasy must have passed to Lynn, for after we left the cubicle, she led me to a small natural amphitheater that was secluded from the campus. It was a bleak March day, dark by then, and we were the only people there. "This place is known as Passion Pit," she said as we sat down. "Usually it's more popular." Without a word she took down the cape of her green corduroy coat. The mane of her chestnut hair could have been her full nakedness for the jolt and gasp that went through me.

What followed, though, was both the apple and the worm. We quickly progressed to what was known as "soul kissing" in that prudent age. But after a few minutes she began to withdraw, making each passage of tongues and hands a little shorter. I felt once again that she was giving me less of herself than she had with just those two kisses on New Year's Eve. Finally, I accepted the message. "You seem to have changed your mind in midstream," I said.

She frowned, stared straight ahead, then put her hood up again. "I'm getting cold," she said. "I've just gotten over a chest infection."

"Let's go then," I said. Looking at her face set obdurately away from me, I didn't know what to say. It was like talking to someone else, someone I hardly knew.

"You should have told me you'd been ill. I could have come another weekend."

"I wanted to see you," she said, though her voice hardly indicated that. She had begun to shiver. I offered to take her back to her dorm. "Maybe that's a good idea," she said.

"I'd hoped we could have a hamburger somewhere before I caught my bus."

This made her scowl. Then she said, as though to herself, "Hamburgers, fries, and a few more lies."

I was as perplexed as disheartened. From angelic, to moody, to weird in less than a half hour. "Are you okay?" I asked.

"Is she okay?" she repeated with a bitter laugh. "Is Marilyn, Mickey, Lynn Ringler okay? Which one are you asking about? They're all overworked, stretched thin. Too many broths spoil the cook." It was as though she had gone into a witchy trance.

I laughed at that. "Well, you may be losing your grip," I said. "But you haven't lost your wit." With that I gave her a playful tap on the forehead. Suddenly I was back in my element, or almost. I hadn't ministered to my mother's moods and drifts for nothing.

Still, her dark mood remained as we walked back to her dorm and said good-bye with a bare touch of mouths. I spent the ride back to Ann Arbor wondering what was going on and suspecting that I knew all too well.

9

Having been a busboy for two summers, I figured that I could handle a waiter's station, but it turned out that I couldn't, not, at any rate, at the Grand Hotel, an expensive Catskill resort that prided itself on having a certain European air and offered a more varied menu than the simple Borsht Belt *table d'hôte*. At lunch and dinner, twenty-eight people, many of them Central European émigrés, ranging from the exacting to the impatient, would gather at my station and begin to make complications: "the salmon salad with no tomato; no French dressing; you will make a vinaigrette for me." By the main course I had moved from resentment through confusion to panic, doing whatever it took to arrive with a medium sirloin that I would have to beg the broil cook to exchange for a medium rare, or with four main courses for a table of five. In time I might have settled down, worked out a system, gotten by, but the Fourth of July weekend was not a good time to break in, the kitchen a madhouse of snarling cooks and frantic captains terrorizing the inexperienced summer staff, mostly waitresses with less experience than I had. After it was over, the headwaiter told me that the chef didn't want to see my face in the kitchen again and that if I was going to be this inept in running my tables I'd better grow a nice pair of tits.

So there I was back in New York, brooding the days away at the United Employment Agency, which specialized in staffing the better summer resorts. I was supposed to have an "in" there because my aunt Belle, a hotel booking agent, was friendly with the owner, Alex Ross, so I hung around day after day, the new self-confidence I'd brought from Ann Arbor leached away by a growing sense of futility. By the end of the week, desperation overcoming despair, I approached Mr. Ross on his way out to lunch and reminded him that I'd be willing to take a busboy job.

"Things are very slow right now, but I'll keep that in mind," he said in a way that indicated it would be filed pretty far back.

But later that Friday afternoon, who should breeze through the door of the agency but Lynn. Wearing a dark green sleeveless dress, her hair falling halfway down her back, my heart falling halfway to my stomach as I gazed at her, she sashayed, without a glance my way, directly to Alex Ross's office as though she owned the place. I was so startled and then joyous that I could barely call out her name. She turned, waved without any apparent surprise at finding me there, and then moved into the inner sanctum, where the jobs were kept. The handsome Ross, evidently a ladies' man, rose to welcome her. They talked for a few minutes, while I, restored to the Ann Arbor me, was floating on a bumpy cloud of exultation and jealousy.

This surge of spirit came from something other than the state of the relationship when we had last seen each other in East Lansing. If I needed practice, for my future literary life, in dealing with ambiguity —the current password of the adept—I was certainly getting it in my love life. Lynn was still the soloist of the relationship, I the accompanist. When she was up, she was so enthusiastic, witty, playful, passionate, that all my doubts would clear up. But then, from out of nowhere, a dark patch would come and she'd withdraw into a sullen space and stay there. To deal with her, at least in my mind, I'd decided that she had a tempestuous Russian soul to go with my brooding one. There were a number of such romances, if you can call them that, in Russian fiction; Dostoevsky, for one, could hardly do without them.

The last time we'd seen each other, some six weeks ago, she'd been at her most distant, declaring that it would be better to work in different hotels this summer. She also announced that she was going to transfer to CCNY instead of Michigan. She wouldn't have to pay tuition there and could probably get into the Clara de Hirsch residence, which provided room and board for worthy Jewish girls.

"Is this the kiss-off?" I'd asked, in the bus station over our usual farewell hamburger.

"A cooling-off period," she'd replied.

"From what? We haven't even slept together. We haven't even come close."

"We haven't slept together for the same reason I need a cooling-off period."

"A cooling-off period sounds like I'm making a lot of demands on you."

"You are too... pressing." She chose the word as though from a list she'd been keeping. "I need some distance. I don't need a boyfriend right now. I need a life without a migraine every week and without holes in my underwear."

"I still don't see what that has to do with me."

"Pressure. You're too pressing. Even when you don't mean to be you are. I can't deal with any more pressure right now." Her pained frown confirmed that. On the other hand, I'd just spent a not-so-hot weekend that I could have used to work on a radio play about the new Civil Liberties Act. "You could have damn well told me not to come up here if you felt that way."

"I didn't know I felt this way until you got here. I'm not all that much in charge of my feelings, as you might have noticed."

"But what have I said or done then? I don't make demands, I don't ask you to go steady. I know you're seeing other people. Claude, for one," I added, pressing on the splinter I'd been carrying around in my mind since my last visit.

"That's what I mean by pressure," she said. "It's in your tone, your expression. As it happens, I'm not seeing Claude." Then she pressed her temples, said she might have a migraine coming on, and needed to get back to the dorm. She got up, gathered her things, and then gave me a warm look. "Don't get me wrong," she said. "I like you. A lot." She touched her lips with her forefinger. leaned down, and touched my lips. "Have a great summer," she said and walked quickly away and, I thought, probably out of my life, leaving me with the words and gesture to obsess about.

Now she had walked back in. Which one? Lynn the charmer or Lynn the pain? It was like waiting for the jury to finish filing in and the foreman to rise. Then I noticed she and Alex Ross looking my way and smiling and I suddenly felt, felt deeply, that I already knew the verdict. Our meeting again was not an accident. It was in the terms of the new identity I had been given in Lido Beach and had confirmed in Ann Arbor. I could lose a job at the Grand Hotel without nullifying it. I couldn't lose Lynn, which was why she had come to the United Agency. Why else was it called that, why else was my heart thumping with relief and expectation?

Lynn came out of the office toward me. I rose, palms spread, a no-fault expression on my face, just in case I was reading our meeting wrongly. She walked into my arms, planted a kiss on my lips, and said, "Take me to Lake George, Fyodor. There is work for us there."

"What's going on?"

"I shall be waitress at the Sagamore. You shall be bar waiter."

I couldn't believe it. Bar waiter was the plum job in resorts: the easiest and the most lucrative. "I've been here for a week and he wouldn't even give me a busboy job."

"Ah," she said regally. "He knew you as friend's nephew, not as my great friend."

"That's hardly what I was the last time we saw each other. *Au contraire.*"

"I have changed," she said. "This summer I vant to be with you."

~

The next day we hitchhiked to Lake George. We arrived in the village near dusk, still a good way from Bolton Landing, where the hotel was. Our next ride took us only a couple of miles, the driver turning off just after a diner and a tourist trap called Steve's Cabins.

On the pitch-dark lake road there was hardly any traffic. In any case, it didn't seem like a good idea to hitch on Saturday night with Lynn in a resort area where there were likely to be lot of joyriding guys out, drunk and horny. And I was roadworn, hungry, ready to call it quito.

I said, "It looks like Steve's Cabins for us."

"Yes…?" she said in a leading way.

Was what I'd been fantasizing about for six months about to come true? Except in the fantasy, I was someone like Mellors, the gamey gamekeeper, but in the here and now I was more like J. Alfred Prufrock. What should I say and how should I presume? Should I be "deferential, glad to be of use," and propose to pay for two of Steve's cabins or try to play Prince Hamlet, though even he was indecisive. I tried out, "Lay your sleeping head, my love / Human on my faithless arm." But I'd been the faithful one. Literature, even modern literature, wasn't helping me out much.

Meanwhile, she was watching me with an amused look.

"One cabin or two?" I asked.

"Save money or save my virtue? That is the question. Now let's see." She put a finger to her temple. "Steve's sign says 'Six Dollars and Up.' Up to what, I wonder. Do you have any idea of what's up at Steve's Cabins?"

"I can think of a couple of things offhand."

"Why don't we go and find out," she said with a jaunty bounce to her shoulders.

"You sure?" I said in sudden disbelief, mixed in with two or three other feelings, as though my mind had gone berserk.

"Do you think I would have gone hitchhiking with you if I didn't think this could happen?" She gave me her crafty smile. "Cold feet, *tovarich?*"

"They're heating up fast, Lynnotchka," I lied.

And so it came to pass. In those sexually benighted times, young people did not begin sleeping together as casually as they began smoking. For many of us it was a momentous event, just short of marriage itself, and, like marriage, combined a maximum of expectation with a minimum of experience. For all her nerve and independence and intermittent ardor, Lynn was a virgin; for me, I had made it only with whores, with one exception, and had enjoyed it only in the ports of the Red Sea, where the girl and I would get high on kif and I could rise above my anxiety and scruples. Otherwise, my only preparation for the event was the condom I carried in my wallet as one might carry a ticket for a lottery whose drawing was in the indefinite future.

As I watched Lynn undress, I was suspended between awe and performance anxiety, in which just enough desire arose to keep them connected.

The awe came from Lynn's naked beauty. Though she was only five foot three, her suddenly bare breasts and fully rounded hips and belly and curly black triangle made her seem immediately larger, physically and sexually. I had entered the cabin with a small lissome girl who in my hands turned out to be a ripe young woman. She was so embraceable and also now, her brunette femaleness in full view and close reach, formidable. As I held her body against me, she slid my boxer shorts off my hips and I stepped out of them and against her, hoping for the best.

And that is the last clear memory until afterward. In between is a tangle of shadowy images, images of my pushing in and her recoiling,

a kind of urgency that was more nervous than erotic, half of me trying not to come, the other half trying to penetrate further, to make
sure I had taken her maidenhead (is the word even in use anymore?)
while she moaned in pain. The moans of pleasure they were supposed
to turn into, according to most fiction and locker room accounts, did-
n't occur and I lost my erection.

Clarity returns in the scene that followed. I see us lying side by
side, completely separate again, under a sheet as thin as a handker-
chief, the plywood walls and dank air of the cabin closing in. Clarity
comes in the sound of Lynn's voice, no longer playful, saying into the
darkness, "Did you ever hear of foreplay?"

"Sure," I said. "It was what we did before we lay down."

"What exactly did we do?"

"We pressed against each other, and caressed each other, and kissed
with our tongues and that sort of thing."

"And we did all that for how long?"

"I don't know. Maybe a minute?"

"That long? I wasn't counting but then again I didn't have much
time to do anything. Before I could even get interested, you were pok-
ing away. As I understand it, foreplay is how you make a woman interested. The emphasis is on play. I thought you had a lot of experience
from those navy days, the girl-in-every-port impression you gave me.
Exactly how many women have you slept with."

"Six," I said. "No, seven."

"And who were they?" What little irony there had been had gone
out of her voice. This was an interrogation and an increasingly angry
one.

"They were mostly whores. Two in Italy and four in the Persian
Gulf. There was also a book designer in Greenwich Village. But she
was older and a little heavy and I couldn't make it with her. So now
you know my whole sordid sexual history, so lay off." I turned toward
the wall, trying to get self-pity to wash away the embarrassment and
dejection.

"Did you have any pleasure with those whores and the book designer."

"Sure I did. Do you think I'm queer or something?"

"Did you give any."

"Any what?" I groaned.

"I'm sorry that this is upsetting you. No, I'm not. You deserve to be upset. You never told me those girls were whores. If you'd told me that you were inexperienced we could have helped each other to relax and get interested."

She turned away. I stared at her staring at the wall. After shame comes contrition. After self-pity, pity. Sometimes. I put my hand on her shoulder. "I'm sorry I gave you such a lousy first time," I said. "I really am."

She pushed my hand away. "You should be. You should know how to give a woman pleasure before you climb all over her. Particularly her first time. I feel like shooting both of us. You for being such a bull-shitter and me for being stupid enough to believe you. I should have trusted my better judgment. I could tell in East Lansing that you were pretty inept."

I jumped at this chance to be angry too. "Then you should have gotten someone else to deflower you. Someone like your friend Claude."

She was still turned away. "Don't think I didn't want that," she said. "I practically asked him to. But he was too… moral. He said he'd be taking advantage of me, since I'd be leaving East Lansing."

Before I'd felt like two cents. Now I felt like one. Like none. Claude even topped me in the moral realm. As I went on lying there, a loneliness came over me and dug in, unlike any I'd ever experienced before, the utter aloneness of being in bed with someone you love who wanted someone else there. It was an aloneness more lonely than being left with just yourself, no matter what, because the false intimacy of our bodies was worse than no intimacy at all; the nakedness I'd craved had turned into the wretched nakedness of my useless, vulnerable body. Tears came to my eyes and I knew that if I lay there any longer this way I'd begin to weep, adding shame to my bereftness.

For that's what I was—not just utterly lonely but bereft of the new Ann Arbor self I'd begun to grow thanks in part to Lynn. That's why I was so miserable and she was just angry—because the part of her heart she'd given to me she could take back and the part of mine I'd given to her I couldn't. At the United Agency and in my happiness since then, I had given a part of myself, the new Ann Arbor one, into her keeping. So I needed to know where I stood, because lying here like this in the dark, just short of weeping, I was being severed from the person I was becoming, so that what remained was only the old one—a mostly inept *schlemiel*.

When I could trust my voice to ask the question, "Why me then?" I found that she had fallen asleep. How could she do that next to someone who was writhing in unbearable silence? Well, I'd always believed she was remarkable. I called her name softly. She mumbled something. I called it again and then broke down, saying, "Please forgive me, Lynn. I don't know who I am anymore without you."

"Okay," she murmured, only half awake. "Put your arms around me."

I was so grateful that I began to feel better. Later in the night we woke up and were tender and even effective with each other, though we didn't try penetration, again because I'd used up my one condom. The tenderness and the rush were so much pleasure that I didn't ask my question. Which was just as well, because the answer was to be long in coming and just turn into other questions.

10

That fall I lived with Murray Gitlin in a rooming house a few blocks from campus that a couple were managing. Both the Colvilles were writing dissertations in the English department. Anne was the intense one, thin as a rake and just as pokey. Every week or so she would invite me down for a cup of coffee and some big sisterly counseling. With her gaunt face, severe bangs, high-flown sensitivity, and aristocratic accent, all packed into a pair of soiled jeans and a paint-specked sweatshirt, she looked like Charlotte Brontë returned to earth as the complete graduate student. After she read my Hopwood story, she sat me down and announced, "You have talent. But whether it will pour, as Gertrude Stein would say, is another question."

Having my story and Gertrude Stein appear in the same sentence was impressive enough.

"You must get away from the Hemingway influence. It's inevitable for male writers of your generation and hence all the more likely to be fatal. Particularly in the case of someone like yourself who has strong intellectual interests. You are not cut out to be a soft-boiled egg inside a seemingly hard shell."

"I'm not sure I know what you mean."

"Oh, I mean that Hemingway runniness once you crack the surface—sentiments, just short of sentimentality, lacking mental fiber. You must read Lawrence, you must read the early Joyce, you must read Kafka. Above all Kafka. He's Jewish, too, you know."

I didn't know. I had barely heard of him. I went to the library, took out a collection of his stories, and saw what Anne meant. How could I not relate to "Metamorphosis," to "The Hunger Artist," especially to the beleaguered son in "The Judgment" who writhes in the hands of such an abusive father? When I read "Letter to My Father," I could hardly believe that anyone so famous could have had an upbringing so much like mine; everything seemed to check out—his overdone niceness to the workers his father mistreats; his hatred of the family business; the accusations in the name of reasonableness and common decency followed by concessions to the father's moral blind spots; and most of all, the underlying sense of not mattering, of remaining as useless as his words. This writer's excavated ruins were only a more extreme version of my own: what my youth would have been if I hadn't had sports and a loving mother.

But to write like him? It never occurred to me to try to do so, for the same reason that I began instead to explicate him, along with thousands of other English majors.

The New Criticism was in full swing around this time as the dominant ideology of what Randall Jarrell famously named "the age of criticism." The great modernist writers of the 1920s and earlier were slowing down or had departed, and their explicators had moved in to take over the remains of their great battles of innovation and iconoclasm and to institutionalize them in English departments across the land. Ann Arbor was a major center because of the presence of Austin Warren, who had one of the most powerful minds among the New Critics. His book with Rene Wellek was a major restatement of literary theory in support of the intrinsic reading of literature. His own book, *A Rage for Order*, was compulsory reading for serious and pretentious literature students, both of which I was.

Pursuing complexity and order, the New Criticism was radically conservative in its desire and ability to remove works from their historical and biographical contexts and, as we say nowadays, recuperate them as pure literature. Because historical and biographical scholarship had dominated English departments for the past half century, the new movement had the aura of a revolutionary cause to join as well as the utility of a kit to open and interpret any literary work. Its conceptual tools of irony, ambiguity, paradox, parallelism, image, symbol, etc. operated like socket wrenches on the nuts and bolts of literary structure and released its assumed purpose in a jet of subtle meanings.

Being a sophomore I was not eligible to take Warren's courses, but I didn't really have to. He was the sun around which the most formidable and ambitious of the literary graduate students and junior faculty circled and, having landed on Anne Colville's planet, I was soon blinking in his light. There was an official literary café in Ann Arbor, the Bull Pit, where he held forth every Friday evening. Taken there by Anne, I listened to the table talk and lessons and mystique of the Master. He was also said to conduct esoteric Christian rituals in his house, with robes, tapers, and incense.

I never got invited to those but, even so, the New Criticism with its High Church overtones—by now the general doctrines had developed terms like *ritual structure, sacramental order, heresy of unintelligibility, the social anagogic,* et al.—was seductive as well as off-putting to a young Jewish rebel looking for a new identity and status and beginning to think about a career. Though I still preserved my sketchy Marxism and sentimental populism, I was now being drawn rapidly to the other antibourgeois ethos, that of modernism (startle rather than overthrow the bourgeoisie) and, being an aspiring English major, to the academic modernism that the New Criticism represented.

That I took to it so readily may also have been a function of my Jewish DNA, in which the interpretation of texts was second nature. One of my two grandfathers was a student of the Talmud, the other a soi-disant philologist whose life work was the study of the similarities between the Old Testament and the Koran. Behind them were the generations of Jews who made not only a practice but the highest calling of reading between the lines of the sacred texts, where the more subtle meanings were kept. My father, though he honored the philologist's learning ("My father could read languages nobody even heard of") took the opposite attitude toward my reading ("Always with his nose in some book"), and it now made more sense to me to think of myself as David Solotaroff's grandson than as Ben Solotaroff's son. But I was also responding, however uneasily, to the Christian cast of the new orthodoxy, influenced by its pope, T. S. Eliot, as well as its synod—major critics such as Cleanth Brooks, Allen Tate, John Crowe Ransom, Yvor Winters, Kenneth Burke, and Robert Penn Warren, as well as Austin. Nor was I unusual: one out of two of the new generation of New Critics seemed to have Jewish names.

As it happened, life did not make this new allegiance easy for me. Just as I was adapting to the hermetic reading of all manner of texts, along came a difficult loyalty test. The Bollingen Foundation had given its prize for poetry to Ezra Pound which was, on the one hand, deserved, and on the other, detestable. Talk about the tensions of paradox, about moral complexity! Pound's fraught career as one of the heroic and tutelary figures of modernism and as the most overt of the literary apologists for fascism led me into a dilemma. Like many of the young writers on campus who troubled themselves about the dilemma, I learned to wiggle around the evil horn of Pound's radio broadcasts in behalf of Mussolini by seizing upon the image of the maverick old bohemian, penned up in a kind of cage by the army and now in a mental hospital in Washington—a kind of ultimate victim of the revenge that society takes on the modern artist. As one of the graduate students I got to know at the Bull Pit instructed me, "Modernism is extremism, the far edge, Mallarmé's *'au-delà'* in all things—political, sexual, moral. That's why so many of them were either outright fascists or communists or active sympathizers."

Someone else at the table added that artists hate privilege but love power. "That's what they deal with all the time—the electricians and dynamiters of consciousness. The power of language and symbol."

"Right," said the first one. "So it's only natural for them to be drawn to the Hitlers and Mussolinis and Trotskys and Stalins who knew how to seize a public on a massive scale, how to get a whole society on its feet cheering and screaming, loving and loathing. So it's no accident you get a Mayakovsky or a Pound hanging around, taking a hand. Or Auden praising the "necessary murder" or Eliot associating Jews with rats. Why single out Pound?"

Heady stuff for a sophomore who was looking for ways to rebel against his early life in order not to be crushed by it, to change the basis of his identity in order to grow a new one. With hardly a backward glance, I emerged from my confusion and conflict to become a defender of Pound and a betrayer of my heritage.

This act was to have consequences that I understood only years later. It separated for a long time my interests and values as a fiction writer from my upbringing, my felt past; the writer I wanted to be from the person whose core was still middle-class Jewish. As Erik Erikson—the astute observer of "twice-born" personalities like William James (who coined the term)—strongly puts the matter: the risk of the twice-born is that of becoming "fatally overcommitted to what one is not."

Each generation is susceptible to the values of the previous one since they are what is in the air during its formative years, and part of finding one's own voice and way lies in developing a resistance to them. With respect to my generation, the voices of the great moderns were so immediate, innovative, challenging, and authoritative that one accepted the values that came with them—originality, impersonality, complexity, obscurity, erudition, etc.—as one's own. As the writer George Dennison once said to me, "We knew what our values were. We didn't know what our experience was."

If there was a common experience that characterized us, it was that of coming after. Coming after the Depression, coming after World War II, and coming after the great cataclysmic accession of new consciousness that was modernism—what Harold Rosenberg, one of the most gifted and provocative of its interpreters, called "the tradition of the new," which came in a bewildering array of modes. Dennison and I came on the scene in the late forties to find that the entire frontier of modernism seemed occupied, even colonized. Little wonder that it would take a decade or more of what Rosenberg called "ancestor camping" before new movements began to emerge.

II

The other influence that pulled me into the arts was that of the newly formed Art Theater Club in Ann Arbor. As with the Lido Beach circle, I was brought into it by Murray Gitlin, whose major may have been in psychology but whose heart was in performance, whether as an actor or a dancer. Along with his deep, classy elocution, he had a leonine head of hair, and together they produced a dramatic contrast to his chubby body and warm, soft temperament. He had that ready presentation of himself, the range of slightly exaggerated expressions, an emotive makeup, that went with being an actor. He tried out for the first production of the club, T. S. Eliot's *Murder in the Cathedral*, and was given the role of one of the hostile barons. I began to tag along to rehearsals. After all, almost all the leading European writers wrote for the stage, which was why they had a theater of ideas and we had Broadway.

This comment came from Strowan Robertson, the director of the Art Theater Club. Strowan was the Stanislavsky of Ann Arbor, an attractive, sandy-haired fellow with a nimble mind and a rakish slouch. In his late twenties, he came from Canada but sported a relaxed version of the Oxbridge manner. He seemed to speak in mostly soft labial puffs. But the puffs usually had a dart in them that sped to his point and made it stick in one's mind. He taught in the speech department, where the drama courses and productions were confined, as he liked to say, and he had recently founded the Art Theater Club to give himself and the local talent a much livelier repertory and a more professional stage.

After a few weeks I stopped feeling that I had just jumped down from the cabbage truck and took my place in the group as Murray's roommate and a green but promising rookie. We usually met at a table at the League, the women's activity center on campus, favored by the intellectual crowd over the macho Union, where I had hung out the previous year. There seemed to be two Universities of Michigan, culturally speaking: the cosmopolitan, contemporary one and the provincial, traditional one, the first attached to the great marketplace of ideas, the second to the Big Ten.

Everything about Strowan smacked of the big-time literary world. He didn't drop names and titles so much as float them among us, as he might our own, usually bearing an idea, a judgment, a provocative detail. Brecht was a bitter clown who happened to be a genius; *The Brothers Karamazov* was a novel of ideas that moved like an express train. That Strowan would launch his theater with a play by T. S. Eliot proved to me both his prowess and audacity. Eliot, like Joyce, was a sacrosanct writer, to be admired from the distance of his difficulty. Strowan brushed off the Eliot aura as though it were so much dust obscuring his visage. That he decided to put on the play in a church rather than a theater was another example of his brio, the last thing one looked for in those deadly earnest literary times. It was also an example of his ability to impose himself, a trait that I resented and was still too insecure to adopt but was beginning to see made the difference between the true artist and the merely talented.

Murder in the Cathedral was a big hit and the Art Theater Club was off and running. Strowan's table at the League or at the company's local pub became a charmed place, located somewhere between Ann Arbor and Greenwich Village. Len Rosenbaum, who would later have a stage and film career under the name of Mark Lenard, had been brought from New York to play most of the male leads. He was a big, handsome guy who radiated sexuality—a kind of Jewish Marlon Brando. Another prominent male actor was Dana Alcar, also large and imposing, who ended up in Hollywood. And there was Nancy Connable, who had what Strowan called a glamorous intelligence. She came from a politically prominent family and lived in a large lakefront house outside Ann Arbor that impressed me almost as much as she did. I imagined, imagined intensely, that she must be having an affair with Strowan or Len or Dana. One Sunday afternoon that fall, I found myself at her house with some of the other members of the company. I sat there drinking Scotch for the first time, listening to a conversation so languid and knowing and polished that it might have been piped in from the banned copy of *Memoirs of Hecate County*, which someone in the group had lent me. I realized how small-time I still was, even how paltry my romance with Lynn was in this atmosphere of midwestern *luxe, calme,* and *volupté.*

~

One evening later that fall, Murray came home about ten, which was early for him. I had seen almost as much of him in Strowan's circle as I had in our room. I'd assumed he was rehearsing until the small hours or sleeping with one of the actresses. He was hardly studying, as far as I could tell, and seemed to have been transformed from a psych major into an actor who was having the time of his life.

But this evening he looked like he had just been mugged—not bloody but shocked and devastated. He sank on his bed and began to weep into his hands, his handsome mane of hair all the more in contrast with his chubby face, as though the man and the boy in him had parted ways. When he could bring himself to speak, he said, "I've just been dropped by my lover."

"I'm really sorry," I said. His face was wet, his eyes had the bewildered agony of an animal being eaten alive. He wasn't just heartbroken. I was seeing someone in lover's hell, someone not just rejected but damned. Who could have done this to him? And so I asked who she was.

"It's not a she," he said. "It's Strowan…"

"Strowan?" I asked in amazement and disbelief, as though the room had suddenly tilted.

"We've been lovers for two months. The best two months of my life. Oh, I knew it couldn't last, that I didn't have the mind or the body that could hold him. But still… why did he need to be so cruel?"

He broke down again, but my heart was no longer going out to him. I was in a shock of my own, my mind like a pinball machine with the word *lovers* caroming off this notion and that, until it settled into its slot at the bottom. Murray was queer, I was rooming with Murray. What did that make me? I felt weird. It was as though Murray had said "lepers" rather than "lovers."

And then I thought of the feeling I had had with the football players in the training room. Maybe it was like that. That made what

Murray was going through more understandable. Still… being queer was weird. Even the idea of two men kissing didn't sit right. Cocksucking? Well, there was something mesmerizing about a big, well-shaped cock—if it was circumcised. But taking it in the ass? Wouldn't that be worse than the enemas I'd hated as a boy? With that image, my speculations shuddered to a halt and I came back to Murray, who by now was watching me.

"You had no idea this was going on, Strowan and me?"

"Did he…" I paused, searching for a more precise verb than *seduce,* which was obvious. The only one that came was *pervert.*

If nothing else, the word made him smile, driving some of the heavy emotional humidity out of the conversation.

"Ted…" he began, in the same way he had when he was explaining wage slavery or Brecht's alienation effect, with his brow characteristically furrowed with sincerity, "I don't have the sexual feelings for women that you do. I have them for men and they are just as strong and just as natural as yours are. I'm gay; Strowan is gay. That's why we were lovers."

"Gay?"

"It's a term we use instead of the ones you use."

"I don't use those terms. If you're gay it doesn't matter to me."

Both statements were doubly false. For I was lying to myself as well as to Murray: what he had just told me mattered enormously, certainly enough to change our relationship. Knowing that Murray was queer (the term that expressed my queasy attitude) meant that I would have to move out as soon as I could decently pretend it was for some other reason. Nor did the news matter less when Murray said a few minutes later, "Don't get me wrong, Ted, I like you, but I have no sexual interest in you." Perhaps he read the apprehensiveness I must have showed as being about that. But it wasn't.

What enabled me now to empathize with Murray—to see him as a human being, however shocked I still felt otherwise—was his relationship with Strowan. We were both in the position of loving and desiring someone with superior looks, erotic power, and the tyranny of moodiness, someone who allowed himself or herself to be loved and desired, and so held the high cards in the relationship. When he wished to do so, Strowan had abruptly thrown in the hand and Murray with it. I lived in the fear that Lynn, in New York now, would soon do the same. If I didn't understand queer sexuality, I did understand vulnerable love. My heart went out to him and I decided to wait until the end of the semester to move out.

12

A few weeks later I returned to New York for Christmas vacation. Lynn was living in a decayed brownstone off Broadway, her single room furnished in immigrant American by someone who had a penchant for burlap and oilcloth. The room was dominated by a bed whose headboard was half again as big as the rest of it and a ponderous dresser. In between was the bare semblance of a kitchen; a sink stained with rust, a stove on legs, and an early refrigerator with the motor on top. When she saw me glancing around and trying not to show dismay, Lynn said, "Don't ask if the last tenant was Emma Goldman. Someone already has. I know it's not much but neither is the rent. Those biddies at the Clara de Hirsch House are still stringing me along."

Someone? I barely heard the rest. She had written me as sparsely and infrequently as usual. But whether or not she was seeing anyone else, she didn't look like someone leading the Manhattan life I had been glumly imagining. Perhaps it was the room, but she looked thinner and older; her hair lacked its shine, her eyes their quick dance. Blake's shadow of experience was in the room and on her face. I had seen her out of sorts many times but never drab. "You don't look so great either," I said.

"I've had a series of chest infections," she said. "Also another problem you don't want to hear about. It's been a tough semester. I even sprained my ankle and had to be carried up and down the stairs here and be driven to class."

"Oh, who did that?"

"My psych instructor. He has a car. Also the muscles. He's an ex-boxer."

While trying to deal with the implications of that, I told her about the interesting time I'd been having in Ann Arbor. She interrupted my account of the Art Theater Club. "I don't get you. Have you become a homosexual too?"

Now what? "Not that I know of," I said. I had just gotten to Murray and Strowan and expected her to be sympathetic or at least shocked as I told her about my discovery. But sympathy for the unoppressed was not one of Lynn's long suits and very little shocked her. I asked her why she asked me that.

"You've developed these swishy gestures and way of talking."

I said I wasn't conscious of them. Which, of course, I wasn't. I'd picked up the mannerisms without realizing it, from my being so impressed and impressionable. I tried to explain that to Lynn.

"Just cut it out," she said. "You're sensitive enough as it is."

"What's that supposed to mean?"

It was a strange conversation. She was annoyed with me for something I wasn't even aware of, which made me annoyed with her. But the more annoyed I became, the more solidly I felt who I was. Then a spark of lust flared up. All the negatives—the sad place, her wanness, my inadvertent pose—went up in a horny rush. Tenderness works for me, but sometimes not as well as anger. I stood up and went over to her, leaned down, took her face in my hands, and said, "Why don't I just show you there's been no change, except maybe for the better."

Which I did, more or less. The trouble was that there was little change in her. During the past summer she'd continued to blame me for spoiling our first time at Steve's Cabins, which for her cast a pall over our lovemaking. As though to prove her point, she had pain after

I penetrated her. I thought that it was probably psychosomatic, a term that was coming frequently to mind with her, though, of course, it changed nothing to tell her so.

Unlike couples we knew who had little in common once they got out of bed, we, who were so uncannily tuned in to each other, who matched up like Tracy and Hepburn, had little in common once we got into it. If I became hard, she would soon go dry; if she remained moist, I would come too quickly. The most satisfying occasions were the *mano a mano* ones.

Before the trip to New York, I had bought a secondhand book on "marital relations," written by a Dutch physician who handled the subject as if it were located somewhere between Calvinism and gynecology. At one point, however, he prescribed for "certain circumstances," that is when all else had failed, what he called "the kiss of love." So, when Lynn began to complain that it was hurting, I was prepared. "Ach, meine fraulein," I mugged, "ich habt der solution."

Lo and behold, it worked. Almost immediately she was moist again and soon overflowing. Instead of the grunts, she was chortling. "What's it like down there," she called. "Nice and rank," I called back. "Like eating my way through a field of wet mushrooms." Enjoying myself, rubbing my cock against the edge of the bed to keep it ready just in case, I kept going, running little experiments in location, pressures, and timing, sailing along though my neck was stiffening, until with little shrieks of delight punctuating brand-new moans, she clamped my weary head so hard in the vice of her thighs, I could barely keep the action going, and suddenly her body drew rigidly together and began to jolt as though I were electrocuting her or ("Oh my God, Oh my God") I was Bacchus himself. Extraordinary.

"Thank you Dr. Van den Velde," I said as I made my way north.

"Who's he?"

"Some dry-as-dust Dutchman who happened to have a good idea."

"You went to a doctor?"

"No, I bought his book."

"Did you bring it with you?"

"Nope. But I brought this."

"Oh, a single-dip ice-cream cone." She leaned down. "Mmm."

"You sure you want to," I said, hoping for the other recourse.

"Well, one good turn deserves another, no?"

"Perhaps we could try the other way again."

"Let's go Dutch," she said, and began to go about it freestyle. And so the consummation occurred. Sort of.

For the next few days we mostly stayed in bed, climbing and sliding off the hills of manual and oral sex, and, in between, talking, joking, revealing, analyzing. Lynn was taking a course in personality by the renowned Gardner Murphy, which led to long discussions of how our respective parents had tried to screw us up, and how we had rebelled in order to overcome the damage, as well as other interesting insights. We turned out to have a natural talent for prompting and explaining each other. We even spent time playing psychoanalyst and patient. But mostly we just talked.

Lynn's escape had been to go to a Catholic high school in Erie, because it offered a better education. "It was like commuting each day between hell and heaven," she said. "I had a crush on one of the priests but the light of my life was Sister Agnes, who was young and very lovely and took a shine to me. I kept hoping that Father Peters and Sister Agnes would fall in love, elope, and take me with them. After I realized that wouldn't happen, I decided to become a nun myself."

"How long did this go on?"

"Two years. Until my senior year."

"Weren't you spooked by all the Catholic business? I mean going to Mass all the time and looking at those outfits the nuns wore and those crucifixes. Did you have to go to confession and eat those weird wafers of theirs?"

"No, I couldn't have taken communion, though don't think I did-
n't think of sneaking onto the line. Jesus was very real to me. I needed
a savior and he was it. Like Sister Agnes, I would be a bride of Christ.
It was easy to imagine."

"Particularly since you hated your home life. But a nun? I mean
those were scary people to me. I thought of them as God's witches."

"That's because you only saw them from a distance and had the
Jewish fear of the Church. The Church is more relaxed in a place like
Erie. Sister Agnes was full of life and fun and was even a great vol-
leyball player. She was very musical, too. She became my piano
teacher. We'd play pieces for four hands. Sitting with her at the piano,
those were the happiest times of my adolescence. It wasn't just an
escape from Jake and Clara and all that Jewish *schmerz* and self-right-
eousness. Sister Agnes opened spirituality to me. The Christmas of
my junior year she gave me a Bach cantata, "Jesu, Joy of Man's Desiring," and I'd play it every night with the volume turned down low and
then I'd pray to him."

The more she spoke, the less bizarre it seemed and also the more
dear, the more precious, she became. My fellow waif. Beyond her
lovely face, ripe body, and quick wit was a searching mind and a passionate soul.

"I can't imagine you as a nun. Not after last night and this morning," I added, trying to make our transports, too, as promising. "What
kept you from converting?"

"Sister had given me a rosary, which I hid in my underwear drawer.
Mistake number one. Mistake two was that I told my mother the
truth when she found it. She said I was a disgrace to the Jewish people and pulled me out of there the next day. I was miserable at Erie
High. But then Sister Agnes came to visit me there."

"Really?"

"No, unreally. She was there first as a presence but then she
appeared. Two different times. Like she might in a dream. Except it
was broad daylight and my eyes were open."

"Like a vision or something? Like the movie *Song of Bernadette*? Was it scary?"

"Startling at first. She didn't speak but I knew she was there to take care of me. To see me through my anger and grief."

I gazed at her face, which was turned away; I was caught in the spell of her memory, her emotion. If the eyes are the windows of the soul, she had raised the shade; an added brightness was shining from them. She looked like she must have three years ago when the vision of Sister Agnes had appeared to comfort her. I wanted to ask what expression the nun had had, how long it had gone on, what did she think had caused it, but the light in her eyes made the questions seem trivial and gross. She was somewhere else now as well as here. Something told me not to go any nearer, that along with everything else, she was a spiritual being. My Lynnotchka. The complete Russian package.

She asked me if anything like that had happened to me.

"Yes and no," I said. "When I was eleven or so, I used to have talks with Lou Gehrig, who I wanted to believe was really my father. He would be up there somewhere, halfway between me and God, and he'd not only advise me how to bat and field but also to behave right, not to clown or bellyache or show off."

"Like your father never did," Lynn said, coming out of her reverie and moving closer to mine. It's known as 'compensation.'

"Yes, he was one of several fathers I've adopted along the way. Then Gehrig got fatally ill with the disease they named after him. All those powerful muscles quickly wasted away. And yet when they gave this day for him at Yankee Stadium, he said, 'Today, I feel that I'm the luckiest man on the face of the earth.' I heard it on the radio, but for years I'd tell people I'd been there. It was partly to impress them but in some deep sense I believed I had been—in the way that he had been for me on the ball field.

Lynn said, "I'm beginning to see why we're seeing each other." She moved closer, putting her head against my shoulder. I began stroking the thick, silky strands back from her forehead.

Floating in tenderness and fulfillment, the man of the hour, I said, "We could be seeing each other every day if you came to Ann Arbor, if we lived together there."

"Uh-uh," she said. "I'm not ready for that."

Even so, "not ready" was promising; a door that I thought had been closed, even locked, opened at least a crack.

We all but lived in that bed that week. Around eleven we would have breakfast there and play and talk and analyze into late afternoon. Then, ravished, we would get up and go to Starks, a hamburger place with a touch of style, and gorge ourselves on the special plate and cream cheese cake. Twice I bought us seats at City Center for the New York City Ballet. Otherwise we walked a few blocks uptown to the Thalia Theater at Ninety-fifth Street, where we saw Pagnol's Fanny and Marius trilogy and Carné's *Children of Paradise*. Then back to bed and into our own fascinating lives again. One revelation after another. I had almost stopped worrying about the muscular ex-boxer until then.

Walking back down Broadway, the final scene of *Children of Paradise*—the love-struck mime losing forever his ravishing mistress in that teeming crowd—vibrated within me. Losing her for the second time, having earlier handed her over to the confident actor and seducer. Before I knew it, I was saying, "I think we should crap or get off the pot."

Foolish and vulgar as my words were, Lynn took me up on them. "You mean, my poet, that you want to marry me?"

"I guess so. I think the sexual problem would disappear if you didn't have to worry about getting pregnant."

"Oh, you're proposing that we have children right away too. All on the GI Bill."

"No, of course not. It's just that the thought of not seeing you for the next five months and not knowing where I stand is tough. I mean we're so close and yet it's all so indefinite."

"Why don't we just let life take its course. As for where you stand, you're someone who can't take yes for an answer." With that she put her arms around me and kissed me in that special way she had, openly, deliciously, and, in this case, to the point.

13

I spent the tail end of the vacation with my family in their new home in Teaneck, a nice town on the other side of the George Washington Bridge. My mother had managed to buy a house there perched on a small hill and with an aspiring English look conferred by its angled wood paneling on the white stucco of the upper facade. The inside needed painting, which Mom and her two-child crew were beginning to attack, but it already bore her touch of taste, frugality, and a bit of disorder.

The meager settlement Mom had been finally driven to accept in order to leave the dump by the railroad tracks made an appropriate final chapter to the marriage—except that it wasn't. The divorce mainly carried on the marriage by other means, Dad's stinginess and neglect arrayed against Mom's passivity and last-ditch dignity that allowed him, in the words of her Weiss family, "to get away with murder"—in this instance by often not sending the monthly child care and alimony check until she became desperate enough to have to entreat him.

So once again, I decided to step in. I phoned her lawyer, but all he wanted to talk about was that my father still hadn't paid him the rest of his fee, which had been part of the settlement. So I made the second call.

I hadn't seen my father for eighteen months, the last time being when he had taken me by surprise, offering sweet talk and a dinner at Newark's best restaurant to get me to withdraw my opposition to the terms he was offering.

This time there was none of that. When I said I'd like to visit, he said, "I'm tied up right now. What do you want?"

"I want to see you. It's an important matter. Otherwise I wouldn't bother you."

"Call me next week," he said, and hung up.

I called him back. "Next week I'll be back in Ann Arbor. Why don't I just show up at The Shop tomorrow around six. It'll only take a few minutes. That's not asking for much."

"Suit yourself," he said. "Now would you get off the line, I'm expecting an important call."

So I took a bus to Newark and another to Elizabeth. As I walked along Broad Street, where downtown Elizabeth turned impressive for a few blocks, its two big department stores, its array of upscale shops, its good movie theater, and its towering county courthouse brought back memories of my outside-the-house life. Broad Street was where I had done my yearning, at the Regent Theater, and my short-lived thieving, at Levy Brothers, the latter being mostly attempts to get my hands on objects—a penknife, a fountain pen that didn't leak, a baseball glove, a slide rule, things that life itself seemed to deliver by way of an "allowance" into the hands of my friends.

But more than envy had driven me. After I turned thirteen, I fell into the grip of a wild streak of delinquency that, along with the department stores, sent me to the detention room almost every day after school and out at night to provoke fistfights or break windows in the neighborhood school. Finally, I had been pulled out of school, taken to the police station, and questioned about the broken windows. That had pretty much ended the delinquency. But the "bad me," whom I called "Little Benny," had continued to lead a life of his own across the street from "the good me," whom I called "the Weiss boy," my Uncle Gil having told me when I was four that I was one and that Weiss boys always kept their head up.

Turning the corner of Broad Street and starting down Elizabeth Avenue was like going from the west side of upper Broadway to the east side at the time, from Elizabeth's glitz to its schmutz. Ten dingy blocks past the bargain stores, the tire shops, the Liberty Theater with its B pictures and marquee that sagged, was The Shop. As always, my spirit dropped as I approached it, my will to be firm with Dad dissolving in the depression that seeped in. Home had its pleasures and laughs when Dad wasn't there and even sometimes when he was. The Shop was the place where I had done time, sentenced to five years of answering the phone and typing letters and bills by his inability to keep office help except for my mother and me, and by his apparent need to make my adolescence as miserable as his had been from having to help his learned father who couldn't handle even a little window glass and shade shop after his partner went into the army.

Though Dad was in the storefront business, his own front remained unfinished, still bearing only the black primer that had been brushed on nine years ago when he had bought the property. The jumble of picture frame samples, cheap frames, and dressing table and wall mirrors in the display windows looked dusty and fly specked, as though no one had touched them since I'd gone into the navy. On a piece of cardboard wedged in the door was scrawled, "Around The Back," with an arrow pointing to the alley. I doubted that he had put it up for me.

In the back things were different and even impressive. The plumbing supply store Dad had shared the space with was gone and his warehouse had been expanded. As I let myself in, I saw that an overhead crane had been installed, the number of tall plate-glass racks had doubled, and crates of window glass and rough-wire and other structural glass were stacked all around. So I knew that Dad had carried out his plan to change the business from contracting to distributing. But, as though it were still the Depression or the war years, there he was bent over the old, carpeted cutting table, cutting glass an hour after his men had gone home. He responded to my hello with a nod and went on cutting.

His tough-nut act. "There's been a hell of a lot of expansion going on around here," I said.

"True," he said. "So what do you want to see me about?"

"Not much," I said. "Anyway, I can see you're busy. Mind if I look around? I can gaze at the fortune I gave up by not going into the business."

"What are you talking about?" he said without looking up from the L-square and glass. "I would never have taken you in."

"You used to talk about it. When you were in one of your occasional positive moods toward me."

"You don't say." He went on cutting.

For all the expansion and improvements, he hadn't bothered to put in a heating system and still relied on a small electric space heater that he'd stationed on the cutting table. Though I was wearing gloves, I kept clenching my hands against the January chill, but he went on, in just his business suit and hat, cutting rough-wire factory window glass to specification.

"Just to satisfy my curiosity, when did you realize I wasn't the son you had in mind?"

"I know that from the day you started working here. I gave you a box of old screws and nails and bolts to sort and you took all morning."

"That's when you told Mom I was green as grass. Do you remember how old I was?"

He shrugged. "What difference does it make?"

"I was eleven," I said.

"So you were eleven. So what?" He finally put his glass cutter down and looked at me directly. "You asked me a question and I gave you an answer. I didn't notice that you became any more useful later on until they taught you how to type. But I could get anyone to type bills. What I needed was someone who could apply himself to the business, which you never saw fit to do."

I wanted to say that he must still be looking; otherwise why was he—probably now the glass *macher* of Union County—doing a cutter's work after hours. The partner who would bring order and organization was a myth. He was a one-man act if there ever was one. As Mom would say, the leopard can't change his spots. One of them was on display, the grimy back of a used envelope on which he had scribbled the order he was making up, one from the many piled wrist deep on his desk in the office.

So instead, I said, "Well, let's let bygones be bygones." I took off my own overcoat and walked over to the crate he was pulling the glass out of. "To stay warm, I'll finish unloading this crate and then load it with what you've cut. It'll be like those Sunday afternoons during the war."

That had been one of my jobs back then, helping him to get ready for Monday morning; such tasks, along with our occasional hikes, had been the only occasions of bonding between us. My gesture seemed to take him by surprise. A chapped smile came out from behind his scowl like a winter sun from behind a cloud. "If you insist," he said.

"I do," I said.

I stacked eight lites of glass for him to work on and then grabbed the pair of pliers and the matchbook he was using. Wire glass has to be cut on both sides and then the excess pried off with pliers, the trick being to do so without chipping the edge, hence the matchbook cover to sheathe the glass. I was pretty good at it from long experience and gradually warmed, literally, to the task.

At one point he said, "I figure by now you've given up your cockamamie idea of becoming a lawyer."

"Who told you that?"

"I knew you would. I may only have a tenth-grade education but I'm pretty prescient." He mispronounced it, as he often did with words he had read rather than heard in his rough-talking world. It was one of the ways he touched me, held on to me as the bearer of what he might have been.

"So what are you going to do now?"

"I'm going to be a writer," I said, inwardly wincing a bit.

"You mean a journalist."

"No, I mean a fiction writer."

He put down the cutter to smile at me. "Well, I always said you were going to suffer."

"That you did. Always. It may be the one way I won't disappoint you."

~

After we finished making up the order, Dad closed up and led me into his office, which was heated, or slightly warmed, by an oil stove next to his desk. I hoped that he would take me somewhere for dinner both to be warm and to get away from this room, where I had been stationed most of the time. He probably knew what was coming, which was why we were sitting there in our overcoats rather than in a pleasant and neutral place.

"How's your new life going?" I said tactically. I knew that he'd married the woman he'd left my mother for.

He gave me a cockeyed look. "Is that what you came here to talk about?"

"No, I came here to talk about Mom's and the kids' home life. It's very hard on her and Sandy and Bob to wait weeks for the monthly check. She's on such a tight budget as it is."

"I've been short of office help the last couple of months," he growled. "So I've been late a few times. I got a million and one other things on my mind beside your mother. That expansion you saw didn't happen by itself, and the money for it didn't fall from the sky."

"It's not like paying a creditor, Dad. It's more like meeting a payroll."

"What do you know about meeting a payroll? It's just a phrase to you. Do you know what happens if I don't meet my payroll? The only union man who shows up here Monday morning is the president of the local and maybe his lawyer. As usual when it regards me, you don't know what you're talking about."

But I did know. After all, I'd typed and read his business correspondence, listened to his phone calls, for years. Even when the money rolled in during the war the check was either "in the mail" or had "slipped my mind." Mom said he got it from his mother.

I had one card left to play, a dangerous one. "Sandy and Bob have had a tough time the last few years. They need a father they can count on. Why don't you be that? You've got it in you."

I thought that he'd either go into a rage or soften up. He did neither. Instead he gave me a canny, appraising look, his head nodding slightly. "You're twenty-three, twenty-four years old, right?

"Twenty-one," I said.

"But you've gotten around pretty good for someone your age. You've been in the navy, you've worked the hotels, you even learned a thing or two here, much as you tried not to. You're beginning to know the score."

"I guess," I said. "But I'm only in the second inning." Who was softening up whom here? I was getting colder and hungrier and more frustrated by the minute.

But he seemed increasingly at ease, fielding the thought I had hit to his position as he leisurely prepared to throw me out. He even took one of his pipes from the top drawer, filled it with Brindley's Mixture, and lit up.

"You talk a lot about my responsibility. What about your own? When an oldest son reaches a certain age doesn't he have some responsibilities too?"

He nailed me again. I had come here as the Weiss boy, my uncles and aunts' star nephew as well as their sister's son, and he, with hardly any effort, had turned me again into Little Benny, the guilty chip off the old block. I lamely asked him to promise to send Mom's checks on the first of the month. He said he would see what he could do, stood up, and sent me on my way. Once again, he'd been able to play me like a flute—knowing were the holes were because he'd put in most of them.

14

Dylan Thomas came to read in Ann Arbor one March day in 1950. A hard wind was blowing that afternoon as I walked over to Rackham Auditorium with my new friend, Saul Gottlieb, a twenty-eight-year-old freshman who had published a story and a poem in *Penguin New Writing*, a leading literary magazine of the war years. "He's sent his wind on ahead of him," remarked Saul, who had heard Thomas read at the Ninety-second Street Y in New York. "He's going to turn Rackham into Fern Hill."

"Fern Hill?"

"That's one of his major poems. You're in for an experience."

Little did I realize. Were it not for the Oscar Williams's *Little Treasury of Modern Poetry*, I would hardly have known who Dylan Thomas was. Each night, my classwork done, I would read it into the early morning, consulting the little oval portraits in back to help me connect at least that much with the difficult poems, to thrill all the more to the dynamite ones. Modern poetry had such a glamour then that I would pore over those portraits as reverently as I had once done with the team picture of the Brooklyn Dodgers, looking for portents and clues of significance between the face and the name, humanizing the gods and goddesses.

So I was all the more taken aback when, after the introduction, a roly-poly clownlike figure wove to the podium of the opulent new auditorium, grasped it hard, and began to peer around as though trying to figure out where he was. The halo of frizzy gray curls, the puffy face that had once been angelic, announced that he was indeed Dylan Thomas, wearing a suit that looked like he had slept in it. Taking a full moment to look around and get his bearings, he said something like "I do not usually read my poems in Radio City Musical Hall. But then again, we are all pigs here, so I'll have a go at the trough."

The words were in keeping with his appearance and completely at variance with the most distinguished voice I had ever heard. And having gotten his displeasure, or whatever it was, off his chest, he let the voice take over or rather joined it in passionate wedlock to the poem he began to read. A year before, Frank Huntley, my advanced-exposition teacher, had walked into class one day and, to change the atmosphere, had read some poems—Blake's "Tyger," Yeats's "The Second Coming," e. e. cummings's "Buffalo Bill"—poems I had never heard of before and that probably made me an English major once and for all. Now, Dylan Thomas took that experience of the power of poetry to the next level. Hearing phrases like "the synagogue of an ear of corn" or "the heydeys of his eyes," or lines like "The force that through the green fuse drives the flower / Drives my green age," or poems like "In My Craft and Sullen Art" was like a reveille to my spirit. My courses were teaching me that literature was texts to analyze; Thomas's imperial voice and cosmic language and mountainous range of feeling declared that literature was a natural religion that in the right hands hallowed the world. Nor was this true only of his own poems, which put Pan back in pantheism. In the cathedral of that intonation and diction, other poems became objects of worship: not only those by Yeats and Hardy but Henry Reed and even a poem of John Betjeman, which he transformed from light verse to delicate art.

After the reading, the audience was invited to go backstage to meet Thomas. It wasn't like a reception; it was more like a tryout for the team with a vaunted new coach. He sat astraddle a folding chair and we sat around him on the floor. Perhaps it was arranged this way to keep him away from the booze a while longer. The questions came from the star graduate students and younger faculty, but I was burning to ask one too, not only to touch the force field of this living presence of Literature but also to find out something.

"How conscious are you of other poets, like the ones you read today, when you're writing?"

He gave me an appreciative smile and some words that are still deposited in my account of memorable moments. "I try not to be conscious of anyone when I'm writing," he said, "least of all, myself."

I was so taken with the second part of his answer (it was just what Eliot said—literature was an escape from your personality) that I failed to grasp and heed the first.

∾

Saul Gottlieb was an unlikely freshman even in those times when many veterans were still on campus. A married man with two children and a soft mustache, he wore a suit and tie to class, instead of the standard army field jacket or navy foul-weather jacket, as though he were trying to get a college education between business engagements. Not very lucrative ones, judging from the seediness of the suit, the frayed shirt collars, the hangdog tie, his overfull head of curly hair. He was still working in the Detroit office of the Joint Distribution Committee, where he wrote mailings on behalf of the flood of refugees to Israel.

That someone who had published both fiction and poetry in *Penguin New Writing* should use his talent to sell refrigerators and stoves, however worthy the cause, troubled me. One of the first things a novice writer learned then was vigilance about "prostituting your talent."

"I'd rather shovel shit," I announced soon after we'd met in Marvin Feldheim's American lit class, where we both were starring.

This brought an ingratiating smile, Saul's characteristic one, enhanced by the moustache that framed it. "But that's exactly what I do," he said. "Except that I use a typewriter. What would you have me do to support my family?"

It hadn't really occurred to me that a serious writer would have a family to support, any more than a priest would, so close were the two vocations in my mind—both requiring years and years of training and self-sacrifice before one could perform the sacraments. Not that a writer shouldn't have plenty of sex. That was one of the inducements. "I guess you shouldn't have bought a cow when milk is so cheap," I said, though you would hardly have known it by me.

"You're still very young," Saul said as kindly as if I'd complimented rather than needled him. Because of that smile, those coyly appealing eyes, the gentle voice, you would have thought him weak, and you would have been wrong. The smile and the manner were used for leverage and to cloak his smarts. He'd grown up in the Bronx, learned the score from the Depression. Like James Baldwin, a friend of his at Dewitt Clinton High, the literary man and the hustler fed off each other.

To Saul, writing was writing. Solicitation letters, ghostwriting, freshman themes, stories, poems, plays—you sat down at your desk and pulled the chain. By a kind of linkage of opposition we quickly settled into our roles: he the versatile freelance, I the putative purist. He wrote relaxed, straightforward prose, perfect-pitch dialogue, and lucid poetry; I weighed every sentence and line of my stories on the scale of Joycean austerity—the Joyce of *Dubliners*—staying away from subjects like my father that might involve me personally and prevent my escape from personality.

This didn't inhibit our friendship but rather fostered it, since I envied and admired his fluency, and he my slow, painful struggle with otherness that was supposed to take me eventually to a distinctive style. When the freshman Hopwoods came around, Saul won first prize in all three categories, three bull's-eyes at two feet for him. He had chosen Michigan mostly because of the many Hopwood Awards.

∾

One Sunday that spring I rode out to Willow Run in nearby Ypsilanti on one of the buses that the university operated between the campus and the vast veterans' housing facility there. My companion was Marvin Feldheim, an engaging younger member of the English department. Sporting a complexion that looked buffed and the most tasteful wardrobe in Ann Arbor, Marvin attracted bright students, mostly Jewish, flirting with the men and charming the women, yet managing to parent both—a remarkable act of moral poise.

I had written a paper for him on Mark Twain that he wanted me to revise to make it a bit more scholarly. He was pretty sure I could get it published. At the end of his comment he'd written, "Whee, fame."

But I had no interest in that kind of fame, as I told him as we rode out to Saul's. "I want to be a fiction writer, not a scholar."

"That's understandable," he said. "But if you don't mind my saying so, I think you're kidding yourself about where your real talent lies."

"In your opinion." Marvin was notorious for his provocative opinions. I pointed out that my first story had won a Hopwood Award.

"I know, Ted, I read it. Herbert Barrows showed it to me. It's sweet but derivative and, if you don't mind my saying so, a bit corny. But the problem is that it has little imaginative power. I'm sure you don't want to know why but I'm going to tell you anyway. I want to save you from pulling the wool over your own eyes."

"Okay," I said, used to his aggressiveness. "I want to hear your words so that one day I can watch you eat them."

"Willingly. But I don't think I'll have to. Saul, for example, is a fiction writer. Willy Wiegand is another. They trust their imagination completely, its individuality, its grasp. The trust is a kind of primal thing that goes deeper than technique, deeper than words, even deeper than talent. This is why even a klutz like Dreiser or a lightweight like Sinclair Lewis can keep the reader identifying, keep him feeling, keep him guessing. You, on the other hand, don't trust your imagination and have to rely on others. What you do trust completely is your literary judgment and insight, which is why your judgments are bold and your insights keen, sometimes even original, as with the Twain essay. Otherwise I wouldn't be wasting my time or causing you pain by telling you this."

I was shaken. He had seen further into me than I ever had and was right on the money. Last year it was Hemingway, this fall Thomas Mann, now Joyce. "Why can't you develop both kinds of trust? Look at Robert Penn Warren or Edmund Wilson."

"I don't think you can develop it. You develop the ways you use it but I think it's either there or it isn't. Like being able to act any role or hit all the notes. It's primal."

The powerful last word brought the curtain down. I was both resentful and stirred. But I quickly discounted the praise, which left me feeling like I'd been talking to a classy version of my father. No sooner did I show some ability or receive some recognition than Dad was trying to discredit it or me. Still, Marvin was certainly right about one thing: I wrote course papers so much more confidently and effectively than I wrote stories; the first written, revised, done; the second written laboriously, revised endlessly. Just like Flaubert, I would tell myself.

~

During his military service, Saul had married an English woman with a young son. Ann was a large, benign person in her midthirties. Their house, or rather housing, was in a row of shacklike structures that made Willow Run, where three or four thousand veterans still lived, seem like a staging area for the postwar world. Anne had done wonders with their place—the fresh-painted walls in cream and green, the waxed floor, the spic-and-span utilities, the modest but modern furniture, the vase of wheat stalks set in front of the ugly hot-water heater, the Impressionist prints on the walls, the two bookcases mounted floor to ceiling and jammed with books—all this gave the main room an air of resourceful comfort and even charm that seemed almost heroic. In this, his own space, Saul lost his harried, tentative look, seeming to brim with the same assurance and stability that Anne did—he was very much the man of the house, the competent, hardworking breadwinner who made it all possible. Along with ten-year-old Michael, a serious boy, very much Anne's son, there was a four-year-old who clearly led the charmed life of an adored child. I kept thinking of what it would be like to grow up in a family like this.

Whatever competitive edginess I normally had around Saul melted that afternoon as we tucked into a delicious and, for me, lavish roast beef dinner. Marvin was terrific with the two children—he had that rare touch of being able to talk to them as he talked to adults. My dismay and perplexity from our bus conversation dissolved in the warm glow of brave *Gemütlichkeit* topped off with the levity produced by the fine wine that Marvin had brought. Here in this household, life was earnest without being grim, the grimness overcome by determination and taste, creating for me a kind of austere glamour. What if part of Saul's writing fluency and the weight of his stories and poems came from leading this full and serious life? Beside his, mine seemed both empty and self-indulgent, full of lonely weekends in which I retouched and reframed descriptions and recast dialogues—mostly the same ones, over and over—slowly emptying myself of confidence and them of naturalness and spontaneity. It was all so provisional and egotistical. Maybe what I needed was a strenuous, devoted—in a word, adult—life, like Saul's, to make my fiction real, my vocation a touch heroic, as it was supposed to be. My model wasn't only Saul. The campus atmosphere was still dominated by the veterans: they made my one advanced course so interesting, just as they made the political coverage and letters to the editor in the *Michigan Daily* so mature and informative. I would often watch them debarking from the Willow Run buses in the morning—serious young family men fanning out like an intellectual occupying force.

Late that spring, the Major and Minor Hopwood Awards came around. On the afternoon of the day before, special delivery letters were delivered to the winners. Around four, Saul called to say that he had just received two letters—awards for fiction and poetry. I tried to be as enthusiastic for him as I could. Just then the doorbell of the rooming house rang and, sure enough, downstairs was a special delivery letter for me. When I tore it open, all set to read it out to Saul, I saw that it was a letter from the chairman of the English department, telling me that I had been awarded the Lucinda Downes scholarship in literature.

"That's terrific," Saul said. But it didn't feel that way. It felt like having the sexiest girl in the class phoning to ask how to do the math assignment.

15

Around this time, I received the following letter from Lynn.

Clara de Hirsch House
May 17, 1950

Dear Ted:

You may find this hard to believe but for the past week or more I've been thinking with such joy of us and the life we might have together in Ann Arbor. No, not to worry, I'm not pregnant. But I feel as changed in my life as if I was, changed for the better without any of the anxiety and regret that becoming a premature Mommy would bring.

Perhaps a better way of putting it is that the scales of self-doubt have fallen from my eyes and I see myself, and us, in a new and much clearer light. I see the family deficits that we have both struggled to overcome dropping behind us, and our particular difficulty and disappointment ending as we succeed in making a new and very different life together than each of us has known. I'm having a great semester here taking Gardner Murphy's course in Abnormal Psychology in which he's singled me out. But I know that part of my progress in thinking well of my mind has resulted from your stimulating interest in me as well as your patience and tenderness. I feel that in serving as your Muse, as you say, I've helped to contribute to your growth as a writer. The thought of living and studying and musing (pun intended) with you in Ann Arbor, of beginning a life together, so vitalizes me that I want you to know it in the

hope that you still want to share it. I want you to know I love
who you are and what you are. And if being married makes
things a bit easier for us—yes, by all means, yes.

Your loving _____?

Though four or five months ago I would have walked from Ann
Arbor to New York to receive such a letter, by now it didn't elate me
or even very much surprise me. I'd hitchhiked to New York six weeks
before at the Easter break, and though we were glad to see each other
and had slept together at the beginning and end, nothing much had
changed in the passion department. Yet we had somehow become a
couple, regarded as such by her sisters, by my New York aunts and
uncles, and by her friends. The capper to that had been when she'd
come with me to Teaneck to meet my mother, sister, and brother.
Much to my joy she had let out all the stops on her charm, joking with
thirteen-year-old Bobby, the family card, who had us all in stitches
with his imitation of his cornball math teacher. To Sandy, a gifted high
school senior, and somewhat at sea, she'd been big sisterly; to Mom,
she'd been a resourceful sous-chef in the kitchen and a prospective
companion at Carnegie Hall and the Metropolitan Museum of Art,
which she had since become. I couldn't get over how she not only fit-
ted herself in but raised the level of morale in the home, made us
almost a happy family instead of, at best, a zany one.

As I was walking her to the bus, I'd said, "You outdid yourself
tonight. Thanks for your forbearance."

She punched me in the arm. "Idiotka, there was nothing to fore-
bear. I enjoyed myself. You're quite a family. Four real minds."

"Inside four waifs," I said.

"That too. I guess that's why I felt so at home."

"You brought us out, particularly my mother."

"You just have to shine a little light on her. Sandy too. And that
routine of Bob's had me in stitches."

She began to mimic his mimicry. Her eyes were alight, her face a bouquet of droll expressions. When she was animated, she was superanimated. "You're too much, Lynnotchka," I said when she was finished.

"Who knows?" she said, giving my hand a squeeze. "Maybe, Fyodor, I've finally found a family worth belonging to."

Since then she had made a couple of weekend trips to Teaneck on her own, even pitching in with painting the dining room a lovely burnt orange, her idea. Along with telling me this, Mom had said, "There is so much that I like about Lynn, her warmth, her style, her wit. Also, unlike myself, she's a girl who will always make sure that the seams of her stockings are straight."

These trips to Teaneck were the closest Lynn had come to attaching herself to me until this letter, which appeared to do just that. Yet I felt no more sure of our relationship than I had before receiving it, only less unsure. The difference between being sure and unsure was one little word—*desire*—which, for all the warmth of her words, was the absentee in this play of feeling. She had sent allusions—"difficulty and disappointment"—chaperoned by aspiration. How would "a new and very different life" turn into passion for me? Wasn't it supposed to be the other way around? If anything, the letter corroborated what I had felt since the previous summer—that she wanted my mind a lot more than my body, the mentor rather than the man. The passion, the full-heartedness, in Lynn's letter were for herself. We were both in love with the same person.

The Lake George question returned in a more fateful way. Why me?

~

After a good deal of walking in the Arboretum and talking to myself that afternoon, I came to the conclusion that I had no answer other than what she'd written. Meanwhile, the doubt I'd felt was turning into a brand-new sense of maturity: like the other veterans on campus, my youth was now over; my adulthood had begun. The image of myself as one of them, of living with Lynn at Willow Run, was much more satisfying than my present image as one of the horde of the guys on campus who lived alone, unattached to anything besides their courses and the Bob Marshall Eating Club, where some of us ate our often solitary meals. Holed up with my labored fiction on weekends, friends with only a couple of other groping writers besides Saul, I had even lost touch with Murray and through him, the Art Theater group.

This loneliness and literary frustration and worrying about who was kissing Lynn now was what the freedom that had been so precious less than two years ago had become. So precious that I'd sacrificed to it my responsibilities as the mature son and brother. Even my mission to The Shop had been a failure, since Dad had continued to stall with the monthly check.

And now an opportunity had arrived with Lynn's letter to redeem myself as a moral person and at the same time solve the loneliness problem, maybe even the literary one, by getting married. She had said herself in her letter that my support had partly enabled her to grow. Solicitude came easily to me; I had been a child star of it. In time, I had grown to resent my mother's need for support, indeed to flee from it, but now I would have the opportunity to improve on my performance, to further re-create myself as the opposite of my father, by assisting in Lynn's growth. I had already taken on a gentle, soft-spoken demeanor, an idealistic politics, a career in which making money would be the last concern; now I would add the most radical counter: the husband who was devoted to his wife's well-being and growth.

16

We were married at the end of summer, a few days after we quit our dining room jobs at the Jersey shore, on the Saturday night of Labor Day weekend. Because of the holiday, we had trouble finding a rabbi, and the one we finally came up with was in the Bronx. We traveled there on the subway with our luggage, which we carried to the rabbi's apartment building and waited in the lobby for the rest of the wedding party to arrive: my mother and Sandra and Lynn's sister Esther and her boyfriend Arnold, who was driving them in from New Jersey.

The night was sweltering and we had to walk up six flights because the elevator wasn't working. The rabbi's wife came to the door with a look she might have given to a group of Jehovah's Witnesses selling *The Watchtower*. As we filed in, I noticed her staring at Lynn's belly. She had no doubt why this *mishigas* was taking place.

After we had filled out the marriage contract, the rabbi led us up the aisle, as it were, from the kitchen to the living room, while Sandra played Mendelssohn's wedding march on an old upright and Mom said, "Not so loud, dear, I don't think that piano can take it." Out of the corner of my eye, I gazed at Lynn, sleek as ever in a green striped silk dress. I hovered beside her, almost a foot taller, her awkward gentle knight. What was she thinking with that wayward smile, half her mind amused, the other listening to her own broadcast. The sheen of her hair, the beautifully cut eyes, the skin, tanned almost as dark as mine, molding the model's cheekbones, the ripe mouth. Half a gamin, half a beauty. My initial disregard for the ceremony faded and for the rest of it, I felt like a bridegroom, entrusted with this precious young woman whom I had hardly begun to know.

Still, there was much to disregard. The bridal canopy, or *huppah*, was a portable one, a small domed cloth with four sticks. Arnold, a man of the people who went on chewing his gum, held two of them aloft, Mom held the third, and the fourth dangled, a trope of the situation. It signified to me all those who were missing from the ceremony: two of our three parents, Lynn's other sister and her husband, and my New York aunts and uncles and cousins, not to mention friends. But that was what we had wanted—a no-fuss wedding that accorded with our notion of marriage as a bourgeois trap. We were taking our vows to qualify for married-student housing and for the additional stipend that the GI Bill paid. Otherwise, who needed marriage? In a catchphrase of the time, we were free, white, and twenty-one (or almost, in Lynn's case).

After the ceremony, Arnold dropped us off at the Marlton Hotel on Eighth Street, the scene of our trysts during the past spring when Lynn was living at the Clara de Hirsch House. The Greenwich Village ambiance was supposed to free up the lovemaking but the Marlton's seamy atmosphere and tacky furniture seemed to take us right back to square one at Steve's Cabins.

I did what I could patiently, gently, even subtly, I thought, but she soon went dry again. I fought against the disappointment. "Let's rub our rings together," I said. "It's been known to produce moisture. Dr. Van den Velde practically guarantees it."

"I could use a few tender moments," she said. This meant that I should slide off, draw her against me, and stroke her brow, the position in which we spent most of our downtime. "I'll be more relaxed when we get to Dale's cottage," she said after a while. "That wedding just about did me in."

"Between the rebbitsin's glares and Arnold's gum-chewing, I didn't know whether to laugh or weep," I said.

"Maybe a little of both are in order," she mumbled against my shoulder. And then there were tears like two raindrops on my shoulder. "I'm sorry, Fyodor" she said. "I'm so fucking sorry."

I hoped she was apologizing rather than confessing something, but I didn't want to ask. By now I tried to accept these sudden mood swings as the expression of her volatile Russian nature. I lay there in the seedy darkness, holding her, pondering the significance of the event. What lingered most in my mind was the dangling pole of the *huppah*.

Our honeymoon was to be at a lakeside cottage near Detroit that Lynn's former roommate was loaning us. But first we had to get there. The next morning we took a taxi with our four suitcases to one of the streets that feeds into the Lincoln Tunnel and stuck out our thumbs.

Soon a tractor trailer pulled over and we climbed aboard. Our trek, our honeymoon, our life together had begun. Two clinging rebels on the lam from their pasts. Bonnie and Clyde meet Hansel and Gretel.

17

The children's ward of the Neuropsychiatric Institute at the university hospital soon became the focal point of our life in Ann Arbor. The first semester, Lynn took a course in learning theory in which she attracted the interest of her professor by an experiment she was designing to explore the relation between ego strength and learning ability. Professor Wilson's wife, Libby, was in charge of the education program on the children's ward and soon Lynn was working for her as a reading and math tutor while she carried on her research. It was a love-at-first-sight job in which Lynn's knack for relating to children, her passionate sense of racial injustice, and her intense interest in her subject came to center on a sexually abused eleven-year-old black child named Louise whose intense hostility made her almost unreachable, much less teachable.

Lynn's accounts of the ward made it seem much more challenging and positive than my job had been with the veterans. I applied for a position as an attendant and after a month or two was called in, closely interviewed by the director himself, and taken on.

The Ward was a remarkable place. The director, known as Dr. R, was a tall gangling man with the craggy forbearance in his face of a young Abe Lincoln. He belonged to the school of "milieu therapy": the development of a total therapeutic environment for children in which all members of the staff participated and closely communicated, from the student attendants and nurses aides up to the psychiatrists and Dr. R himself.

The Ward was a high-energy place, fed by the liveliness of the kids as well as the ardor of the staff. So engrossing and intense was Lynn's daily three-hour stint in the afternoon and my eight-hour shift thrice weekly in the evening that our courses and doings on campus became secondary to us. This was particularly true for Lynn, who threw herself into her work with a dispatch and effectiveness that her self-doubts stood in the way of whenever she had to write a paper for her courses. Here, especially, I was all too ready to help her out of her procrastination, which she would accept and then resent. Ironically enough, or not so ironically, it was working with disturbed kids that rescued our marriage after a mutually disappointing first three months and gave it much of its juice and joy. Our experiences there, the kids themselves, the weekly staff conference in which one of them was discussed in depth, the personalities and performance of the staff, particularly the brilliant Dr. R—all gave us something better to talk about than her emotional problems and my shortcomings, a more stabilizing and stimulating place to share than our bed.

～

Early one evening shift I emerged from the nursing office on the Ward to find a new face waiting for me. It was the face of a boy hurtling through adolescence—hurtling through something—a round, Buster Brown face, if Buster Brown were Jewish and manic; his eyes were popping with animation, as though every neuron in his brain were firing. 'Hi, *landsman*," he said. "Hi, jukel. Hi, fellow kike. You didn't expect me to know that, did you? I'm Morrie, who knows everything. Who has access. I know you're an English major, I know you're married to the glistening Lynn, the newly crowned queen of my masturbatory fantasies, I know that you're the attendant I'm supposed to pal up with. Milieu therapy and all that crap."

"Hello, Morrie," I said. "I've been hearing about you, too." And so I had, from Lynn, after his first day there, but earlier from others once it got around that he was coming back. Morrie was a Ward legend, a fifteen-year-old schizophrenic with a prodigious intelligence and amazing acquisitiveness, who had been one of Dr. R's success stories. He had been placed in a good boarding school for disturbed children in Cincinnati, but after six months or so had had "a schizoid break" and had been shipped back to the Ward. From the looks of things, he was breaking still. "Since you know so much about me," I said to him, "I'll tell you one more thing. I don't like people who use the words *kike* or *jukel*."

"Ah so," he said, putting a finger to his forehead, looking for the all the world like a juvenile professor. "Someone proud to be a Jew. Unlike myself. But the point is, Big Ted, we live in a democracy of which I happen to still be a member, ostracized but still a member... Speaking of members, how big is yours?"

"The word *kike*, Morrie, has a lot of blood on it. The blood of six million people recently."

"That's a metaphor," he said. "Or a simile. Sometimes I have trouble telling the difference. It might also be a metonymy or an oxymoron. That's the trouble with this place, it's filled with morons. There are the oxys like you and me and R and your wife, the glistening Lynn, my new Homeric epithet for her, and maybe one or two others and the rest are the morons, especially the doctor they've given me."

All of this and more was delivered in a rapid-fire way, like an untended machine gun on automatic, jolting back and forth as it fired away. Meanwhile his eyes were locked onto mine, their attentiveness disconcerting, to say the least. He was looking for admiration but there was something else there, some fear that was keeping him in overdrive, spritzing through his inner graveyard. He was off-the-charts expressive and utterly desperate.

So began a relationship. After a few more days of sedation Morrie began to calm down, to act like an exceptionally driven Jewish kid with a dulled body and a hyperactive mind. The case history in his file said that he came from an intensely Orthodox home ruled by an authoritarian maniac of a father. I'd enjoyed working on the ward before but Morrie's presence gave me a personal stake that grew and deepened. In his brightness, clownishness, energy, and vulnerability he reminded me a touch of my quick-witted, mercurial kid brother, who was about his age. But unlike Bob, Morrie had little boundary between self and world. Also he was close at hand three days a week. Close indeed. In my hair, as we used to say.

On Sunday evenings we would take a group of boys to the pool in the Michigan Union. The practice there was to swim in the nude, which usually turned Morrie's manias back on.

"I'd like to suck Mr. Bunting's cock. It's so big and juicy. Do you think I'm turning into a homosexual? On the other hand, I'd like to have his big juicy cock so that I could fuck Joanna with it. Don't you think she's got the greatest pair of tits for a fourteen-year-old girl you ever saw? Don't you want to at least lick them and to hold Don's cock? I don't mean to be personal, Big Ted, I'm just trying to figure out if I'm queer or just totally horny. Anyway, you haven't answered my question. And don't tell me my question is out of order. I have a right to ask inappropriate questions. It's in the schizophrenic Bill of Rights. I'm a little schitzy but not psychotic. Right?"

The last was a variant of the question he often asked me, even though I gave him the same standard response, that I wasn't qualified to answer it. There were no prescribed responses for the others. So I said something like "As you can tell from consulting your own equipment, Morrie, you're an adolescent, or, as you like to say, pubescent. You've got all these new hormones rushing around inside you and one of the things they do is make you horny. And teenage horniness doesn't make a sharp distinction between male and female. So I'd say generally horny."

"What about wanting a shlong the size of Don's? I'm trying to grow one by steady exercise. Is that delusions of grandeur? I'm still developing so I have a chance but you're never going to get there."

I told him that I had to pay attention to the other kids in the pool. "Why don't you go for a swim, Morrie, it will help you to cool off."

"You're evading my questions, Big Ted, which could have a negative effect on my rapport with you, which is mainly what you're being paid for. Milieu therapy and all that crap."

Part of Morrie's precociousness was that in a calm phase, relatively speaking, he had the face of a mature deadpan comedian. Since he almost never smiled, it was difficult to know when he was putting me on and when he was serious. To ask him was out of the question, because if he was serious, he could take the question as an instigation to riot. Nothing set him off as explosively as being misunderstood. Then you would have to wrestle him to the "quiet room," which was hard for me to do, emotionally well as physically—his pale, puffy body in a frenzy of strength, his voice a screaming whip of invective. Many of the other kids on the Ward "blew" from time to time and one learned to handle it, usually with another attendant, as part of the job. But with Morrie I'd feel like the "Kapo" he kept telling me I was.

This happened only a few times in the fourteen months I was to know him. The rapport he spoke of was real, indeed potent. I had already encountered several people with whom I communicated intuitively and at a high level because in being with him or her I was carried closest to the person I wanted to be. Morrie's strange, brilliant mentality called forth and empowered my guardian spirit, the Weiss Boy, or in his adult version, the good Ted, who could live on easier and more effective terms with his imagination than the writer in me could. That's what "kindred spirits" do for each other; each objectifies and brings out the other's better self. This was true of Lynn and me when it wasn't bringing out the worse one.

～

Lynn and Louise also proved to be kindred spirits. A scrawny twelve-year-old from the Detroit Tenderloin, Louise had the temperament of an alley cat. After their first week together, Lynn said, "The trick isn't teaching her to read. It's getting her to stop glaring at me." She tried one tactic after another to little effect. On a beautiful March day, right after a snowstorm, she took her for a walk in the Arboretum. She'd brought along an old hat and scarf, two pieces of coal from our bin, a carrot, and a tomato. It went something like this:

"We're going to make a snowman."

"Maybe you is. I guess I's just gonna have to freeze my ass off."

"Not if you move around. Here's what you do. You start with a snowball."

"Snowball's for throwing."

"Okay. We won't make a snowman. We'll have a snowball fight." Which they did. For a while. Louise making and throwing three for every one of Lynn's. "I surrender," Lynn said. "You're a snowball-making machine."

For the first time in Lynn's presence, maybe in Ann Arbor, Louise smiled. "I think it was a smile," Lynn said. "It was more like a pucker. As though she had never used those facial muscles before."

But whatever it was, it proved to be the start, the inchoate dawning of trust in a child who had had so many reasons to distrust. Six months later you would hardly have recognized Louise from the alert, sly, pretty teenager she had become. Her mind had blossomed along with her person. She was reading now only two years from her grade level and doing better in math and her other subjects in the Ward school. Once scrawny, she was now slim; once haggard, she was now stylish, once a loner, she was now at the front of the older girls' cohort. If Louise had blossomed, there was no question who had been the gardener. Lynn had taken her to thrift shops to buy her stylish clothes. She had gotten the ward psychologist, who was black, to take Louise with her to the beauty parlor. But mostly it was her knack for relating to Louise, of being right there in word and gesture and feeling, that had drawn the abused and withdrawn child, step by step, out of her hostility and the fear and shame that it was defending.

The bonding seemed to be mutual: her work with Louise brought out the Lynn that I associated with her East Lansing days when she was lively and independent, harried but self-confident, drawing sustenance from her involvement with Claude and the others. The maverick was back. The first semester in Ann Arbor she had been "besieged by self-doubt," one of the ready phrases of mine that come back from that stormy, benightedly earnest time, in which I began to take over as her therapist. Now she was cocky.

Too cocky. For she was making an enemy of her patron, Libby Wilson, a commanding, efficient woman who had hired Lynn for her smarts and spirit and come to resent her way of deploying them. Lynn's main method of reading therapy was taking Louise to the local library, finding a book that spoke to her, then reading it together. So it became Libby Wilson's reliance on the latest methodology versus Lynn's intuitive ability to reach and motivate Louise. But, of course, there was no parity, and Lynn was put on notice.

If Louise had steadied and energized Lynn, the conflict with Libby enraged her, drove her. It became the center of her life, our life. I tried to get her to back off a bit, to temporize, to do a few more phonics exercises and make a few less trips with Louise off the ward.

"You don't mean temporize, you mean compromise. Never! I'll beat Mrs. Treachery at her own game." Her Russian blood was up; she was like Natasya Filippovna in *The Idiot*, Grushenka in *The Brothers Karamazov*—those proud women, already a handful, now aroused—the blazing egos, the demands, the scheming. She went to Judith Abernathy, the black psychologist, and tried to enlist her to tell Dr. R that his whole concept of milieu therapy was being undermined by his teaching supervisor—Lynn's version of "if only the Czar knew." When word of this got back to Libby Wilson, Lynn was fired.

That night was hellish. It went on and on, beginning in fury and recrimination. After Libby Wilson, she moved on to "two-faced Judas Abernathy," and then on to me for my insufficient outrage. "A real man would be standing up for me. A real radical would be organizing a protest, even a strike. You haven't even said you're resigning in protest. You can't support me financially. You can at least support me emotionally. Well, the hell with you, the hell with your fucking Ann Arbor, this capital of liberal hypocrisy. I'm going back to New York where there are at least a few people who I respect and who respect me." She then smashed around in our one closet until she had dragged out her suitcase, and both ablaze with fury and wet with self-pity began to throw clothes into it.

I tried to reason and sympathize with her but that failing and her abuse getting to me, I fell into my usual ranting to her raving. "If you weren't such a heedless arrogant bitch this wouldn't have happened. I warned you but would you listen?... Do you ever listen?... Go to New York and give me some peace for the first time in nine months."

But this time the usual outcome of our sleeping at opposite ends of the bed wasn't the end. In the middle of the night I was awakened by Lynn kicking me and screaming. What she was screaming was "Rats! Get rid of the rats!" She was standing on the daybed, her night-gown clutched at her knees, her eyes shut. I jumped up and turned on the light, thinking she was having a nightmare. She went on scream-ing about rats, about the room being full of them, swarming all around the bed.

I tried to shake her but she writhed away and began to scream again, holding her hands over her eyes, insisting that the room was full of rats.

This wasn't a nightmare. A nightmare you can be woken from. I turned on more lights; I tried to take her hands from her eyes to show her the room. Her strength was astounding, but I finally moved her hands away and she looked and began screaming, "They're so big! Black! Hideous! Oh God... Oh my God!"

Should I slap her, like in the movies, and bring her out of it? Sup-pose it didn't; I'd just feel brutal. Besides, this wasn't the movies. This was real craziness.

Which somehow settled me. I told myself that from the veterans' and the kids' wards, I knew how to deal with sudden craziness. I did-n't, beyond getting another attendant and in the worse cases, a ward psychiatrist, but the illusion gave me a bit of calm and an intuition, which told me that she didn't need to be slapped but held. I pulled her body to mine and held her until the shaking stopped. Then I said, "They're gone, I've gotten rid of them." She let me take her hands away from her eyes, and draw her down onto the bed. I began to stroke her forehead and down into her hair. It was what we often did when we wanted to be close, in our "tender moments." My stroking her forehead was our most fulfilling form of lovemaking, perhaps what we each most needed: she to feel loved and I to feel loving. And so I went on stroking and murmuring, "It's all right, Lynn. Everything's all right. I love you, Lynn. I'll protect you." After a time she said, "You've gotten rid of them. I believe that," and soon fell asleep.

I got up and went to the kitchenette and poured myself a big glass of wine. With the crisis over, my first realization came back with shocking force. I felt overwhelmed. Never—not on the veterans' ward, not on the children's—had I been this close to the black vertigo of insanity. The ambiguous markers along the course of our relationship fell dismally into place: the weird remarks in East Lansing, the various ailments, the immobilizing depressions when a paper was due, her occasional thumb-sucking in her sleep, the crazy idea of trying to enlist Judith Abernathy, now this. "You've wanted your life to be like a Russian novel," I said to myself. "Now, look what it's gotten you into."

∾

A few days later, I was sitting in Dr. R's office, having come to plead with the Czar. When I'd called his office the day before to ask to see him, he had said, "Yes, of course," which indicated that he already knew and this put me as much at my ease as I could be, which wasn't much. He was not only the one person who could help us, but also being a brilliant psychiatrist, he could see around the psychic corners and already knew more about Lynn than I did.

It was the end of the day and he was sitting back in his chair, one of his long legs up on the typewriter panel. It was first time I had seen him without his white coat. But even relaxed, his collar open, he was still a daunting figure of clarity and force.

Still, I gave it my best shot, speaking the opening line I had searched for and rehearsed for two days. I said that I wanted to talk to him because Lynn seemed to have been fired for doing her job too well.

He said, "Tell me about it."

"I say it for two reasons. One, the purpose of the Ward is to help disturbed kids get better, and, well, look at Louise now. Lynn has had a lot to do with that."

"I realize that," he said. "She's certainly been a healing presence for Louise."

Which, for the moment, made the situation a lot easier. So did his gaze, which regarded me, as though I were a junior colleague who had come to consult with him, rather than a college kid working as an attendant and the husband of a big problem. "And secondly, Lynn feels that she's been acting according to your milieu therapy, making herself an integral and positive part of Louise's milieu rather than just a reading therapist."

"So she has." I expected him to go to say that nonetheless she was part of a team and that she had to accept having a supervisor or that she hadn't focused enough on Louise's reading skills. But he didn't. He said, "How has Lynn been taking this?"

What could I say? Though he asked in a kindly way, it was the last question I wanted to answer. It was also the first question I would otherwise have wanted to ask. Sitting across from me was a psychiatrist who would understand what was going on, who could tell me what to do if it recurred. The landlady had already complained about her screaming and had threatened to call the police the next time and then to evict us. But hoping desperately that this was only a more extreme version of her crisis behavior and would end if I could help her get another job on the Ward, I couldn't tell Dr. R that along with her other problems, Lynn was hallucinating. It was as though I'd been marooned on a dangerous island for the past three days and now this expert sailor in a big boat had come near. But there was no way I could ask him to pick me up.

Meanwhile, Dr. R was waiting for an answer, no doubt taking in some, maybe all, of my dilemma, with his X-ray psychiatric vision.

"She's pretty upset," I said.

"I'm sure she is," he said. "She has every right to be."

"She put her whole heart into her relationship with Louise. She loves working on the Ward. It's like a calling with her. She's going to be a child psychologist."

"I hope she does," he said. Then he said, just as levelly, "Has Lynn had any psychotherapy?"

His question was matter-of-fact and therefore all the more formidable. So I sat there with my dilemma in my hands or rather, at my throat. For the past two days I had so much hoped he would see me and let me plead Lynn's case to the point of her being offered a job as a female attendant. Now I only wanted to be out of there, to get off this spot where I might soon break down myself and tell him everything and betray Lynn myself.

Perhaps I shrugged as an answer. In any event, he spared me. "I think very highly of Lynn," he said. "I think very highly of both of you. If Lynn needs help with this, she might want to see Dr. Charney at Student Health." He wrote his name on a prescription pad, tore off the page, and handed it to me. "Let's talk again when you're back from summer vacation."

So the Czar already knew that, too.

18

Halfway through my junior year, a friend who was an editor of the *Daily* asked me to write a review of a collection of stories by William Carlos Williams. Wishing not only to see my name in print but to star, I gave it the big-time treatment. "These twenty-odd minor stories, the detritus of a major poet's oeuvre, are marked by the modernist's impassive compassion." What they were really marked by was a mill town pediatrician's directness of eye and heart, but hot for paradox, I couldn't let that get in my way. When the review was turned down by my nonplussed friend, I took it to Herbert Barrows, who had been one of the judges of the freshman Hopwood Award and whom I'd since drawn close to.

A soft-spoken, diffident man with a singular wit, Barrows wasn't a New Critic. Far from it. He seemed to enter class directly from the pages of a James novel, an observer from the sidelines of life but, like Lambert Strether or Ralph Touchett, with his own fine force. I once asked him what it was like to have Auden teaching in Ann Arbor; Herbert said that he'd come there after Auden but "you could pretty well figure what it was like by the trail of sulfur he left."

The closest Herbert came to making a dogmatic statement was to say that a good prose style was like a simple, expensive black dress that you could make expressive in your own way. He may have told me that in his office the afternoon I brought my review of the William Carlos Williams stories to him. What I clearly remember his telling me then was that reading it made him feel like "he'd been hung up by his suspenders for five minutes." And then, "I don't know quite why you want to write this way, except maybe to be in the swim." He pointed out that when you wrote for a general audience like the *Daily,* the burden of interest was on you; or, in his words, "'Impassive compassion' is not exactly hot stuff on fraternity row." He wound up saying that he was teaching a course in "practical criticism" next fall that I might find useful.

The first weeks were hell. At the beginning of each class, Herbert would read a passage of fiction or a poem that we were supposed to respond to by writing a paragraph or two about what we found interesting or not. Habituated by now to search for complexity, I was left at the starting line every time. After writhing for most of the ten minutes we were given, I'd scribble some desperate gibberish that I once had to read aloud, shaking my head at my own words. The guy with the department's principal undergraduate scholarship had become the class dunce.

After the first few meetings, I approached Herbert for help. "Oh, you'll get the hang of it," he said and immediately changed the subject. It was strange to be put off by him, so much so that I sought out the voluble Marvin Feldheim, whose office was down the hall.

"Herbert is probably just letting you stew in your own juice for a while," he said. They had been Ph.D. students at Harvard together and were close friends, though Marvin was so outgoing and Herbert so indwelling.

"It feels more like boiling oil," I said.

"Well, maybe it should," Marvin said. "Maybe you're being punished for trying to pretend you're a Gentile."

"Me a Gentile?"

"Wasn't that how you became a Critic? With a capital *C*?"

"You're just baiting me now."

"No, I'm not. I'm just making a connection between the person who sat here last year and told me why he was for Ezra Pound and the person who's in the quandary you are in now."

"So all this has to do with my Jewish problem?"

"No, with the problem of finding one's own way of being literary. You opted for the New Criticism. But its ideology makes you feel like a fake goy, right?"

"I don't feel particularly Jewish anymore. But I don't see what that has to do with the trouble I'm having in Herbert's course."

"Do you feel particularly Episcopalian? Who are you for, Burbank or Bleistein?"

Suave, even a bit of a dandy, a man whose synagogue was the theater, Marvin was the last Jew on campus I would have expected to bring up the Jewish question in this intellectually crass way. "I'm not for either," I said. "Are you trying to shock me?"

"Not at all. I'm just suggesting you think a bit. You may not want to right now but someday you'll know what I mean. I hope it's not too late."

"In the meantime, why am I having so much trouble in Herbert's course? You told me last year that the reason I was going to be a critic was that I trusted my judgment instead of my imagination."

"That's right," he said. "Except that you've stopped trusting your own completely and are trying to imitate Cleanth Brooks's or God knows whose. You should try being a responsive Old Critic. It's worked for a long time now."

"How would it help me in Herbert's course?"

"One of its approaches is that a poem or a story is a highly individualized voice talking. If someone came into Herbert's class and started talking about himself or some other subject he was intense about, you'd listen and form an impression of him and then if I asked you what had gone on, you wouldn't have much trouble telling me. You'd have an impression and, if you were really alert, a crystallization of the impression known as a characterization. That's all that Herbert's asking you to do. That's why it's called practical criticism and once you stop faking yourself out with the fancy moves you'll do it well."

I bought the advice and let the insight go. Jewish solidarity—which was what I thought he was talking about (it wasn't; the force of his point wouldn't register for another five years)—seemed to me just another mode of Jewish groupthink. But in the meantime, I began to pay attention to what I was hearing and feeling and to try to characterize it.

I got a major assist from an older student in the class. By late 1951, he was one of the last of the veterans and his response was almost always arresting. At first I thought the hearing aid he wore might be a recording device that enabled him to replay the words that Herbert had read twice. But his advantage was his knack for finding words, often an image, that characterized the text, so that it emerged from his mind as freshly and expressively as it had entered. I remember his saying of a poem or story that it was like a calm stretch of sea where two mighty ships had just fought and gone down, which was just right.

At the end of Barrows's course I wrote a review for the *Daily* of
e. e. cummings's new collection. This one was published.

19

The hallucination of the rats did not return after we left for the summer, which we spent working at a hotel in the Borsht Belt. Because
there were no rooms for couples in the help's quarters, I slept in the
waiters' shack, Lynn in the waitresses' one. It wasn't a hardship but
respite from our problems. We behaved like the other young couples
on the staff who were just having a summer romance. At one point,
after we had made love at night by the lake, Lynn said, "You know
something? I'm beginning to really like you again." We talked the
matter through and decided that when we returned to Ann Arbor, we
would cultivate our independence from each other.

With Lynn this took the form of not asking for a job on the Ward;
with me, of going back to work there, which was a big step, given the
history. Because of our savings from the summer, she didn't have to
work and soon became engrossed in a course in Renaissance art. Also
she changed her style. "I'm tired of looking like a psych major," she
said and adopted a more arty look with a lot of black, like the actresses
in the Art Theater Club. But our new regime of "separateness," such
as not meeting for lunch, soon foundered in the old rut of analyzing
her problems.

This took a new turn in November when she began to awaken me
at night, saying that there was someone in the room.

The first time I was scared myself, the second annoyed, the third
alarmed. I called Dr. Charney, the psychologist at Student Health
whom Dr. R had recommended, and he began to treat her. Unlike
during the rats incident, Lynn did not become hysterical; the apparition that would appear was indistinct and passive, a haunter rather
than a stalker, though no less frightening for that, like the indistinct
face in the photograph in *Diabolique*. Except that Lynn's apparition

had no face. She said he was like a "three-dimensional shadow." I called him the "Night Intruder" and tried to speculate and analyze and even to joke him away. But a few nights later he would be back again, more foreboding than before. For he was stationed now closer to Lynn when she awoke, and his presence was becoming more distinct. A figure in a dark coat or cloak, his face turned away.

Lynn was under a moderate sedative, enough to get her to sleep but not enough to knock her out for the night. Dr. Charney believed that the apparition was a process that would work itself out and that to "plow it under" with drugs could be dangerous. He saw no reason to hospitalize her. "I don't think your wife is prepsychotic," he said. "Try not to make too much of these apparitions of hers."

I tried. It was hard because she developed a chronic twitch of her head in the evenings and also often slept with a thumb in her mouth. By day we went our separate way to classes and such and often didn't meet up until evening. I held on to my four-to-twelve shift on the Ward, biking home as quickly as I could, often to find Lynn in good spirits, unfazed by having spent the evening alone. But then the twitching might start. She was almost never depressed during the day and often elated. As part of our declaration of independence she was making friends of her own on campus and was bowled over by Marvin Eisenberg, the dynamic young professor of her Renaissance course. Also she had fallen in love with the sculpture of Donatello and was engrossed in researching a paper on his statue of the aged Mary Magdalene, writing about, as Lynn put it, "how Donatello made an old woman's face tell the story of the amazing thing that had happened to her." Eisenberg's lithe eloquence (he virtually danced as he lectured), the relief from the terror of her nights, the awakened passion for Donatello, the intensity of her identification with Mary Magdalene—all this could have the remarkable effect of creating a glowing daytime Lynn, whom I would meet at the League for lunch after Eisenberg's lecture (I was taking no chances) and find her so transformed from the cowering girl of the night or two before that the hands of Jesus himself might have been laid upon her. My brother, who studied in Ann Arbor a few years after we left, told me that Marvin Eisenberg still hadn't gotten over looking at Lynn in his course. "All in black, with those eyes! That hair! My God, what a figure she cut!"

In the talks we had about the possible identity of the Night Intruder, I had settled on her father, the phantom of her guilt about joining her mother during her adolescence in putting him down. Also, like the gentle Jake Ringler, as the figure drew nearer, he became less ominous, his turned-away body indicating he meant no harm. Her fear now, thanks to Dr. Charney, was not of what he'd do to her but of what he'd reveal.

One night Lynn awoke to find that the figure had moved to our bed and was sitting on the edge of it, still facing away but slowly turning toward her. Lynn woke me with a scream. It was not her father; it was not a man at all but a woman, dressed in black, her head covered by a kind of cloak. We turned on all the lights and clung to each other. Adopting Dr. Charney's attitude, I'd begun to feel like someone watching a particularly interesting, subtle horror film. But now I felt that I was in the film myself, for the fact that the Intruder was suddenly a woman with an identity to reveal made her more real, more to be reckoned with. "It's like she's come for me," Lynn said. We knew that she wasn't Lynn's mother; their relationship was so overtly hostile that it left nothing to the imagination. "Let's get out of here," I said. "I feel like I'm being asphyxiated by my mind."

"That's what it's been like for me all along," she said. I got us dressed and led her out into a windy moonlit night. There was nothing open at three in the morning, but a few blocks away was the university stadium. A deep, gigantic bowl, only the top of which was visible at street level, it offered some shelter from the wind. Normally, it would have been weird to be huddled in a stark empty stadium in the middle of the night, but its very vastness made it seem like a refuge from that little bedroom where the apparition had been sitting at the foot of the bed. Like the night of the rats, I was out of interpretations; I was out of my depth and unable to touch bottom. So I held Lynn against me and quoted poetry to her, until she said, "It's all right. We can go back there now."

The next visitation proved to be the last one. I didn't learn about it until the next morning, when I awoke to find Lynn already dressed, sitting at the kitchen table with a cup of coffee and a cigarette. She looked both stunned and stunning, the brightness back in her eyes, but contemplative as well. She looked like the Mary of an Annunciation as Caravaggio might have painted it. In all the gallery of her expressions, I'd never seen this one before. She turned to me as though from far away and said, "The Night Intruder came back last night. I saw her."

"You saw her?"

"Yes, she's a nun. The hood I thought she was wearing is a wimple. She turned to me and I could see she was a young nun who was smiling. There was nothing to be afraid of."

"Sister Agnes, I'll bet—the nun from St. Mary's."

"No," she said. "It was me."

"You?!"

"Me. Don't ask me what it means. And please, for once, don't try to tell me."

20

Morrie Fishkin continued to be the other fascinating person in my life, a trial and a gratification rolled into one. As he forged on into his treatment and his adolescence, the demonic choke in his brain appeared slowly to adjust itself, so that I was more often able to have a calm conversation with him.

This usually took place at our apartment, where Dr. R allowed Morrie now to come for dinner once a week. The presence of Lynn helped to gentle him and to keep the conversation from running out of bounds, where he still sometimes tended to carry it on the Ward, in his ongoing effort to get a rise out of people, especially me. Arriving on the dot of six, freshly showered, combed, and beaming, he'd announce that he had beaten his record in walking from the ward to our apartment and then would ask if we were glad to see him. On such repetitions did his fragile sense of continuity depend.

He had an equally strong effect on us—he changed the chemistry between Lynn and me and made us a family instead of a couple who often seemed to be staying together for the sake of their hangups. With Morrie there would be a kind of team spirit; helping him to feel at ease and appreciated seemed to do the same for us. He gave us more adult roles to play than we handed each other.

One evening he arrived while Lynn was listening to the *Saint Matthew Passion*. I got there a few minutes after he did to find the two of them sitting side by side. After the last record in the stack had dropped and played, he said, "I never heard anything like that before. What's it all about?"

"It's mostly about Jesus Christ's last days," I said.

"I wish you hadn't told me that." Jumping up, he began to pace about, going into his rapid delivery of words and spittle when he was upset. "JC freaks me out. Do you think that's because I'm Jewish, so Jewish, so Jewish I can't stand it. JC's so weird! I mean whenever I see JC on his fucking cross I get this weird, dizzy feeling in my brain, like my brain wants to throw up. You should have told me and I wouldn't have listened because I'm getting really upset."

His face was flushed, his eyes wild. I'd seen him blow a couple of times and it would go on and on until he was sedated. He had no stopper. I got very worried, very fast.

But Lynn stepped into the breach. She walked over to Morrie, put her hands on his shoulders, and said, "I know how you feel. I feel the same way about him sometimes. It's natural for us Jews. It's very natural."

And repeating that, patting his back, stroking his neck, she calmed him down.

That was the only time there was any trouble. Mostly he was on his best behavior, though that's off the mark because in time I didn't feel he was willing himself to be good but rather that a shy love rose from where it had been kept deep in his nature and took over.

After dinner, we would play Hearts, which he often won, much to his delight. He would always position himself so that he gave the three cards at the opening to me and not Lynn to cope with. He played with a combination of strategy, memory, and intensity that kept him ahead, but now and then I'd catch him slightly misplay a hand so that Lynn would take it.

On the ward he was the oldest child now, a complete loner, and often bored. He continued to want more of my attention than I could give him, and as time went on, he sometimes became sulky with me, telling me to leave him alone. Dr R said it was actually a healthy sign; Morrie would be leaving the ward soon and this was his way of separating himself.

The memory of our parting is reverberant and elusive as though I have just dreamed it. Morrie and I are standing on Hill Street, somewhere between our flat and the hospital. One of us is about to leave for good, though whether it's me going to New York or Morrie to his next placement, I can't recall. Though Dr. R allowed Morrie to come for dinner by himself, I had to walk him back to the ward. This evening he stopped there on the street and asked me to let him walk the rest of the way by himself. I said that I couldn't, that it was part of the deal.

"I'm asking you to," he said. If he'd said it in his sulky ward-behavior way, I would have put my foot down and risked a scene that would have been hard to handle. But he'd asked me in a calm, together way that impressed me. I didn't know what to do. I needed to consult Dr. R but, of course, I couldn't. Except in my mind. When I did so, he immediately told me to let him go, that it, too, was part of the separation.

After a last hug, he turned and started walking up Hill Street. I stood there, meaning to watch him as long as I could. After about twenty yards or so he turned to me. There was an expression of such loss on his face that I started to go toward him. But by the time I was halfway there, it had changed and he had a little smile. He held up his hand, whether to stop me or wave good-bye, I don't know. Then he went on his way and I went on watching him, until he turned off Hill Street toward the hospital. I went home, called the ward just in case, and then began to try to separate from him.

21

For my Honors thesis I chose to write about the pleasure/pain paradox in three odes of Keats, though given its resonances you could say the subject chose me. It took me back to the collection of his poetry that my mother had given to me as her blessing; it took me forward to an observation post of the New Criticism for what would prove to be a last look around; it took me inward into the emotional crux of an existence where pleasure and pain went together like gin and vermouth.

The thesis, along with the e. e. cummings review and a term paper that used Aristotle to criticize Coleridge, enabled me to graduate with honors, to win an undergraduate Hopwood Award, and to receive a scholarship to the University of Chicago. The writer and editor Baxter Hathaway, a Hopwood judge, wrote that he saw a critic in the making and invited me to contribute to *Epoch,* one of the leading literary journals of the day. So much for the pleasure from writing; its pain came when my stories went down for the third and final count in the Hopwood fiction contest and when I was turned down cold by the writing programs at Iowa and Stanford, which were the only ones going in 1952.

All of which was substantial evidence for the case that Marvin Feldheim had made about where my talent lay and where it didn't and also for the career I should choose. My previous life—in my father's glass business, in high school, and in the navy—was that of three different environments connected by a losing struggle to fit in and succeed. From the first day in Ann Arbor, I knew I was finally where I belonged and soon found my way to the front of the line. The University of Chicago looked to be even more right for me. It had a dual reputation for intellectualism and bohemianism; it featured its own school of Neo-Aristotelian philosophy and literary criticism, the latter being the leading adversary of the New Criticism. Aristotle and hip: how could I turn it down? It wasn't hard once I decided that what I really needed to do was to strengthen my will to be a fiction writer by following Stephen Dedalus's instruction to himself of "silence, exile and cunning." And so I persuaded Lynn to go off to New York with me to lead a life that I already had diverse evidence I was not cut out for. Or, given the original cutter, all too well cut out for.

PART TWO

Among the Fishes and the Flies

I

The Paris Employment Agency was located at 80 Warren Street, a six-story warren of them, ten or twelve to a floor, that catered mostly to the lower depths of the New York labor market—janitors, delivery boys, porters, dishwashers, manual laborers, and sweatshop workers; there was also a smattering of the skilled trades as well as waiters and waitresses who mostly worked as "extras." Warren Street agencies were typically hole-in-the-wall affairs, a desk or two behind a railing or partition and a few rows of benches in the larger ones which, given many of their occupants, seemed a little like chapels in a Bowery shelter. Each had a bulletin board outside festooned with cards scrawled in black crayon that described the jobs available:

Waiter. Full-time. Midtown. Excellent tips.
Clean Cut and experienced.

The job might exist but usually it did not, having been filled a week ago by another agency, but the sign was left up to rope in someone for a luncheonette in Canarsie or a job for the day. The Paris Agency was one of the better ones—more active, better jobs, less devious agents, as well as furniture and an atmosphere bordering on the respectable.

Having worked summers as a waiter as well as a stint at the Michigan Union dining room, I'd decided that a well-paying lunch job would be just right for an aspiring writer. At the Paris Agency I got one right way from a dapper little man named Maurice, who quickly let me know that he was really a cantor, and that he could see I was something else, too, But mainly I was "clean-cut," which was at a premium at 80 Warren Street.

The job, in the Wall Street district, was indeed the perfect lunch job—affluent clientele and a fast turnover. The trouble was that the turnover was a lot faster than I was, and two days later I was back at the Paris Agency. Maurice returned my fee, as he had to by law, told me that I had damaged his credibility, and henceforth treated me as he did the unclean-cut who hung around the Paris. After a month of losing another steady job and of cruising the other agencies to little avail, I became a regular extra.

So, while some of my literary contemporaries around this time were hanging out at the *Paris Review*, I had the Paris Agency, where I did a lot of my reading.

One morning I was settled into a chapter of *Ulysses* when a small, bald waiter dropped into the chair next to mine and gave me a hard once-over. We had worked together at the Glen Isle Casino one Saturday night without making a connection, which was not unusual, since temporary waiters tend to be turned inward, either guarding or deadened by the reason they've come to this pass. My seatmate was gaunt but otherwise exceptional looking. Starchy instead of sleazy, he wore a pristine white dicky rather than the usual wan, frayed, stained white shirt; his alpaca jacket was brushed instead of haggard, his tuxedo pants sported an actual crease, his shoes a shine, and he wore a sash. Also, he smelled of aftershave rather than booze or coffee, the Warren Street waiter's cleaning fluid. His heavy beard was shaved so close that it seemed like a beady shadow.

"I see you're reading that phony," he said by way of greeting. "Unless you're just trying to make an impression."

"1 imagine if I were, it would be pretty lost around here."

"The subjunctive too. Right. One phony reading another."

I might have gotten angry at that but this was the first informed, however peculiarly, conversation I'd had in the time I'd been hanging around there. Also his appearance piqued my interest. He didn't seem like a waiter but rather like someone who was dressed up as one. That is, like myself. Except that he looked like he expected to be sent to 21 and I to nowhere. "What have you got against James Joyce?" I asked.

"Decadent shit," he said in his vehement way. The phrase, too, was singular. I'd never heard anyone who knew the word pronounce it with a long a. On the other hand, I knew now where he was coming from.

"You sound like some of my old friends at YT'SL." I said.

"So you had a radical college experience. Right. You were for Henry Wallace but then you chickened out. Right." He used the word as though in his mind every single thought checked out. "You were a fellow traveler, now you're an internal émigré. Right. I can spot someone like you from a mile away. Go stuff your mind with more false consciousness, what do I care?"

"Why false consciousness?" I asked. "Give me an example instead of a diatribe."

He threw up his hands in disgust. "An Irish novel whose main character is a Jew. What are there, ten of twelve of us there? An ad salesman who's supposed to be Ulysses because of the wandering angle. That's not false consciousness? What did he think Ulysses was, a fucking spear carrier? Also, show me a Jew who likes kidneys, pork kidneys no less. That's as far as I had to go and I did plenty of skipping to get there too."

With that he returned to his sulk and I to my book. But a few minutes later he muttered, "Okay, I'll admit the funeral scene wasn't bad. At least you begin to get some social reality, some sense of the class structure of those Irish fucks."

"I thought you said you only went as far as the first Bloom chapter."

"I said that's all I needed to read. So I skipped ahead too. What's the matter with that? You think you're better than me because you pore over that decadent shit? Because you look up every word that no one ever uses except him? 'Ineluctable modality,' now what the fuck does that mean? Go ahead, tell me. I'll bet you can't.

I was trying to when our names were called and we continued the conversation, if you can call it that, into the subway and on uptown. "No, you've got nominalism all wrong," he said at one point, surprising me again.

We had been sent to the Harvard Club. "You're in your element here, aren't you," he sneered after we had set up and were waiting for our first customers. "What're you writing a book or something? *Down and Out in Manhattan?*" He invaded my privacy at will but rigorously patrolled his own. When I asked him what else he'd read of Orwell, he replied, "Nothing I want to go into here." Find out anything about him and the steel shutters would drop. When I asked him if Harvey was his first or last name, he replied, "What difference does it make?"

We worked a few other jobs together. One was a banquet at the Brook Club for Admiral William "Bull" Halsey, the George Patton of the Pacific war. We were given white gloves to wear, set the tables with actual goldware, and served the meal "French service," which I'd never done before. I came out of the kitchen wobbling a heavy tureen of turtle soup on a silver salver. Harvey, who had just finished serving one of his tables, rushed over to me and took the salver, tureen, and ladle. "Why didn't you tell me you'd never done this before?" He sent me back to refill his tureen. We then continued to work as a team, I delivering, he serving. He was terrific, without losing more than a degree or two of his chilled demeanor.

Afterward we walked together to the subway. The atmosphere was somewhat easier between us—two guys who had come through, thanks to the resourcefulness of one of them. I thanked him again.

"I'd probably be under arrest by now for assault with a scalding tureen."

"Bloated capitalists. War profiteers. Right! They deserve a lapful of their fucking turtle soup. One of their forks cost more than we were paid tonight."

"So much for the labor theory of value," I said, partly in jest, partly striking one of my thawing matches on this frozen pipe.

But there was no jest in Harvey. "You know why you say that? Because it's just an expression you've heard. When are you going to stop being so glib about life?"

"Life? What does my life have to do with the Brook Club? What does yours?"

"Plenty." Harvey looked left and right on the empty street as though there might be informers in a doorway of these East Side townhouses. He lowered his voice and explained to me how what we had been part of tonight was a "perfect but minor example" of the labor theory of value. "Marx would have taken the Brook Club and its warrior stooge for granted. To understand what you saw tonight you have to go to Gramsci or Veblen. You've heard of the theory of the leisure class, I assume, since you've heard of everything, though you've understood next to nothing."

By now his voice was back to its normal growl, his sudden volubility having triumphed over his strange furtiveness, also a tone of erudition over his usual irritableness.

"You sounded for a moment like a teacher I used to have."

"Ex," he said, again lowering his voice.

"Why ex?"

"That's for me to know and you to find out."

Baffling. One minute a didactic explainer, the next a childish game player. But there was something more than childishness in his response. There was fear, or if not quite fear, then suspiciousness. I hadn't come across anyone like him except maybe Dostoevsky's underground man. I didn't know from just what height, but I knew now that he'd fallen and was still, emotionally speaking, in pain.

One of the few things Harvey had told me about himself was that he lived with a sister in Brooklyn. It seemed like a lonely way to spend the rest of Saturday night, and I asked him if he wanted to stop off at my place on East Twenty-eighth Street. We could go somewhere for a drink or he could come home with me and meet my wife, whom I thought he would like.

"I'll take you up on the second," he said. "I don't like going anywhere in this monkey suit."

We were living in a "studio" in a small building that housed mostly sweatshops. The room was about twelve by sixteen with no windows and a skylight that didn't open. Which we didn't miss given the minimal heat supplied on weekends. Lynn was home from her job at Longchamps Thirty-fourth Street and met us at the door in jeans and a turtleneck, her hair piled up in a towel. Guests tended to turn on her glow. "Come into my boudoir," she said with a flourish of her hand. "You can take your coat off or keep it on. As well as your hat."

We sat around the kitchen table. With an electric space heater and the oven on, the room was only moderately chilly.

"How can you live in a place like this?" said Harvey.

"We pretend we're Eskimos," Lynn said. "You wouldn't by chance be the guy who thinks Joyce writes 'decaydent' shit, would you? Or are you the Dadaist?"

"I see my reputation has preceded me," Harvey said. "I'm not the Dadaist. That's Schein, another of us Warren Street regulars." Gone was the gruffness, gone was the wariness, replaced by a look I had never seen before, could scarcely have imagined—that of the youth he had been—shy, vulnerable, already a bit smitten.

An hour and several glasses of jug wine later, Harvey had put the cards he'd held so closely, faceup for Lynn's inspection. He'd been a history and economics teacher at a Brooklyn high school and had been

forced out in the purge three years ago. He told us how it had begun
with the faculty at CCNY and Brooklyn College and then had swept
down into the high schools, propelled by the Rapp-Coudert hearings.

Lynn and I were both still left-wingers who trekked to rallies at
Madison Square Garden to support Alger Hiss and William Rem-
ington, to save the Rosenbergs and Willie McGee—the early 1950s
version of the Scottsboro Boys. We subscribed to the weekly news-
letter of the brilliant, indefatigable I. F. Stone, whose investigative
reporting and judgment seemed the last hope of the left, and to the
Daily Compass, a mediocre tabloid somewhere between the defunct
PM and the *Daily Worker.* Reading it was to be made conscious of
how much further the radical left had diminished in the five years
since the Wallace campaign, how it had gone from the margin of
dissent to the edge of oblivion, its identity contingent mostly on its
victimization. Without Joe McCarthy and HUAC, without Whitaker
Chambers and Judge Irving Kaufman, who had eagerly sentenced the
Rosenbergs to death; without the Hollywood Ten and J. Robert
Oppenheimer, what would there be beside a kind of organized know-
ingness, nostalgia, and pathos?

However, it was one thing to think that and another to experience
the persecution and pathos in personal full force, which I did that
evening with Harvey. For he was one of the victims, and as with his
first seeing Lynn, once he began talking about his wrecked career, a
different person, the teacher he had been, emerged from behind his
barbed-wire defenses.

He was obsessed with Sidney Hook. He said that Hook's famous
essay, "Heresy, Yes—Conspiracy, No" had led directly to the Rapp-
Coudert Committee, which had purged hundreds of teachers in New
York City alone. "He got the public to believe that anyone with a communist perspective was ipso facto a Soviet agent. The argument behind
it was a disingenuous disgrace but because Hook knew how to argue he
got away with murder. Or, in this case, mass character assassination."

His gaunt face animated, his bald head nodding vigorously, his language on its best behavior, his right hand chopping the air, Harvey laid out the varieties of American communism—agrarian populism, trade unionism, even black nationalism—that had often resisted the Leninist-Stalinist line. He showed how Hook had fudged the issue of McCarthyism by joining its attack on what Hook called "ritualistic liberalism."

Through it all, Harvey remained articulate and cogent. Had he been like this in his classroom at his Brooklyn high school? It was easy to see him so—his gruff fervor driving his points home, piercing the thin, blasé attitudes that high school students brought into social studies classes. If he made converts (and what good teacher didn't?), he would likely make more adversaries and many more interested spectators. He belonged in a real suit rather than the monkey one he was wearing, standing in front of a class rather than serving from the left and taking from the right. I thought I could see now why he worked as an extra; it was his way of not giving in to the bastards, of staying in touch with the other person he'd been, with the fading potential he still possessed.

The evening wore on. Now in his cups, Harvey began talking about his present association with a Marxist study group that was reading Gramsci and applying his theory of class dominance to contemporary capitalist society. "Really eye-opening stuff," he said. "You two should come to one of our meetings." As he talked on, he made me think of a story by Isaac Rosenfeld, whom I was just then discovering. Titled "The Party," it deals with a splinter group of a Trotskyite splinter group. The meetings are hardly attended; the mimeograph machine is broken. "Why do we go on?" the narrator asks; and then answers himself, "We go on because we have been given a great promise. Someday the whole world will fall into our hands. The whole world! Then where would we run?"

~

Another of the Paris waiters was Frank Schein, an experimental poet who often scribbled alongside me while I read. Frank was my age and as sweet-natured as Harvey was dour. He was so sweet-natured that he didn't mind my response to his poetry, which made no sense to me, had no point. When I told him that the first time, he chortled as affably as if I'd said I loved it. "The point is that there is no point," he said. "I'm trying to activate the ninety percent of your mind you don't use, pique your sense of language, not just confirm it."

"But all those run-together phrases and dropped words and some words in red and some in black and the word *rhyme* at the end of each stanza and the form being that of a single parentheses… it's more like a puzzle than a poem."

"Great," he whooped. "You've opened the door to the great Dada. Now just keep your eyes open and let Him work on you." He opened the canvas briefcase he carried with him and peeled off two or three mimeographed pages from a thick sheaf of them. "Try these now," he said. "Have fun."

Fun? Poetry as fun? It was like saying truth or art was fun. Because of Eliot's dominion and the New Critics' preoccupation, poetry was the queen of literature, to whose austere rules and regulations the other genres were supposed to aspire. A well-written "modern" story was like an extended poem—every noun and verb and modifier mattered, each was putatively part of an intricate underlying circuitry so that only with the final lines that threw the switch would the whole light up with meaning. Fiction, like poetry, was an act of revelation, what James Joyce, my current mentor, called "an epiphany." Dada, of course, was also part of modernism, but nothing could be further from the religion of it than what Frank was doing, other than committing the "heresy of unintelligibility."

Which is why I admired him. He was leading the life of total devotion to his writing impulse that I wasn't, was taking all the risks associated with modernism instead of being burdened by its late protocols of taste and significance. Who was to say he was misguided? Were these pages that looked like typing run amok any less intelligible than the abstract cartoons of Miró or the black-and-white hullabaloo of Franz Klein or the shrieks and grumbles of Elliot Carter or the weird tunelessness of Ornette Coleman? Whatever value his writing would prove to have, Frank was engaged in the great enterprise of making it new. The payoff was that, though he lived and worked as meanly as I did, he had the cheerfulness and purposefulness of someone who was fully taken with his task. He was like a kid lost in play while I was like one who has played hooky only to find the day stretching emptily before him or else was sitting at his desk after school writing "I shall not be me" a hundred times.

2

Sometimes I would walk over to East Twelfth Street and hang around in the vicinity of the *Partisan Review* office, hoping to see Isaac Rosenfeld or Delmore Schwartz come out. Both of them wrote with the common touch that might make them approachable. What drew me to them even more was the sense of vulnerability that rose from their work like a prayer; that sense was precisely what I was trying to get into my fiction, or, as I would put it, "achieve" with my carefully calculated sensitive characters.

Especially Rosenfeld, and especially his story "The Hand That Fed Me," which deals with a young writer, Joseph Feigenbaum, in the aftermath of the 1930s, the era of which I seemed to be living a proxy version. The WPA Writers' Project has folded; the beginning of the war effort has passed him by; the last six women he approached have turned him down. He receives a Christmas card from a Russian (!) girl who flirted with him three years before, took him home for lunch, and then dropped him. Touched, wounded, hopeful, bitter, he writes one letter after another, none of which she answers. He becomes more desperate, even goes to her house and is thrown out by her brother. He sends a final letter to her, which ends:

> For after all what is humiliation? It does not endure forever. And when it has led us underground to our last comfort, look, it has served its purpose and is gone. Who knows what newer heights may not appear? I believe some men are capable of rising out of their own lives. They stand on the same ground as their brothers, but they are, somehow, transcendental, while their brothers are underground. Their only secret is a tremendous willingness—they do not struggle with themselves!

Sometimes you read a story or poem that sounds such deep personal chords of situation and sentiment that it feels like it was written by you. Such was "The Hand That Fed Me." At last I had found someone who understood what I had gone through (was still going through with Lynn), who was telling me what I needed to know, and who even gave an eloquence to my situation:

> Be gentle to the unfulfilled, be good to it. We are accustomed to sing the joys of the happy, the fulfilled men. Let us also sing the joys of the desolate, the empty men. Theirs is the necessity without fulfillment, but it is possible that even to them—who knows—some joy may come.

This heart-flooded ending that somehow managed to soar—at least in my lofty mind, busy with its own unwanted offerings—became a kind of personal anthem of consolation at Warren Street, at the bum jobs, at my desk. As though I were being ushered to my rightful place in the community of the unfulfilled, the Paris Agency sent me forth to meet other of my fellows.

~

One Friday in early November I was sent to Brighton Beach to work in a delicatessen. Though the weekend had come to this neighborhood of retired garment workers and commuting beachgoers, the news hadn't reached the Breakers Delicatessen and Restaurant. Judging from its dilapidated kitchen, its smoky walls and pitted linoleum, nothing had energized it for a long time. The woman who owned it was also the cook; the other worker was her daughter, who sold franks, fries, and soft drinks at the counter. As I set up the tables for dinner, my eyes couldn't take in enough of her. She was possibly twenty, demure, a bit dreamy it seemed, finely featured, and stacked to perfection, a Jewish Gina Lollabrigida, the beautifully divided tops of her breasts leading an alluring life of their own as she went about turning the franks and shaking the french fries and drawing the Cokes. She was doing all the business. The tables, it turned out, were mostly used by the elderly street customers, who brought their hot dogs to the table to chat with Mrs. Kalish, the owner.

At one point the daughter and I chanced to meet in the kitchen. "Hello, Mr. Waiterman," she said in a way that wasn't demure at all, that seemed to be giving me a ticket to the rest of the two moons. There were the teenage oafs crowding around the counter, trying to make time, to whom she was indifferent, and there was Mr. Waiterman to whom she wasn't. She was so delicious and I was so hungry.

By eight-thirty I had made maybe two dollars in tips, the worst gig in my career. Mrs. Kalish, who had spent most of the evening with her friends at the tables, asked what I would like for dinner. "I'm sorry you didn't do better," she said. "I thought this would be a good weekend because of the nice weather. But at least I can give you some nice pot roast. With latkes and applesauce? And a bowl of borscht and sour cream to start? And my cherry blintzes to finish." She could have said Spam and navy beans once she told me, "Melanie will be joining us."

So that was her name. What else could it be with all that sculpted softness? And candlelight, no less. "It's Friday night," Mrs. Kalish explained. But we don't bother anymore with the *bruchas*. You know what I'm talking about?"

"I know," I said. "*Shabbos*."

"He's Jewish," Mrs. Kalish said. "I told you so, Melmy."

Melmy nodded. "That's nice," she said, without appearing to take it in.

From that point on, Mrs. Kalish did most of the talking. Or rather questioning. "Maybe you two would like to take a nice walk on the boardwalk after dinner? What do you think, Melmy?" Melmy affably shrugged her shoulders—a response and a half.

The beach was probably chilly. On the other hand, there was the boardwalk with the soft sand and darkness underneath and the heat we could generate. On the third hand was the fact, arriving in my mind as sudden, late-breaking news, that I was married and hadn't come close to an infidelity, except in my fantasies, where I did so more or less nightly.

As we made our way from the borscht to the pot roast, potato pancakes, and red cabbage—all deliciously prepared—I began to realize two things: that Mrs. Kalish had a lot on her mind and Melmy very little. What she wanted to impress on me was that we were sitting in a place that had once been a gold mine. "This time ten years ago, they'd still be waiting for a table. By now we'd have done fifty, fifty-five, dinners with another hour to go. We had three waiters, a busboy, and two countermen. But mainly we had Lou Kalish, my late husband, may he rest in peace, who knew how to make a customer feel at home. You've heard of Nathan's of Coney Island. Well, let me tell you that around here it was The Breakers of Brighton Beach. And it wouldn't take much to bring it back. A man who knows the business and has a way about him and some money to invest. You look like someone who might have a *knipl* put aside."

Her open, rather hectic face had turned shrewd. She even gave me a calculating wink. I expected Melmy to have a reaction, one way or the other, to this pitch, but she maintained the same expression as before. Except it wasn't coy, I could see now, or even demure. It was vacuous. Lovely, zaftig, but probably retarded. My heart sank with sympathy and relief. The dead husband, the slow daughter, the decrepit restaurant, the disappeared clientele: that she could think of someone like me as a possible savior suggested a desperation without end. Did every temporary waiter who came here for an evening of standing around get the same meal and the proposition? How many had tried to take advantage of it? Why not me?

My lower part was saying, Yes; my upper part, Think it over. What would Joseph Feigenbaum do? The last six women hadn't turned me down, only the one that I was married to. The secret was not to struggle, to be one of the "transcendent men" who would take Melmy, her full body and slow mind, for a roll under the boardwalk. How many guys who came this way would be as gentle with her? To her and maybe even to Mrs. Kalish, who knows, a half hour of joy might come.

Such were my thoughts but they weren't the ones I had over the blintzes and sour cream. Without much more inner debate, I put Mrs. Kalish straight—I had no money to invest. I wanted to become a writer, not a delicatessen owner. I even added that I was married, so both of us would be sure to get the point of what a strictly moral person I was, how little I had to struggle with myself.

3

Our neighbors at the windowless room on East Twenty-eighth Street were the Gerundalos, Leon and Beth, he a pianist, she a painter who supported them by working as a welfare investigator. Wearing an old pair of tuxedo pants, Leon would stay home all day practicing his repertoire; wearing mine, I would return from Warren Street to practice my austere style on another new beginning—both of us preparing for our debuts. On the wall of the landing hung one of Beth's paintings, which appeared to be abstract but was an enlarged cross-section of a stone. "A perfect symbol of what's going on here," Lynn remarked.

Lynn was also waiting tables. Working five lunches and two dinners a week at Longchamps Thirty-fourth Street she wasn't quite supporting me but coming close and, unlike Beth, didn't see any reason for doing so. We got a cocker spaniel, mostly to have someone to talk to and touch when we weren't doing either to each other, and called her Nada, I to honor the waiter's version of the Lord's Prayer in "A Clean, Well-Lighted Place," Lynn to express our situation. Finally, unable to stand the comparison to Leon anymore, I found steady work as a typist in an ad agency. After a month or so, nothing else had changed except that working full-time I produced even less. By January we had had it, and hoping to get a life, we used Lynn's savings to fly to Berkeley and enroll in graduate school there.

Getting out of that room on East Twenty-eighth Street, however, soon proved to be an insufficient reason for me to buckle down to Middle English and "Principles of Literary Scholarship." I started a story about the Gerundalos but mostly watched my cut classes mount to the point of no return, while Lynn did the same with her philosophy courses, the latest tack of her ambition.

That summer we waited at adjacent gambling houses, the CalNeva and the CalVada, at Lake Tahoe. There I began fooling around at the craps table, and after winning two hundred dollars, I was hooked and wriggling. When I'd lost a night's tips at the CalVada, I'd take my last few bucks to a small joint known as the Bucket of Blood, where you could gamble for quarters. Twice I came back to the room we'd rented and stole some of Lynn's tips while she was sleeping and went back to the Bucket of Blood. After the second time she hid her money and resumed her New York attitude, leaving me to my obsession.

Lake Tahoe is one of the most beautiful lakes in the world, but the only green that drew me was the felt of the big table; the only blue, the azure dollar chips. When I wasn't gambling I was replaying the previous night's action: the crucial passes I hadn't made, the fabulous runs I had gotten off of too soon, the failure to follow my resolution to quit when I was a hundred dollars ahead and not try to get even all at once. With a desire run amok, a fixed idea that I was living for, I had again managed to enter but good the Dostoevskyian world.

What drew me back to the tables was something akin to the excitement of a date with an irresistible woman. What kept me there was the fulfillment of other powerful desires. One was "surge" when the dice came around to me and I took them, blew on them, and threw them. Not only my hopes but those of most of the others at the table were riding on me. If the players didn't throw the dice I doubt that I would have gambled at all; I had no interest in blackjack or roulette for that reason. I would always seek out the "hot" crowded crap tables where the heavy action was. Now and then I would hit a streak of six or seven passes, and by the fourth one the table would have gotten behind me with side bets and the surge would come and I would just know that I'd throw a natural or make my point or have a long sevenless run in which I'd make my side bets and everyone else's and feel like not just a winner but a star.

One afternoon we were lying on a blanket at one of the lake beaches when Lynn said, "There's something I need to talk to you about."

I thought that she was about to say she was going to leave me if I didn't stop gambling.

"I'm not telling you this to hurt you but rather to help you. But in any case, there's something you need to know."

I was hardly listening, immersed in reading *Invisible Man*, which had recently come out. Another underground man but coming from a wholly new place. It made me want to write again. So I didn't want to get into another of those interminable discussions about what was wrong with our relationship, beginning and ending with me. But she immediately got my undivided attention.

"I know I've not been much of a companion to you," she said. "I have my own obsession. And I think you may have picked that up without realizing it and now you're paying me back with this gambling."

"I don't know what you're talking about," I said. Because I truly didn't. "How could I be paying you back for something I was not aware of?"

"I don't mean consciously," she said. "A good deal of marriage takes place in the unconscious, you know."

"So do most things these days," I said. "What are you leading up to?"

"I've had my own obsession," she said again, with a little imperious glint in her eye that told me that my worst fear was about to come true. "I've decided to tell you. But I don't want you to interrupt me."

And so she did. A short account of how she had come to be "secretly married" to someone else since our last months in Ann Arbor. He had been the teacher in her course in symbolic logic, which she'd aced while getting incompletes in two of the others. He was a short sturdy guy, probably in his early forties, with a buzz cut and a hard, dry manner of teaching. Bill Hamilton. Very Gentile, as I almost pointed out.

She described how he had developed a presence in her mind, first as a mentor, then as a friend, then as a lover, and then, once away from Ann Arbor, as a husband. She could summon him and he would be there in a moment, not just the thought of him but his presence. He made her happy, balanced, and most of all, hopeful. "Whenever any shit is going on with you or someone else, I can turn to him. Whenever one of my dark times comes, he leads me out of it. Whenever anything beautiful happens I can share it with him. I haven't had any suicidal thoughts since I've known him."

As she went on talking, her tone changed from imperious to descriptive to soulful. And my reaction changed from jealousy to curiosity to a kind of dry-mouthed sympathy. He had only taken her out for coffee a couple of times and then told her that since they were both married, they'd "better get off the train before it crashed." And that had been that. For him.

"So now you know," she said, lifting rather than breaking the spell, coming back to me, sort of, halfway. "I thought you'd be more upset," she said. "You were so jealous of Claude."

"I'm surprised myself," I said. "I guess I'm getting used to…" I was about to say "your intense fantasy life" but drew back because it seemed wrong and even dangerous to say that, as though I'd be treading on her spirit by comparing Bill Hamilton to Sister Marilyn, as we called her apparition. Hamilton seemed mostly like a do-it-yourself form of therapy. And the truth was that she had been less depressed, healthier, easier to live with. No more intimate but no less: there were still the three or four times a month when she would warm to me, though, of course, I now knew whom she was thinking of. But then, too, I would have my own fantasy to spice up things. though a more promiscuous one.

So we sat there on the blanket, the beach almost deserted now, the late August shadows descending from the mountains, where summer was already ending. Then, her eyes suddenly brimming, she said tenderly, "You think this will help your with your gambling?"

"I hadn't thought of it," I said. "I don't think it has anything to do with you, anyway." The mood had lightened enough for me to say, "Each to his own madness."

"So you're not going to leave me?"

"Not unless you're planning to go back to Ann Arbor."

"I want to go back to the Village," she said, "and make a go of it this time. I want you to have another chance at writing and I think I'm going to study acting. What do you think?"

"Well, you certainly have the imagination for it," I said. "My very own Alla Nazimova," I added, putting my arms around her, drawing her, willing, down to the blanket for a consoling tender moment.

And then it happened. A look came over her—her eyes narrowed into an unmistakable leer, her mouth grew greedy, her nipples hardened, she began to shiver, her body became heavy. "I want you to fuck me," she said. "Really fuck me." And so we hurried to our room and I did so, three times, soup to nuts, this way and that. Best of all, we achieved our first mutual climax. For once, I knew enough to keep my mouth shut. Also, I had to because the fantasy that came raging through my mind each time, making me feel virile and masterful, and then got me off, was that I was Bill Hamilton.

4

Back in New York we got lucky and walked into the apartment of our dreams—mine at least—a cold-water flat on Macdougal Street. Thirty dollars a month for three rooms with its own new toilet. Otherwise it needed a lot of work. Inhabited by an Italian family for the past forty years, its windows were rotted under their newspaper insulation. But windows were something I knew about, and we set to work repairing, plastering, painting. The work would make the place our own, make us Villagers who had earned the right to be there; true Bohemians who didn't mind a sixth-floor walk up. Also it was close to the roof where Nada could do her earthy business. She quickly proved to be a Village dog who looked for any opportunity to bolt down the six flights of stairs and out into the smells and generosity of the mixed Italian and tourist street life, leaving me to walk up and down Macdougal Street calling, "Nada, come!" like a demented nihilist.

The climb and the repair work were a small price to pay for the Village glamour and the neighborhood contacts—the "Syndicate," as it was called then, owned many of the nearby nightclubs and jazz clubs, which they staffed with local talent. With the patronage of Tommy Corallo, a friendly neighbor and fellow waiter who was related to the famous Tony Ducks, I put my Italianate complexion to use and soon had a steady weekend gig at Cafe Society Downtown and two nights a week at Eddie Condon's, the only waiter in either place, as far as I could tell, who didn't have a police record.

What I came to like about Macdougal Street was its day life as an Italian neighborhood. The well-kept tenements, the pungent food stores, the serious tradesmen shops, the espresso parlors, gave off a robust, dark, foreign sobriety that stimulated and settled me. But by evening and especially on weekends, the neighborhood would be transformed. I would sometimes sit on the windowsill I had managed to restore, and gaze down at the flocks of tourists, striding and craning, hoping, just as I had a few months before, to breathe the air of liberation.

I was no more liberated than before but because of them, I made lots of money in clubs, which put me right in the middle of the prevailing atmosphere; for what the neon lights along West Third Street and around Sheridan Square signified was the new commerce of cultural pretense. Whatever the Village had once stood for, it was now mainly a fashionable place to live, to shop, to date, to cruise, to booze. As the lofts and studios were demolished and replaced by high-rise or midlevel apartment buildings, I sensed the ending that was taking place, just as I did on Saturday nights at Cafe Society Downtown, where a sly, sensual Josh White held his uptown and suburban audience in awe (the men) and rapture (the women) with "Jelly, Jelly, Jelly" and his other sexy ballads, leavened by an occasional sharecropper, chain gang, or other protest song that had made his earlier reputation. At Eddie Condon's, an artist like Lester Young or Art Tatum had to compete with the table conversation.

Under the spread of affluence, even tenement-lined Macdougal Street was not what it seemed to be. The sculptor across the street, who had designed sets for Piscator, now spent most of his studio time giving lessons to women members of the ILGWU to pay for his house in Woodstock. The Cuban painter downstairs had poured more than five thousand dollars into his twenty-two-dollar-a-month flat. The wild-looking guys I watched drinking at The Kettle were not painters but mostly neighborhood construction workers or movers; and at the San Remo the haggard urbane types weren't the free-floating café writers I had taken them for but teachers at NYU, book editors, or even ad writers.

After work, I would drop in at the San Remo, where I was told the writers in the Village did come—those who weren't at the White Horse, on the other side of the Village. I sat at the bar and nursed a bottle of beer for a number of evenings without any particular literary action occurring but attentive to the moves of two lithe black girls whose cheeks were tinted green and who seemed to know a lot of the men there. One night I heard a conversation going on among a small group of men at a nearby table in which the name Wystan was dropped once or twice. They were playing a game in which each would quote a familiar line of poetry and then his own next line. A beefy, blond fellow with a petulant mouth and a commanding voice, who reminded me of Strowan Robertson, knocked me out with "Full fathom five thy father lies, / Among the fishes and the flies."

He caught my chuckle. "Why don't you just sit down here. You're practically leaning into our conversation anyway."

I got down from the stool and joined them. "I was wondering if the Wystan you keep referring to is Wystan Hugh Auden."

"How do you know his middle name?"

"'I Wystan Hugh Auden and Louis MacNeice / In the twentieth year of the Western peace,'" I quoted.

"Go on," he said. I did, for another ten lines or so.

"Impressive," he said. He told me his name was Chester and introduced me to the other three. One was a robust, friendly guy about my age named Arnold; the other two were older and more uptown stylish.

"Auden is one of my gods," I said, to say something bright, to get out of my waiter's self-image. But I wasn't just trying to make an impression. My copy of his *Collected Poems* was coming apart from heavy use, though I wasn't keen about the current Auden, who had forsaken his role as the public poet of the age and entered *his* Anglican period.

"We were wondering about you," said Chester, who seemed to be the master of ceremonies. "You look like a Bronzino. Are you Italian?"

"I'm taken so at Eddie Condon's, where I've just been working," I said.

"You're Greek?" asked one of the others.

"No."

"Lebanese or somewhere around there?"

Normally I didn't like such questions, since they had an ethnic belittlement attached to them. In the navy I had been called "Ayrab" and resented it. But coming from these literary guys, I was flattered. No one had ever compared me to a painting before. They made me feel exotic. "Black Russian," I said, to keep up the impression.

"Do you come here often?" Chester asked.

"Sometimes. I live down the street," I said.

"Would you like to meet Auden?"

"Do you know him that well?"

"Pretty well," he said. "I live with him. Come over some afternoon. I'll introduce you and also play you *The Rake's Progress*."

I had heard him being called Chester but I hadn't put one and one together. "Then you must be Chester Kallman," I said. "I just read two of your poems in *New World Writing*." All at once the literary life of New York that I had been vainly pursuing was coming at me with open arms.

I started talking about one of his poems so that he wouldn't feel I valued him just because of his connection to Auden but he didn't seemed interested in my view of them, which made him seem all the more august. The talk in the next half hour was mostly about Virgil or Glenway or Christopher or other members of literary high society, and my head spun as I tried to put last names to their first ones, to locate places like Ibiza and the Marais.

At one point one of the lithe black girls passed close to the table, her fingers trailing close to Arnold's, and then his eyes met mine on our mutual return from watching her fine chassis. "You interested?" he said.

It was one of those moments when the ground on which you stand suddenly becomes a gorge; you can make the leap or you can turn back to being who you were. On my own, I would have turned the possibility down—as I had done the few times a clear one came up since I'd gotten involved with Lynn. But circumstances had changed. I was now entering the literary life, where one was supposed to be promiscuous or at least liberated—saying yes to Arnold seemed as much a credential as knowing Auden's poetry and having a strong position about his change of direction from politics to religion. As for the morality issue, wasn't I owed one from Lynn's secret marriage to Hamilton? Underneath the rapid calculation going on was a bounce of sexual confidence that had continued after that night at Lake Tahoe. So I jumped.

∾

By the time I got home it was 3:30 A.M., normally a safe hour to arrive. But Lynn was waiting at the kitchen table. It was as though one of my lungs had stopped working. Lightheaded, unreal, I sat down, and putting on a big rush of excitement, I told her about meeting this guy who lives with Auden and some other writers, trying to talk myself back to myself. "I've spent the last three hours in the literary Big Time. You know how I've waited for this. So I couldn't tear myself away."

The more I told her what we'd talked about, the stonier her face became.

When I finally stopped, she said, her nostrils flaring with disgust, "Your friend Chester uses a very raunchy perfume. When did you decide to become queer?"

"I'm not queer and you know that better than anyone else. I came home a little late, so don't go apeshit."

"I don't even need the perfume. As soon as you walked in, I knew you'd been unfaithful. Now I learn, or maybe relearn, that you like men. Anyway, I don't know you anymore. And what's more, I don't want to know you."

"What's that supposed to mean? Have you freaked out again? Is that's what's going on?"

"No, I haven't freaked out, if that's what you're hoping. But go ahead. Be hateful as well as unfaithful and dishonest. Throw your whole rotten character at me. You bastard!" At that point she began to scream it.

This time, of course, there was no holding her until she quieted down. So I shouted, "I haven't been unfaithful to you so shut the fuck up before we're thrown out of this place too."

That didn't work either. Nothing worked. Afraid that the rats would return, I said, "If you stop this nuttiness I'll tell you the truth."

With that she stopped screaming, poured a glass of wine from the bottle she'd been hitting, and lit another of her Viceroys. "He'll tell me the truth," she said and suddenly began laughing, as though sharing the joke with someone.

"The truth is that I picked up two girls with another guy, a playwright, and we went to his place but I didn't... I couldn't. I felt too guilty. So now you have the truth. So now you can scream or laugh or ridicule me some more."

She went silent, cold silent. After a time she said, "Washed in self-pity, the rat tries to become a lamb."

"Have it your way." I was too miserable now to respond.

"So you couldn't get it up," she said. "Who was she?"

"They were sisters who hang out at the San Remo. Negro. Sort of exotic floozies."

"Hm, I thought exotic floozies were just your speed. Isn't that what you told me the last time you put me through this hell?"

"I'm not putting you through any hell. You're putting yourself through it. So I strayed, or tried to. So is that really more destructive than you being shacked up in your mind with Hamilton for a year or more?'

"Don't you dare!" she shouted.

"Dare what? Take his name in vain?"

"That was a fantasy. It kept me alive. It kept me sane."

"A fantasy. And when you were too tired again or had another of your opportune headaches that was a fantasy too."

"Don't hand me that old shit of yours. We finally have something together and look what you've done to it. It's the timing, you bastard. Can't you see that? How could you after we finally could make love the way we both wanted, the way you told me so fulfilled you? How could you?"

Which was how she got me by the short hairs of guilt. And would hold on to them.

~

I never did get to meet Auden or receive his co-librettist's tour of *The Rake's Progress*. A week or two after the debacle with the girls from the San Remo, I ventured into the Minetta Tavern and there was Chester. But this time he paid no attention to me, for he was giving all of it to two sailors, very much now a rake making his own kind of progress. So seeing that his interest in me was probably no more literary than it was with the two gunner's mates, I decided that I'd had enough of the Big Time for the time being.

But I continued to read Isaac Rosenfeld and to look for writers and artists in the Village who lived mainly for and through their work and who might father or brother my ambition to do so and possibly even set me straight, show me how to put my writing back in touch with my élan instead of my depressiveness. It would only take one, I thought, but the evidence of their existence was scarce. The *Partisan Review* group, the one I was particularly attracted to, was scattered among various universities: Rosenfeld and Bellow at Minnesota, Rahv and Howe at Brandeis, Kazin at Amherst, and so forth. One of the regular features of *PR*, the onetime center of "alienation," was a "Letter from the Academy"—the very place I'd recently left. Even more unsettling to me was its symposium, "Our Country and Our Culture," which I came upon around this time, two years after it appeared, to learn, in Philip Rahv's words, that American writers and intellectuals had "ceased to think of themselves as rebels and exiles"—the very two things I had moved to New York to become. The terms now were *adjustment* and *reconciliation*, and the sense of new opportunities and well-being that came from embracing American society was almost as apparent in the pages of the symposium as it was at Cafe Society Downtown.

As for alienation, I had been learning about that not from writers but from my fellow waiters—the alcoholics, the compulsive gamblers, the devitalized refugees and survivors of the Holocaust—and by now I could see that it was either a posture, fastidious and superficial, or else a fate—a slow crushing of the social nerve, a cold remoteness and self-centeredness, of which no one could want more than his lot and which only some genuine achievement of art or intellect could possibly redeem. Two such cases had come into my view—Beckett and Genet. In the light of their intransigent deviance and vagrancy, their strategy of constituting the self in the midst of its nullity, of grasping existence at its bleakest extremes, I began to regard my running around New York in my dingy uniform as a particularly demoralizing form of self-abuse. Beckett and Genet were what it meant to take alienation seriously, to live it out, to invite in its demons. I had merely cut myself adrift, a professional type without a profession.

5

Thinking once again that we might get out of our deepening rift by changing its venue, Lynn and I rented a cabin in Maine—two hundred dollars for the summer and as long as we wanted to stay thereafter. It turned out to be the pastoral equivalent of a cold-water flat—a two-room ramshackle cabin with a few sticks of furniture, a truckle bed with an old tick mattress, and no plumbing at all. We fetched water from a well and heated it on a gas stove whose oven didn't bear looking into, much less using. The cabin was surrounded by major trees and a wide inlet, which, when the tide was just right, you could swim in for a minute or two. The owner, a disgruntled writer who had stopped publishing ten years ago, lived nearby, but once he had handed us the key, a can of kerosene for the lamps, and an axe, maul, and wedge, he returned to his lobstering and drinking and left us to our own rural devices. "Good," I said to Lynn, picking up the axe and heading for the minuscule woodpile, "Emersonian self-reliance. Just what we need."

"Don't chop off a toe," Lynn said. "We may want to get out of here after sleeping on that mattress."

We stayed until the day after Thanksgiving. I wrote another sensitive story in which nothing much happened except for the burst of consciousness at the end; it was about another of life's displaced persons—this time a cousin of Lynn's who had dropped out of Brooklyn College to support her mother and regarded us as though we had come directly from the Sorbonne. But otherwise I happily chopped wood, abetted by a hurricane that toppled trees one scary night, retaught myself Latin, started German, and read all the Dreiser, Faulkner, and Fitzgerald in the public library in Bath. We had a '42 Plymouth on the last of its bearings and springs, so we used it only for our weekly trip to Bath and walked the two miles through the woods each day to the general store/post office in Robin Hood. We stayed away from the summer crowd and took up with a young electrician down the road who taught me how to fish, chop wood, and change my own oil, while his wife was rusticating a surprisingly compliant Lynn.

An hour or two each day she would rehearse one or another speech from *The Seagull* for her forthcoming audition at the American Academy of Dramatic Arts. I'd be outside chopping wood and I'd hear, coming up from the bay, "I am a seagull. No, I am an actress…" She was good, already professional in her projection of Nina's moodiness, and her husky, mellow voice was made for the stage. Her new interest gave her spirit a lift, refocused her mind. Away from the Village and its dire memory, she began to turn to me in the truckle bed instead of coldly coexisting there. We did a lot of berrying, and at night, the Maine fall coming on fast through the chinks, I'd happily sing "Hey huckle, buckle, Come truckle with me." By October she was pregnant.

Once we were sure of that, everything began to change. It was as though while we were walking our wobbly tightrope someone had put in a floor: that is, a steadying reason for us to be married. Back to New York, I gave up the Village club jobs for the Oyster Bar in Grand Central Station, which got me into Local 1, with its medical benefits. When the word went out that the union was looking for volunteers to picket the Stork Club, I went on the line. Picketing this bastion of celebrity and privilege soon lost its thrill in the December cold, but I kept at it, having being told that it was the best way to put down a marker at the union.

So it proved to be. I soon found myself working at Blair House, a famous steak house in the West Fifties where the menu was simple and expensive and no one was in a hurry. The manager, Connie Immerman, had owned the Cotton Club in Harlem, managed gambling houses in Havana, and was now in his vivid sunset years: a tough Jew with a lot of Broadway color. His brother-in-law had been Benny Friedman, ("the greatest of the great Jewish quarterbacks, kid, and I don't wanna hear about Sid Luckman, who couldn't run a foot") and when I told him that I had gone to Michigan, he began to take a shine to me, which brightened further when he found out that I wrote in my spare time. "You're going to write my memoirs, kid, and we'll split a million bucks. Guaranteed." Meanwhile, he threw some of the "live ones" my way—Fred Allen and Billy Rose; Dan Topping, who owned the Yankees; and David Sarnoff, who owned RCA. ("Take good care of him, General, he's the only Phi Betta Kapper we got here.") Thanks to Connie, the money poured in.

Between the lunch and dinner shifts at Blair House I would go to the Horn and Hardart's on Fifty-seventh Street where you could sit for hours over a coffee and a piece of pie from one of the little glass cages. Instead of the torpid silence of the public library, which only added to my own, I wanted to be surrounded by the hum of life and the rhythm of the day produced by the quick snackers, the rendezvousers, the tourists, the indigents, the lingerers. My instinct was right but its practice remained barren: what connected me to my experience seemed to evaporate when I tried to put it into words on a page. I could tell my stories of being a waiter—indeed I would do so to anyone who would listen. But they remained stuff to drink with or dine out on. None lent themselves to my touchy style; instead of turning rich and strange they became dull or noisome. Chester Kallman's improvisation—"Full fathom five thy father lies / Among the fishes and the flies"—summed it up perfectly.

As I sat in the cafeteria one afternoon, I thought of Sir Philip Sydney's famous instruction for writer's block. "'Fool,' said my Muse to me, / 'Look in thy heart and write.'"

As usual, nothing happened. In time, two lines of Yeats came to mind. They were about the Irish rebellion but they rang my bell: "Too long a sacrifice / Can make a stone of the heart."

The words had the terse gravity of an epitaph. I wrote them down, closed the notebook, went out of the cafeteria, and walked over to Central Park. It was a warm afternoon in early spring, one of those days when even Manhattan bears a tenderness to life. Even the muddy, littered path down to the lake spoke of renewal, the fresh chance, that I didn't feel at all. On the contrary. The stony heart in my consciousness reminded me of a saying my father had handed me when he was complaining about his marriage: "Alone is like a stone." It sounded like something translated from the Yiddish that probably his father, another misplaced and locked-up man, estranged from even his own family, had passed on to him. "He knew about everything except how to make a living," my father had said with the bitterness of the fifteen-year-old glazier he'd had to become. My mother had been close to "Poppa" and had always said I took after him. Would I, then, end up as some Greenwich Village version of him—the man who sat in the back of his glass shop in Elizabeth with his Zionist correspondence and his translation of the Koran while his only son went out and replaced broken house windows?

I had been in New York for most of three years now. What would I be like in ten if I stayed here? Probably no different at all from the Village types I drank with in the San Remo and Minetta's—interesting failures five or ten or twenty years further along. I had seen how bitterness was collecting like rust on Harvey's spirit so that it seldom moved anymore. Frank Schein was another story, but his energetic self-publishing already had a sense of permanent futility; thirty years from now he would still be writing his cult-of-one work and supporting himself in one marginal way or another. Or else he would adjust, as I needed to do.

For soon I would become a father, perhaps of a son. What example would I pass on to him? Everything in me that had wanted to be, like the young Henry James, "just literary" seemed to collapse against those hard words of Yeats and the bitter ones of my father. Then a phrase came to mind by a much older Henry James—"the madness of art"—along with the famous description of the literary vocation. I intoned the words to myself: "We work in the dark, we do what we can, we give what we have. Our doubt is our passion and our passion is our task. All the rest is the madness of art." I was full of doubt, but where was the passion for the task? I'd had it at the start; where had it gone? Probably into the stories I hadn't allowed myself to write, hadn't given what I had—not just those from my present life, but also those from my early one, such as the Saturday morning on the way to The Shop—I was eleven or so—when my normally obdurate father, complaining of his marriage, had told me that "alone is like a stone" and later had broken down and wept in his little office while I watched from the glass racks outside and saw him anew.

I sat there on a bench in Central Park beside the small lake, scummy with new algae, and tried to understand, really for the first time, the "block," the "sieve," the "abyss" I had been cultivating as well as deploring. No doubt part of the hole in my mind, down which my writing thoughts fell, had always been there; indeed, it was what writing was supposed to fill. During the first year in Ann Arbor of Romantic feeling and expression and self-discovery, writing had filled it. This had led me on, committed me. But then I had opted for "art," for T. E. Hulme's "dry feeling," which didn't merely fill the self but fulfilled it, made it admirable, redeemed it.

I began to grasp the grievous mistake. Why hadn't I written more than two scared paragraphs of the story of that funny and sad evening at the deli in Brighton Beach? Was it merely because Chekhov would have done it better? Or Isaac Rosenfeld carried it further? So what? That's what apprenticeship was for. Wasn't the truth that I didn't *want* to write about it because I would have to go into my own life, to bare myself, or a character close enough to me, to present my dreary circumstances as well as my lust, my ambivalence, my evasive moralism, my habit of standing in my own way—truths I would have to cope with. Wasn't the basic truth that what I wanted from writing was another self that wasn't my divided, sad-sack one that had failed to screw exotic, green-faced Bonnie and then failed to keep it from Lynn? Weren't the qualities of style I aspired to precisely those that had enabled me to avoid the coarse and uncertain and troubled life I'd mostly known as a youth and now had managed to resume without its hope? What other heart did I have to look into? The impassive tone, the fiddling with sentences, the barely visible conflict, provided an illusion of mastery—control without confrontation, refinement of surfaces, mere gestures of bloodless good taste. As Saul Bellow had said of writers like me, they want to be praised for the offenses they do not commit; or as the poet George Barker put it, "They handle the bit and the snaffle all right, / But where's the bloody horse?" No wonder I was plagued by the guilt of being an impostor. There *was* an impostor in me, a false self that wished to stand above my groping existence and be admired for its artful cunning and grace. No wonder the rest of me had become so unsure, my writing feelings so dried up.

For the next month or so I tried to put this new insight to use, to break the habits of literary constraint and false pride. It was a desperate experience, dogged by the sense of wasted years, of having run out of time. The balled-up sheets of yellow paper and Lynn's growing belly were obvious signs of that. So was our flat at the top of the six flights of stairs she had to climb, and whose dinginess we had not been able to carpenter, plaster, or paint over. I didn't want this life anymore, and certainly not the future it led to. It was all right, it was possibly destined, for my father's son to become a waiter; it was not all right and certainly not destined for my child's father to remain one. It was time to resume the other life while I still had time.

A nice elderly woman taken to Blair House for Mother's Day asked me what I did "on the side." Formerly I would have been eager to tell her, but now I said, "Very little."

"I thought you might be continuing your education," she said sweetly.

"That's so," I said. "I'm saving up for graduate school."

6

Lynn breezed through her audition at the American Academy but soon found the classes silly. "This is a school for kids coming to New York from Kansas with stars in their eyes and air in their heads." She particularly had it in for her acting teacher, an enervated Englishman, whom she summed up by his signature phrase, "In the professional theater, my dears…" After a month she dropped out. "They treat me like I'm an escaped convict hiding out there. Imagine what it will be like when I'm walking around with my big unprofessional belly."

The role she stepped into with ease and full-heartedness by the second trimester was that of expectant mother. It was as though the affection and attention that she had lavished on Louise in Ann Arbor now regathered around the "bump that's already kicking" in her stomach. I'd come home from Blair House to find her engaged in a humorous meditation/conversation with "Nina" about the world she was coming into, the family members she'd have to cope with, the plans Lynn had for her. Also there was a physical happiness that contributed to the psychological one. As her breasts enlarged, she became very proud of them, wore clothes that enhanced their new heft and curve. They also reassured her: she was "growing two jugs," which meant that she would be equal to motherhood, would indeed make a major go of it. To see this volatile girl turning into a calm, uncomplaining madonna was all the more inspiriting.

By the eighth month we needed to leave the walk-up and I heard that the union was trying to organize a new million-dollar beach club in Lido Beach and was looking for waiters to work there. I jumped at the chance to move us, to make a big killing, and to give our infant a wonderful start in life by the sea. I found us a cheap place for the summer in nearby Point Lookout. It was a kind of seaside tenement, but Lynn and the baby would be at the beach a lot and we would save that much more money for Chicago, where I'd decided to go to graduate school rather than return to Ann Arbor, where life would probably be easier but, as I decided, too banal.

We moved to Point Lookout in mid-May and Lynn went into labor a month later. In the middle of the afternoon. Which meant that we were some thirty miles from Doctors' Hospital in Manhattan and reached Southern State Parkway in the middle of the rush hour. Jammed in between cars, alternately cursing the traffic and myself for getting us into this precarious situation, I tried to monitor Lynn's contractions and keep us from getting banged into when I desperately switched lanes or rode the shoulder and tried to get back in before the turnoffs. Visions of screams and gore and umbilical cords barreled through my mind. Except for the contractions, Lynn meanwhile was almost serene: emergencies often did that to her.

"We should be flying a sign," she said. "Instead of 'Just Married,' 'Almost Delivering.'"

"What we should have is a police escort."

A few minutes later, she said, "I think your wish is coming true." Parked on the shoulder ahead of us was a patrol car with a state trooper standing alongside and motioning with his thumb for us to join him.

I explained the situation. He wasn't impressed. "How you doing, honey," he said to Lynn.

"I'm a bit uncomfortable."

He nodded. "Your first, I betcha."

"Stay in your lane," he said to me. "You'll get there in plenty of time if you don't have an accident."

Which proved to be true. More true than either of us wished. By the time we reached Doctor's Hospital on the Upper East Side, Lynn was in serious labor, but her ordeal and my vigil were just beginning. Through the early evening I waited with the other prospective fathers. And went on waiting while each of them got the happy news, including those who had arrived well after me.

Around 2 A.M. Lynn's obstetrician finally came by. A handsome man with a Clark Gable moustache, he was normally very much the Doctor's Hospital courtier; the place catered to the wealthy and the famous. But when he walked into the waiting room he was still wearing his scrubs and looked like a butcher at the end of a long day. "Everything is all right," he said. "We've had a difficult time because your son was in a transverse lateral position."

I asked to see Lynn. He said she was still asleep and suggested I go home and get some sleep myself.

"I want to see my wife," I said. "I want to see both of them. I won't leave until I do."

He shrugged in stone. Another kind of cop.

I finally managed to convince a nurse that I had to be at work far out on Long Island the next day. Lynn was still sunken in anesthesia, pallid, her Lynness almost all drained out of her. I stroked her brow and resolved all over again to do better by her. The infant who was held up to me through the nursery window was remarkable—somehow fair, smooth-faced, his eyes open, with what seemed to me a "Hey, I'm here" look in them. I took him in and took him in, and as I did I felt myself being transformed. The great change I had been anticipating and working on for years had come at last, unexpectedly but unmistakably. It was not into a literary artist but into a father.

Driving back to Point Lookout in the middle of the night, I kept bouncing on the seat, sighing and stating and sometimes shouting, "I'm a father. I'm a father of a son. What do you know?" At some point along the South Shore I took a wrong turn. But so oblivious was I, so lost in my joyous realization, that I didn't realize until the car suddenly lost speed and traction that I had somehow driven directly onto a beach. And there I stayed and watched the dawn come up on my new life.

PART THREE

The Ivory Basement

⧗

I

Live and unlearn. By the time we got to Chicago that September of 1955, we were down to almost nothing. The new club in Lido Beach had everything but members and after a brief flutter at the Memorial Day opening, the dining room became what waiters call a blizzard—tables occupied only by their white cloths and place settings. The only job I could find in the area was at a pizza restaurant and bar in Long Beach, but during the week I did more waiting around than waiting, which gave me plenty of time to rue the move from Blair House. By the end of the summer, with Lynn pitching in as a waitress on Saturday nights, we saved enough to buy a car that would get us to Chicago and to pay for a quarter's tuition. When we arrived there, we found that I had been accepted too late to make the married-student's housing list, and the tuition money went for a month's rent and security for an apartment that was closer to the Black Belt than the campus.

Since I'd won a scholarship to the university three years before, I decided that my only chance was to see if I could get them to renew it. The "them" was an English department dominated by the Neo-Aristotelian "Chicago Critics," who I assumed had been impressed by the essay in which I'd used Aristotle to take Coleridge to task. But the next day I learned that most of them, including the department chairman, R. S. Crane, were gone—either into retirement or elsewhere. The new chairman was a Mark Twain scholar named Walter Blair. After some reluctance, the department secretary phoned him. "He wouldn't say," she told him. "He says it's a very important matter."

Mr. Blair proved to be a short, crusty man who seemed to have adopted his subject's famed deadpan face and sepulchral tone. I went into my number that was to end with my admiration for Aristotle and maybe Mark Twain but he cut me off at the pass. "Let me get this straight," he said. "We gave you a scholarship to come here three years ago, which you turned down, and now you're here and broke and want it back. That about the size of it?"

I said it was, though there were some extenuating circumstances such as the shortage of married-student housing and a new child. He asked me how I'd been supporting my wife and child. I said I'd been a waiter in New York. "Well, we've got some pretty fair restaurants here in Chicago. Why don't you find yourself one and when you've saved up enough for your tuition you let us know and we'll consider you for next year."

"What about next quarter?"

Back came the hard eye and voice. "I thought I said next year. I thought I said it pretty clearly."

"You did. But I'm twenty-six years old and I have a wife and baby boy depending on me and I can't wait another year."

He nodded, the first sign that he was giving any thought to what I said. "I guess that doesn't impress me as much as it does you," he concluded.

"Could I get a student loan?" How different all this was from the way I'd been treated at Michigan.

"We generally like our students to be here for more than a day or two before we give them a loan. But there's a bank at Fifty-third and Woodlawn you could try." While he waited for me to leave, he added,

"If you go there and talk to the bank officer, you might try using the word *Sir* now and then. You'll make a better impression."

He'd missed his calling. He should have been the deck officer on my destroyer. As it turned out, he was my teacher for one of the two required courses for entering M.A. students. It was called something like Principles of Literary Interpretation. There was nothing Aristotelian about it; there was nothing even vaguely theoretical; there was nothing vague. Mr. Blair (no teacher was called *professor* at Chicago—they were above that) taught it mainly to disabuse the entering graduate students of any fancy ways of reading they had picked up as a lit major. His main, seemingly only, principle of interpretation was the topic sentence. "In *Heart of Darkness* Conrad..." After you completed the sentence you supported it by *objective* (Blair's emphasis) evidence from the text.

Still bearing Barrows's reliance on intuition, impression and style mixed up with the New Critics' penchant for complexity and order, I needed a lot of time to open up a text and inspect it. On the final, I spent more than half the allotted time trying to cram alternative possible approaches into one topic sentence after another. My grade was a B, and I added another in Methods of Literary Scholarship, which ended any chance for the fellowship I would need the following year. Fortunately I wrote a paper in the third course that prompted my professor to ask the dean to grant me a tuition scholarship.

Which kept me in school the next quarter, along with our getting into one of the little villages of erstwhile ROTC barracks carved up into two-room units that still dotted the campus. I'd been a bust as a student for the first time since the tenth grade, but I now had a foothold at least on my climb upward from nowhere. In any case, I had no alternative to going on at least to an M.A. and a job teaching in the city junior college system. My New York union card had created about as much interest at the waiters local as I'd drawn from Mr. Blair, and hanging around the hall for extra jobs, I felt like I was back on Warren Street. Finally, I was sent to the Conrad Hilton as a steady banquet waiter—at eight dollars a banquet. There proved to be an average of four of them a week. On this we paid the rent; kept the car running; subsisted mostly on corn flakes, powdered milk, tomato soup, and spaghetti; and bought Similac for our son, Paul. Three or four times a month I got a Saturday night or a Sunday dinner at a restaurant, which helped to pay back our bank loan for tuition. One such job was at a huge restaurant on the North Side that was very faux-medieval, very Chicago—big steaks and small tips. Yearning for meat, for protein, I lost my last compunctions, slipped inside my jacket two nibbled-at porterhouses and one prime rib, trimmed the edges when I came home, and the next morning told Lynn that I had gotten them intact past the checker.

"We're living like we're in one of those Italian movies," she said as she reheated the steaks.

"Early de Sica," I said, trying to humor her. "*The Steak Thief.*"

Trying to humor her is what I did a lot of. The Barracks looked much more inviting from the outside in early September than from inside in a Chicago December. Its tacky two rooms were heated by a kerosene stove that had darkened the walls and were furnished in left-over GI—olive green table, four folding chairs, a pillowless couch, bunk beds. To me, it was "functional," to Lynn "a hovel." She was going through a bad patch—physically and mentally. Her gastritis was at times severe—an old malady that she now attributed to "the six flights of stairs on Macdougal Street." I didn't argue; I was still afraid that her apparitions might return—in housing where you could hear the sinks running in the units on either side.

What made our life in the Barracks at least plausible was that many of the young families there were living in the same hand-to-mouth way. I'd meet a guy at the unit's kerosene drum and share our gripes and tips about getting by. So would Lynn with the other hollow-eyed young mothers as they hung out the diapers they washed in the sink to freeze-dry in the winter wind and then thaw inside. Moreover, there were a few new and soon deep friends, with whom we regained the selves we were when weren't toeing the mark in class or buying baby food and soup bones at the Co-op.

The friend who mattered most was Jay Aronson, a strapping, bearded fellow who had played tackle in college (though with his droll nature it was hard to imagine him smashing into anyone). He soon took to calling Lynn Lynnochka, as I used to, and he had only to phone to say he was coming over for the cloud on her face to dispel.

Jay, too, had come to Chicago because of its double aura of intellectualism and radicalism, only to find, as I had in the Village and now here, that the train had left while we were still making plans. The university was in the hands of a chancellor very different from Robert Hutchins, the Voltaire of American higher education in the thirties and forties. Lawrence Kimpton's administration seemed mainly concerned with regaining the support of the pre-Hutchins alumni, erasing the College's iconoclastic reputation, and gentrifying its neighborhood by a vast program of "slum clearance," a euphemism for Negro clearance. All three developments were only initially under way but the mood in the air was that of the Counter-Reformation and Hutchins's name in the English and other departments evoked a smug smile or a shudder.

His radical innovations, it turned out, had been in the College where many now famous intellectuals had started out as students or teachers. The Hutchins College, built upon three years of general education in the Great Books, was still more or less in place but encircled now by the orthodox academics in the graduate departments and divisions who had been waiting for two decades to dismantle it. Among the other remaining vestiges of the Hutchins era was the Basic Program in the Downtown College—a Great Books curriculum that was taught mostly to earnest adults by a circle of long-term graduate students who had formed around the figure of Leo Strauss. That was where Isaac Rosenfeld, one of my main reasons for choosing Chicago, taught, and since Jay was on the fringe of the Straussians, I thought that through him I would sooner or later meet Rosenfeld, whom I was still too awed by to contact directly.

Except for his work with Hans Morgenthau, Jay was as unhappy academically as I was. The political science department was filled with what he called the stats men, heavy on voting behavior and other quantifiable data and indifferent if not hostile to the philosophical and moral issues of politics that Chicago had been known for. He often dropped by toward the end of the winter afternoons when we were both eager to get away from the day's *chazzerai* we were feeling stuffed with. Every now and then he brought something with him he had "just discovered": Constant Comment tea, espresso made in a little pot that he happened to have with him, a half-dozen scones ("they were on sale"). On Saturday nights, if I wasn't working, we would provide the spaghetti, he the half gallon of G&D, "the class of the jug wines," and we bantered, argued, and slowly sipped our way to eleven o'clock and the one reliable high point of the week—Studs Turkel's *Midnight Special*—an hour of the great folk-music artists. Such were the joys Jay brought with him. Now and then I would catch Lynn gazing at him and so did he. Behind the bright witty talk he brought out in her a certain avidity. He always phoned before he came over to make sure I was there.

Though Jay was a liberal, he had the sharp, realistic political mind of his Boston background that allowed for few illusions about the democratic process and the current state of liberalism. He liked to argue against the grain, as it were, to say that if our admirable and eloquent Adlai Stevenson had won in 1952, we might well still be fighting the Korean War and contending with an even wider spread of McCarthyism. I said that Eisenhower had the political mentality of a high school civics teacher and that what a democracy needed, particularly this politically retarded democracy, was the political educator that Roosevelt had been and that Adlai Stevenson would have proved to be.

"With this Republican Congress, Stevenson would be dead meat. He'd be spending all his time trying to cover the Democrats' ass for harboring communists and dupes and losing China."

"No, he'd have done two years before to McCarthy and McCarthyism what Joseph Welch did at the hearings. He'd have 'talked sense to the American people,' as he did in his campaign when he came from way behind to make a race of it. He would have also put an end to this total bullshit about losing China."

"That more than half the country believes. I'd say about 70 percent. An elite liberal like Stevenson would just be pissing into the wind. You'll see next fall when he runs against Eisenhower again. This time it's going to be the full landslide." Which, of course, it was.

2

Our own situation became more grim once the Chicago winter set in. The wind coming off Lake Michigan drove the chill factor down to near Arctic levels, so that you didn't go out unless you had to. Which meant that the usual stresses and strains of a broke young couple with a sickly infant were magnified by being cooped up so much and having a car that often didn't start. I, who was normally healthy, developed boils on my hands, which made it hard to take notes in class and to work as a waiter. We appeared to have reached rock bottom, but we hadn't.

After the winter quarter began, Lynn said that she would go completely crazy unless she got away a few hours a day, and since I wasn't working lunch anywhere, she got an afternoon job in the admissions office and I looked after Paul. But her stomach pain and her dark mood persisted and finally she went to Health Service, where a psychiatrist told her she was suffering from severe postpartum depression and a surgeon said that the X-rays were ambiguous but that she might well have a hernia that could have resulted from carrying Paul; he recommended repairing it.

So did I. Though I could devote hours of attention to Lynn's psychological problems, I had little patience with her physical ones. So I took the decisive male approach—if something's wrong, fix it. As for doubting the surgeon, he was the chairman of the department. Since the waiter's union medical plan would cover the expenses and I was hoping to leave it by summer for a teaching job, I wanted her to have the surgery sooner rather than later. As she procrastinated, I become more importunate.

~

That quarter I was taking a Dickens course with Morton Dauwen Zabel, who loomed as my best hope of hanging in at Chicago. A former editor of *Poetry Magazine*, the editor of *The Portable Conrad* (the writer I thought I would work on for a Ph.D. if I got there), and a contributor to *Partisan Review,* Zabel was the most congenial figure in the English department. That is, on paper. Up close, he was an unusually formal, buttoned-up teacher who seemed to discourage questions, let alone advances, from his students. He came into class, read his lectures in a sonorous but monotonous voice, and left. Now and then, as a kind of aside, he asked a question such as, "Do any of you know what other character Dickens modeled even more closely on his father?" then waited through our answers until he got the right one, nodded, and went on. Usually the question involved a fact.

One particularly bitter afternoon as I was being blown toward his class, I noticed a collie following me. To complete our disarray, Nada, our anarchic cocker spaniel, had gone into heat in the middle of February and we now had the male dogs in the area who were free and up to it coming by and waiting hopefully before the cold or I drove them off. They weren't that much of a nuisance; the nuisance was on the other side of the door, constantly whining and scratching to get out to them.

The most assiduous of Nada's suitors was this scrawny collie with a dignified air despite his patchy coat of black and gray, whom we had named the Aging Roué. As I approached Wieboldt Hall I told him to get lost, threatened him, and threw pieces of frozen snow at him, which had no effect other than to make my boils sting all the more. He continued to hang around, giving me the once noble and now slightly imploring look of Uncle Vanya.

I waited outside until no one else was entering the building, then gave him a parting shove, pulled the door closed, and beat it to my class.

Zabel had already begun this day's lecture and he did not suffer interruption readily. Staring me to my desk chair, he resumed: "In November of 1850, Dickens began to sketch the vast social canvas that would become *Bleak House*..." Scratch, scratch at the door. Zabel went on, but so did the scratching. Finally, he walked to the door and listened for a moment. "Does anyone know what that is?" he asked in his usual fact-finding way.

This was not one of his questions that I was dying to answer correctly. So I didn't. But I might just as well have, because when he opened the door, the Aging Roué came bounding into class, down the row of desks, and right to me.

"Is this your dog, Solotaroff?"

The only thing I could respond with was the truth. "No, but he's sexually interested in my dog."

Which broke up the class, in which solemnity normally reigned. Without losing a drop of it on his side, he asked me to remove the dog.

Cursing the hound all the way to the door of the building, I opened it. My rage and frustration giving me the strength of ten, or at least two, I picked up and threw the Aging Roué well into a snowbank beyond the door. "Come back," I said, "and I'll kick your fucking ribs in."

Laughs being in short supply in the English department, and shortest in Zabel's course, my reentrance into class created the sort of stir of expectancy that might have met Lenny Bruce. Zabel broke off from where he had picked up and said, "I think we have had enough of a disturbance for one day."

But, of course, we hadn't. Soon there came the scratching again. Zabel broke off to say, with some alarm, "The dog is back."

More unwanted laughs. "Solotaroff, would you remove him for good."

I hurriedly pulled my things together and slunk out of the room. The Aging Roué eagerly followed, as though he had become my best friend.

So together we set forth as far from Zabel as we could get. But halfway toward home, it all became too much. There on an expanse of ice and snow that could as well have been a half mile from Lake Bakal as Lake Michigan, the total absurdity of the situation, of my situation, came home to me, and thinking about Zabel's "The dog is back," spoken as though he were a criminal loose in the building, I burst out laughing and couldn't stop. Nada, the Aging Roué, Zabel, my big dreams about the university and my dashed hopes, my boils, it was all too much—the comic absurdity at the heart of things. "Nada, de nada, puis nada. Our nada who art in nada…" I intoned what Hemingway's waiter knew in his bones, what Sartre had arrived at in his head, and what the dog and my boils were telling me. When I got home, I told Lynn what had happened, culminating in my wild laughter.

"You look like someone has taken a fifty-pound pack off your shoulders," she said. "You look really pleased for the first time since your classes started."

"I'm getting there," I said. "But let's maybe spread the joy around." I went to the window. The faithful Aging Roué, all alone, was running up and down in front of the unit, no doubt to keep himself from freezing. "He's still hanging in," I said. "That much hope and persistence deserves its reward." Lynn shrugged warmly. "Why not?"

So I walked to the door and was about to deliver Nada to him when Lynn said, "Why don't you invite him in. It'll be nicer for them."

After managing to get them into the john, I put Paul in his playpen by the stove, then walked to the door of the other room and beckoned. "Our turn," I said.

Ten weeks or so later Nada had a litter of five puppies, which we hardly needed. That afternoon, playing the human version of the bitch in heat and the Aging Roué, Lynn and I had the most fun we'd had since Maine. A month later we celebrated the end of the winter quarter with our new scenario and accidentally created the last thing we needed.

3

For Zabel's course, I wrote a term paper in which I made out a case for Arthur Clennam, the melancholy businessman in *Little Dorrit*, as the first modern protagonist, because his consciousness, rather than his actions, is central—the protagonist not as actor but as patient, the victim of urban anomie and Victorian repression. The idea was not entirely original: Edmund Wilson had suggested some of the basis of it in his treatment of Clennam, as had Zabel in his lecture. I also benefited from Isaac Rosenfeld's essay on Sartre in which he distinguished between the genuine alienation of Dostoevsky's underground man and the malaise that afflicts Sartre's characters, who act out and proclaim their neurotic disgust with life, as viewed from the café, that is typical of much modernist fiction. I quoted him to set up a general context in which to view Dickens's most notable sad sack:

> The symptoms are the standard neurotic ones—contactlessness, the emptiness and superfluity of existence, the sexual miseries and perversions, violence and self-destruction. But because Sartre is an existentialist… the ordinary syndromes which we would otherwise discount to sickness, become on this inflated interpretation synonymous with subjectivity, crisis, anxiety and other existential categories, and we read as ontology what we should recognize as disease.

As Zabel pointed out in the margin, I was bringing "a pretty elaborate range finder to bear on poor mild Arthur Clennam." But the thesis was really about me and the painful reevaluation of the prestige I had given to the idea of being alienated, which had helped to turn me into a patient of the neurotic choices I had made in its behalf. And like a patient, I was hurting all over, acting out my father's prophecy rather than my own declaration of independence from him. Unable to carry off the Stephen Dedalus role, I was on the way to becoming a younger version of Leopold Bloom, the model of the passive, incessantly self-conscious outsider. I worried that Blazes Boylan was hovering in the wings.

In the spring quarter we saw less of Jay. I knew that he was getting more involved with the Straussians, but when I needed to torment myself, I explained his absence by my suspicion that he was keeping his distance from the friend he had betrayed. Lynn was certainly aware of his absence, though not in a way that indicated she understood it. Meanwhile, his place in our lives was being taken by Elizabeth and David Tornquist.

Elizabeth reminded me of Virginia Woolf—thin, freckled, shy, serious—literary to her fingertips—but all of her warmed and humorized by a Southern wit that could, as she would say, take the paint off a house. Like Flannery O'Connor and Carson McCullers, Tennessee Williams and Truman Capote, she was one of those highly developed sports produced by the rigid norms of southern gender behavior. Also like many southerners, she came from a family and community of tightly knit eccentrics who gave her, also typical, story-telling talent the material for a thousand and one nights.

Her husband David was, like me, a writer who hadn't been able to get his act together. While Elizabeth was sailing through the M.A. program, David was taking a course or two and studying Russian on his own. Eastern Europe was his mecca. He was the son of a wealthy entrepreneur and his contempt for American capitalism was such that alongside him, I felt like William Buckley. David was a handsome guy with long artistic hair and a taste for simple primitive living that not even the Barracks satisfied. For now he was Thoreau in Cambridge. A decade hence he would be legion.

We got through Lynn's surgery mainly because of them. The operation itself was a disaster in the making. The important surgeon did a brutal job. When he was finished he said to Lynn, pointing to a jar, "There's your hernia." In the jar was her navel. Three days later when she was released she was still in a state of semishock.

Meanwhile, David or Elizabeth had been babysitting Paul so that I could go to the hospital and to the classes and banquets I couldn't afford to miss. By now Paul had come through his colitis stage and was a bouncing ten-month-old charmer who had a remarkable range of pre-speech sounds. Elizabeth called him "the orator trailing clouds of glory" and couldn't get enough of him. Nor he of her. Which was well. He needed all the attention he could get when Lynn came home. As did she, of a different kind.

I don't remember much of the next month or so, except that whenever I needed them, the Tornquists were there. Lynn was barely speaking to me and when she did it was usually to let me have it. I had pressured her into the surgery. I hadn't even gotten a second opinion. I hadn't asked the surgeon what he intended to do. I even refused to acknowledge that she was now hideously disfigured for life. Except for the last point, I knew she was right and that I had been derelict. On the other hand, so had she, because she had not asked the surgeon to tell her about the procedure or insisted on getting a second opinion herself. That was left for me to take care of, along with everything else that had gone wrong in her life. Yes, I had pressured her, but after four years of frustration and indignity at mostly low pay, I had come to regard waiting tables as the swamp of my spirit and to believe that once out of it, I would be myself again, the person I had been in Ann Arbor. "You are what you do," Camus had advised and I now believed; it seemed to be the one belief I had left, or rather, it cut through all the others. So Lynn's continuing resistance to the surgery had become the symbol of her lack of concern for me rather than of concern for herself. That is what codependency does: the other becomes responsible for the mutual weakness that maintains it—a circuitry of covert need and overt blame.

Once or twice I ran into Jay when he was with the Straussians and thought they were bad news for him. In their company he lost his strong poise and even became bashful and eager, particularly when their leader, a swanky Jewish intellectual prince named Allan Bloom, was holding forth, which he usually was. What says it best is the Yinglish expression "schlepping after," which was too cruelly pointed to say to him. I hated to see him doing it; he wasn't in their league of erudition, nor was I, but I quickly had my doubts about whether it was a league worth playing in, for they had all the trappings of a cult.

Most of the Straussians were bachelors who supported themselves by teaching in the Basic Program of the Downtown College. Since that was where Rosenfeld was teaching, I tried for a few times to hang around Jay when he was hanging around them but Rosenfeld never showed up except in the amused, superior stories that the courtiers tell of the court jester, Rosenfeld being incurably playful.

An extracurricular feature of the Basic Program staff was its access to a goodly number of bored or lonely women who were enrolled in it. So there was a good deal of *de haut en bas* kissing and telling and deriding. According to Jay, Rosenfeld overhead one of them characteristically erecting his behavior into a principle—that of the inherent superiority of the male sex. Part of his proof was the basic sexual position, the man on top, the women on her back, submissive, imploring. At which point Rosenfeld began to laugh. The Straussian wanted to know what was so funny. Rosenfeld replied that he had a pretty reductive idea of the positions but even in the missionary one, while it was true the woman was on her back, the man was on his knees.

The story made my passion to know him that much keener, my faith that much stronger that Isaac, as everyone called him except me, would recognize my writing hangup and set me straight. But by May he still hadn't shown up in my life, so, looking for a teaching job, I decided to apply for one in the Basic Program.

The director, a suave man of few words, asked me, right off the bat, "What is your view of *The Republic*?"

His haughty pose, my sense of being put in a position to make a fool of myself, my already brimming antagonism to "the Strauss pack" (the phrase I used to taunt Jay), my instinct to punch my way out of a corner—all conspired to cover as well as to evoke my ignorance. "If this is to be an exam," I said, "I'd like a more specific question."

"All right. How would you teach *The Republic*?"

I knew that if I hesitated I'd be lost. "As a conservative utopia," I said.

"So that is your view? Of one of the monuments of human intellect?"

"Well, he calls it *The Republic* but it's really an oligarchy. And it's certainly an ideal one with a rigid class structure."

"And its philosophical underpinnings?"

"Of course I'd have to talk about his theory of Ideas and the dialectical method and the central analogy of the individual and the state. That goes without saying."

I was improvising like mad, not having read the dialogue since my freshman humanities course. I was also Wily Coyote approaching the cliff, so I slammed on the brakes. "That's about what Aristotle thought of *The Republic*," I said.

"Oh so you're an Aristotelian," he said.

"You might say that." I was taking a course from Elder Olson, the brilliant theoretician of the Chicago Critics, and was working with his principle that literary form was primarily a generator of power rather than of meaning. So I began to talk about teaching *The Republic* in terms of its potent rhetoric.

But he declined the gambit. "Why do you want to teach in this program anyway? Wouldn't you be better off teaching English composition or a course in the novel?"

I could hardly tell him the real reason. I said that I would be working on a Ph.D. in English, which was a pretty narrowing experience, so I thought that the Great Books would be a good antidote.

Around this point he said that there weren't any openings right now but he'd keep me in mind.

So that was that. About a month later I was helping Jay to move into a new apartment. He was in a peculiar state of mind, both elated and yet a bit embarrassed. I thought it might be because he now had this handsome two-room place and we were still in the Barracks. After we had finished and were sitting over a beer, he said, "I have some news but you may not like it. But then I have something else to tell you that you will."

"Why don't we start with that. Good news is at a premium in my life. The last I can remember was daylight savings time when I got an extra hour of sleep."

He had been teaching that year in Gary at an extension of Indiana University. He said he was leaving there but had put in a good word for me with the director, who was looking for someone to teach two sections of composition and two of humanities. "He wants you to call him," he said. "I really sang your praises and it looks good."

"Terrific," I said. "Now the bad news."

"It's not really bad, it's just that you interviewed for the job in the Basic Program…"

Still elated, I jumped to the climax. "You got it," I said. "Great. He told me there weren't any openings but we both knew I was *phumfing* through the interview."

"There wasn't an opening," he said. "I got Isaac's slot."

My heart sank some. "I hope he's not leaving Chicago," I said.

"You haven't heard?"

"Heard what?"

"He died. About a week ago. He had a heart attack. I assumed you knew."

Other than casually pumping him now and then about Rosenfeld, I had kept my love to myself. So Jay had no way of knowing the force of the blow he had just delivered.

"You look like you just had the wind knocked out of you."

"No, the heart," I said and began to try to tell him.

4

I ended up getting a job at the Indiana University extension in East Chicago rather than the one in Gary. It was a smaller school, housed in a single building off Route 12, a major trucking route for the oil refineries in Whiting and the steel mills and factories in East Chicago and Hammond. The modest yellow brick structure looked like a high school except that it backed into a huge expanse of asphalt, where students parked their cars, pickups, and motorcycles. Most of them came to class either before or after full-time jobs—the guys mostly in the refineries, mills, or other industrial-grade jobs that enabled East Chicago to call itself The Work Bench of America. All but the lab courses met only once a week: three hours for humanities, two for English composition. So though I taught two sections of each, I only had to make the twenty-five-mile trip twice a week; on the other hand the long classes weighed heavily, as though teaching Homer or paragraph organization were a form of shift work too.

In other respects, Humanities I in East Chicago was very different from the Humanities I that had turned me on so in Ann Arbor. We only read half as many texts, but they seemed twice the length. Each of my sections had about thirty students, of which perhaps ten, mostly girls, seemed prepared. Hunched behind their copies of *The Odyssey,* the other students stared and frowned at the text as though it were still in the original Greek. Teaching basic literary structure, the only thing I could think to teach them, I would ask a question, call on a student, and watch it buzz around his or her mind like an annoying fly.

"How does Homer begin the Circe book? Mr. Gigiakos?"

Mr. Gigiakos taps the crown of his sleek, pomaded hair. When nothing comes, he asks, "Begins?"

"Okay, starts. Like a car. How does Homer start this new book and get it rolling?"

"Can I use my book?"

"Yes, just so it's the right one. The one by Homer."

Mr. Gigiakos checks the spines, gets a laugh, and then finds his way to the Circe episode. Finally, "He kills this big stag?"

"That's not the first thing, but let's start there. Why does Homer have him do that?"

"Because he's hungry?"

"Okay, he's hungry. But he doesn't cut off a leg and roast it on the spot. What is the function, Mr. Gigiakos, of this incident?"

Mr. Gigiakos peers, touches his temple; his face turns increasingly blank as silence again descends.

"Why does he carry this heavy animal back to his men instead of sending two or three of them to lug it back to the ship? Ever try to carry a big buck on your shoulders?"

Delighted to have a question he can answer, Mr. Gigiakos relaxes and slides back into himself. "Nope," he says.

I ignore as long as I can the same four or five hands that are usually raised and call on Mr. Barrone, who, hulking in his high school football jersey, looks like he could carry such an animal, no problem. "What's the function of Odysseus's action in terms of one of the Big Three—plot or character or theme?"

A new silence. Mr. Barrone stares straight back at me as though he hadn't been called on. "Are you waiting for a hint, Mr. Barrone?"

A few laughs, very few. "Sure," he says with the little smile of the all-county middle linebacker eyeing the guard who has been trying to block him. "Give me a hint."

But the hints didn't work much better than the questions. Or the pep talks or the threats. Nothing seemed to juice their attentiveness.

The composition course went a bit better because it was shorter and seemed designed mainly to crack down on the Six Gross Illiteracies— sentence fragments, comma and semi-colon faults, dangling participles, etc. In one of my classes there was a student, John Dovitch, who brought his own juice. He sat in the first row, small and wiry, his motorcycle boots sometimes lifted over the writing arm as though to avoid the flow of bullshit I was delivering. With his DA haircut, his comb sticking out of the back pocket of his blue jeans, his khaki T-shirt with the Camels rolled in the sleeve, he would arrive late for class, give me the fish eye for most of the hour, and break in whenever he chose to. Particularly when we were discussing one of the weekly themes I'd dittoed up.

"How come you can't use just simple or compound sentences if you want to?"

"Because it's lazy writing. Because it becomes monotonous. Because it spares you the effort of writing more precise and flexible sentences, which college-level work requires."

"Who says so? I mean besides you?"

"Most people who care about language. It makes sense. Repetition is boring; variety is the spice of life."

"How come this guy Hemingway you like so much repeats himself all the time and writes compound sentences like mad."

"That's different. He's doing it for literary effect."

"Yeah… so?" delivered with the full cockeyed look.

"He does it for rhythm and emphasis."

"So how do you know we don't too?"

His writing was similarly blunt and subversive. He came from Calumet City, Illinois's den of iniquity just across the state line, and his compositions were usually more about the wild side of his adolescence than the assigned topic. One dealt with boosting tires or maybe just hubcaps: its vividness was riveting despite all the compound sentences, repetitious diction, spelling errors and Gross Illiteracies. I gave him an A for content and a D- for mechanics. After class he came to see me, his expression even more dubious than usual.

"You want to ask about your grade…" I said, steeling myself.

"It's pretty screwy but what I want to ask you is something else. Where you from anyway?"

"I'm from Chicago."

"Yeah, I know that. You're one of them graduate students. But where do you come from? Where did you grow up?"

"I grew up in Elizabeth, New Jersey."

"No shit." I'd finally said something that interested him. "That's a lot like the Region, right?"

"That's right. Lots of refineries and factories."

"So how come you talk like you grew up at Harvard?"

It was less a taunt than a curious question. In any case, it lodged in my mind as a serious one that I took home with me and brooded about.

The first day of classes I had turned from closing the door to face the twenty composition students sitting expectantly before me, and as soon as I began to speak, I felt that I had come into my own. I was wearing a new suit, the first that I had bought since getting married, and for the first time in my work life I was in charge. The two new facts seemed to have equal weight, which startled me—the suppressed middle-class me suddenly asserting himself. In any event, I was no longer a waiter taking orders or a graduate student having to knuckle under but a teacher who instinctively knew what to say and how to proceed. I was amazed by my confidence and pleased by my performance.

But by the second week the only enthusiasm in the room seemed to be my own. How could that be? My approach was clear and coherent, my comments witty. Then the first compositions came in: they were eye-opening and mind-deadening: such crude, vacuous, tangled, and error-ridden writing (the Six Gross Illiteracies were only the beginning of the problem). I didn't know where to start or end in correcting and commenting. To get through the pile, I told myself that I was teaching in an academic slum and would have to make the best of it. I adopted a mildly sarcastic teaching persona and correcting style to prod both my students and myself.

But now, as I began to see, Dovitch was telling me to wise up, to realize where I was. Why the sarcasm? Mainly because I was so wrapped up in my new role of teaching writing and literature as though I were selling Omega watches at Woolworth's that I had lost sight that I was teaching people. I tried to look at myself through their eyes and saw that my irony was a form of arrogant impatience. Along with my literary notions of style and my insistence on teaching structure, it was no wonder that I sounded to Dovitch like I had parachuted in from Harvard. And meanwhile, there was the other side of me who knew these kids, had gone to high school with them, had buddied with them in the navy. They were rightly interested in their lab and accounting courses, their prenursing and teacher training programs, for they led to jobs that would deliver them from the refineries and factories, the typing pool and checkout counters. But what did using precise transition words or understanding peripety and discovery mean to them? Clearly the burden of interest was on me.

After this moment of truth came the slow groping process of settling into the work and seeing my way, which turned out to be the common ground that existed between us. We tried to imagine what the dawn of language was like—how a grammar naturally came into being as a way of sorting out the chaos of phenomena, and how writing must have evolved to clarify and strengthen as well as to refine speech. Instead of the dicta of correct usage we played with etymologies and synonyms, clichés and other predictable phrasing. In the humanities course we compared Ulysses to Davy Crockett, a pop-cult figure at the time, to see what an epic hero was. We put together a modern scenario of *Agamemnon* with Douglas MacArthur as the tragic hero cut down on his victory march through San Francisco. We tried to understand why Socrates wasn't just a sucker to stay in prison and get executed when the fix was in; why the laws in East Chicago had a lot to be said for them. Much of the time I simply plunged in, letting a line of inquiry develop of its own course. I free-associated and improvised, stimulated by those faces in front of me that I wanted to interest, to wipe the dull stare of boredom from their eyes. Also I found that I was teaching and stimulating myself by going back to the basics and making them interesting.

The next semester, John Dovitch turned up in the second half of the humanities course, both his feet on the floor but his skepticism still evident. "To what do I owe the privilege of teaching you again?" I asked.

"You fit into my schedule, " he said.

5

The rest of the week I was a full-time student in the Ph.D. program. Lynn grew big with our second child, whom she had named Nina to reconcile herself with bearing it. Though I was now earning sixty-five dollars a week, almost twice our income from last year, and we had been moved by the university into a genuine two-bedroom apartment with steam heat, we resumed the struggle to make ends come close enough to be able to borrow the rest from a bank. (Student loans were minimal back then.) What I was now even more short of than money was sleep. I'd had no idea of what I was getting into by teaching four courses for the first time and taking three.

But you are, as I kept reminding myself, what you do. I'd come home from East Chicago after eight straight hours of teaching and seeing students and then the twenty-five-mile drive, which would take me to around 10 P.M. After a bowl of soup and crackers, I'd start in on the assigned reading in *Beowulf* or one of Emerson's essays, and after a half hour I would be reading in a daze. Thinking it was all too much, I'd start for bed but first stop in Paul's room, and then often lie on the mattress beneath the crib he'd begun to climb out of. I'd listen to his breathing and bask in the odors and sometimes fall asleep, but other times a rush of fresh energy would come, as though the talc and baby oil and sweet breath was a form of Dexedrine. I'd return to my book with another hour of work left in me that took me to the middle of my assigned reading, which I would finish after I got up with him at six.

But it was a struggle. Toward the end of her pregnancy Lynn developed sciatica and could barely stand. So I had the household to keep going as well. Then, just before the Christmas break, I came down with a strangely odorous bronchitis. Then the bottom fell out: a psychiatrist called me from Ann Arbor to say that my brother was suicidal and to ask if I was prepared to assume responsibility for him. I called Bob, who tried to assure me that his doctor had overreacted. I wasn't reassured and asked him to come to Chicago for a few days. After putting down the phone, I said to Lynn, "Well, with both of us in bed, no food in the house, a neglected infant, another coming, and a suicidal brother on his way, we've finally become the Marmeladovs," the most extreme of Dostoevsky's woebegone households.

While I waited for Bob to arrive, I finally called my mother and asked her to stay with us until I was better and the baby was born. She had helped us out before, being very willing but not very able because of her severe arthritis. But she had recently sold the house in Teaneck, moved to New York, and seemed to have a new lease on life.

In recent years I had stopped feeling guilty about the rudderless family I had forsaken to go off to college. For they no longer were. By the time I graduated, Hy Enzer, one of Sandy's professors at Hofstra, had already come alongside and taken the three of them into his stout boat. A former bomber pilot, journalist, now a sociologist, and every inch a mensch, virile and gentle, Hy was like a worker sent directly from God's social service: to husband fragile Sandy and to rescue troubled Bob and scattered Mom, who were sinking together. Still in Ann Arbor, I'd demurred about my nineteen-year-old sister marrying a man almost twice her age but soon saw how wrong I was. Thanks to Hy's efforts Sandy was now a stable young mother in her first year of graduate school; Bob, at least until that phone call, appeared to be a going concern as a sophomore at Michigan; and Mom was living in Manhattan where she had enrolled in a good music school and was receiving the piano instruction she'd always dreamed of as well as the training to become a piano teacher.

When Bob arrived he proved to be in better shape than I'd been imagining. He had been undergoing an onslaught of anxiety so prolonged and severe that he had had to drop all but one of his courses and had finally told the psychiatrist that he was thinking of suicide as a way of escaping his terror. But as he talked, he seemed too full of life to be in danger of ending his. As he said, "I was always going to hang around to hear one more quartet or piano concerto."

He then dug the car out from where the snowplows had buried it and did our shopping. The next day it was Mom's turn to arrive and pitch in. Her children's illnesses had always mobilized her and she immediately hired a cleaning woman, took over the care of Paul, and set about in the kitchen. She also insisted I go to Student Health and find out what was puddling in my lung.

It turned out to be a major lesion. Feeling sicker and more anxious by the minute, I was put in a wheelchair and taken to Billings, the university hospital, where the admitting resident told me that such lesions were rare, serious, and could take six months to cure. My worst fear—of proving to be unequal to the situation, of letting down Lynn and Paul and now a second child—appeared to be coming true. Put in a private room, I undressed and got between the cool, crisp sheets, and suddenly all my anxiety melted away into a great peacefulness, a letting go of all my responsibilities as though I had been wounded in action and the fifty-pound field pack Lynn had mentioned was taken from my back and put away.

Thomas Mann has sung the praises of a moderate lung disease (which mine became after two days, thanks to massive doses of a new high-powered penicillin): the contemplative slow time that is induced by attending to one's breathing and being, enhanced in my case by going off cigarettes, was like a retreat for my spirit. Under its spell I put aside *Beowulf* and Emerson, my students' final exams and freshman themes, took up *Joseph and His Brothers*, and descended into Mann's well of time, the thickly braided sentences taking me down to the Canaan of 3,200 years ago, far away from the educational bunker on the truck route and the grim classrooms of Wieboldt and Classics and even from the pathos at 5649 South Maryland, where Lynn, hobbling past her due date, and Mom were struggling to keep things together.

A few evenings later, on Christmas Eve, still in the midst of this sweet surcease, I picked up the phone by my bed. It was Lynn's obstetrician calling to tell me that an "eight-pound boy apparently named Ivan" had just been born. As I lay in bed, exultantly cradling that news, a group of carolers came down the hall, going from room to room. When they reached mine, they were singing "Three Great Kings." Which was about how I felt. One son had newly stationed me in my life; now the second had arrived to enlarge the space. Together they would make sure that I went places.

But a week after I was released from the hospital, I was still so weak that I could barely drive to East Chicago and had to cut short my classes. One subzero day, my recuperating lung couldn't take me across campus. I sat gasping on a bench and thought I was on my last legs. But I wasn't: after a few minutes I got up and made it to class. Nietzsche was right: what doesn't kill you makes you stronger; and once fully recovered, I had the sense of being indomitable. My life had become hard and exacting, but so had I. It was as though the heavy-duty antibiotic I'd taken and a week of contemplation had destroyed a lot of my self-pity as well, that some of Chicago's big-shoulderedness had settled into mine. For I was now the father of two sons.

This accession of can-do-ness was pretty quickly tested. Soon after Ivan's arrival, Paul developed asthma. Along with the harrowing monthly attack during which he had to be carried and comforted for hours until it became certifiably grave enough to bundle him up and take him to the emergency room for a shot of adrenaline, there was the nightly spasm, which began around one in the morning when he woke up and needed to be taken into the bathroom until the wet steam and Theodur, the bronchial dilator I spooned into him, enabled him to breathe freely again. A two-, a three-, a four-year-old in this condition is a trial of your gentleness, calmness, and most of all patience, particularly if you're exhausted yourself. Since Lynn was nursing Ivan, I had to handle it and, in time, it became a kind of ritual of bonding, my holding him, at first in my arms and in time with my words. Theodur and Theodore. I got up for him and for myself.

Fortunately, Ivan soon slept on through it all. Nursed by a calmer mother and blessed with a sturdy constitution and a second child's self-sufficiency, he grew in his crib like a healthy plant until the day he climbed out of it and, having been neglected, began to go his own way.

6

The Hutchins era had created a subculture of dropouts made up of those who had either passed though the College or fallen by the wayside of its graduate schools but went on living in Hyde Park. Either they had found something worth doing there or, more likely, they couldn't think of anything to do elsewhere that would make up for the loss of the community's ambiance of democratic elitism, ubiquitous intellect, and stimulating dissipation. These were conferred by its various bookstores, the Co-op market, the foreign film and the university drama theaters, the strip along Fifty-fifth Street of bebop and classical jazz clubs, and three bars tended by talkers and wits like themselves. This *Gesellschaft*, as they would say, was all the more clung to as the cranes and bulldozers moved ever closer to the honkytonks on Fifty-fifth Street, which was scheduled to be transformed into an upscale boulevard.

In the first group were young writers and artists trying to get their legs under them before they headed to New York and, most notably, a group of gifted young directors, actors, and comedians who had found one another through campus theater and a mutual interest in satire and improvisation. Known as the Compass Players, after the name of the Fifty-fifth Street bar where they performed, they included Nichols and May; Shelley Berman; Barbara Harris; and my favorite, Severn Darden, renowned for his extraordinary lectures under the name of Professor Walter von der Vogelweide, a Dadaist polymath, or better, a U of C *philosophe* run amok:

> For centuries, philosophers have told us that thought cannot be seen. It cannot be felt, read, cannot be tasted. It is not in the key of G. Or F. It is not blue. Nor is it mauve. It is not a pot of geraniums. It is not a white donkey against a blue sky. Or a blue donkey against a white sky. It is not a little girl singing an old song. Nor does it have aspirations to become archbishop. It is not a saffron-robed monk, pissing in the snow.
>
> In other words, philosophers can tell you millions of things that thought isn't, and they can't tell you what it is. And that bugs them.

Playing in a club with a $1.25 minimum, the Compass Players dispensed their high-octane smarts and hilarity in the form of set scenarios and sketches but mostly in impromptu comic scenes and parodies at the drop of a suggestion from the audience, say a meeting between Mayor Daley and Dorothy Day or a dramatic monologue by a periodontist in the style of Robert Browning. They were the community's mode of uplift, Saturday night's R&R, sustaining our morale, stimulating our weary minds, restoring for a few hours our vanishing community.

In the second group were the older intellectuals and talkers who glumly watched the years go by since they had given up on their dissertations, who typically worked in the bookstores or tended bar (the Compass was owned by one of them), or taught in the junior college network to make their rent, child support, and bar tabs. They weren't bohemians so much as home-loving people without a home who had made one of the neighborhood. A good example of the type was Fred Winkle, who taught a section of composition at East Chicago and otherwise worked the night shift typing briefs at a big downtown law firm.

Fred's non-going dissertation was on Sir Thomas Wyatt. The Elizabethan courtier and cocksman of "They flee from me who sometimes did me seek" was not someone you would easily associate with Fred, who had the paunchy, rumpled, pallid look of someone whose lovers were Johnny Walker and Philip Morris. But as with most of his Hyde Park colleagues, there was more to Fred than met the eye.

One evening I came back late to the faculty room to find him sitting at one of the desks in his overcoat and hat with the ear flaps already down, staring into space as though he had received some very bad news on his way out.

I asked him what was the matter and saw that what I'd taken for sadness was fear. "I got a phone call a few minutes ago," he said. "There are two people outside in the parking lot with baseball bats waiting for me."

"That's just student humor around here," I said. "Come on, I'll walk you to your car."

He didn't move or look the least bit relieved. "They're not students. The one who called said he was Joey Romano. From Cicero."

The Romano gang was to Cicero what the Capone gang had been to Chicago twenty years before. "Fred, that's just part of the stupid joke of some student you've pissed off by giving him a low grade. You must know who he is."

"I know who he is. He's Joey Romano."

"Come on. What in the world would someone from the Romano mob have against you?"

"I've been sleeping with his wife," he said, his normal sheepish self-irony returning to consort with his terror.

On the one hand, it was almost impossible to credit. On the other, I got pretty apprehensive. "How did you manage to do that?"

"We work at Pratt and Pringle together," he said. "I thought we were just friends but then Junie and I started having a late-night snack together. Then one night after I got home from teaching, she showed up at my place. It was snowing hard and she looked like she had walked all the way from the Loop to tell me she couldn't stand her life anymore. So I got her to take a hot shower and she put on my bathrobe and…" He opened his hands in a what's-a-guy-gonna-do way.

Fred Winkle and Junie Romano—what really makes strange bed-fellows is sex. There was even something touching about this shambling, lapsed Elizabethan scholar getting together with a housewife from Cicero who no doubt was looking for something finer in her life. Also it was very Chicago—the barbarian land culture that extended for miles and miles to Cicero meeting the strip of civilized water culture that lay along Lake Michigan—another idea I owed to Isaac Rosenfeld. But what it mostly was, was frightening. "What are you going to do?" I asked. "I don't imagine they're going to wait all night for you to come out."

"You sound like Nick Adams in 'The Killers,'" Fred glumly pointed out.

"I also feel like him. 'Implicated,' as I said, teaching the story."

Fred roused himself a bit. "What would you think about getting your car and driving around to the front. I could be waiting there and jump in."

He had said two men and had used the plural *bats*. I couldn't drive a getaway car as fast and skillfully as Joey Romano undoubtedly could. Far from it. "I have a better idea. Why don't you just call the police?"

"I don't want to get Junie involved in this," he said. "It's a point of honor."

I pointed out that this was no time to be Sir Thomas Wyatt, that we lived by a different code. As did Joey Romano. "The cops are your solution," I said and began to pack up my briefcase.

Fred stood up and grabbed his. "I'll go with you," he said. "You're big and strong and look Italian yourself. I'll leave my car here. He can take out his wrath on it."

Clearly, his peculiar mind was set. What should I do? I had a wife and two children now. Did that enable me to tell him he couldn't go with me? Somehow it didn't. Instead it told me that having sons now, I couldn't punk out. The male ego prompts in strange ways. You can't let a buddy down even if he isn't your buddy. You can cross to the less ominous side of the street but you still have to walk down it.

As we went out Fred said, "Don't put the lights out. I don't think he knows what I look like, so I'll lie. I'll say the guy they're after is still inside. But it would be better if I got in your car in case he's identified mine."

Strangely enough, his voice was calm, as though he'd been through situations like this before. I remembered that he had been in the army, had seen combat.

There were still five or six cars in the parking lot. But no doors opened, no lights came on, none of them moved, as we walked quickly to my car. My car was old, the engine balky, only so many tries in the battery. So I had to let it warm up for a minute or more. Another car's lights came on and moved toward us but then out to the entrance. "Maybe he's not even here, maybe he's still in Cicero," Fred said.

Which is how it turned out. Fred continued to get menacing phone calls and one time he came out of work at the law firm to find the doors of his car open and the interior light on. Again nothing happened except to his nervous system. Meanwhile, I'd told the story to my friend Art Geffen, who tended bar at the University Tavern, whose two owners were "connected," as Art put it. He advised me to tell Fred to talk to one of them.

As Art was to tell the story: "When Fred came in I called Sam over and he asked him what his problem was. Fred was sweating bullets, you felt really sorry for the guy, but then Sam tells him, 'It's pretty simple. For a hundred, they'll warn this guy to lay off. For five hundred they'll break his arm. By the way, why is this guy coming after you?... You were messing around with his wife?... Uh, oh. I don't think I can help you. The People don't like that kind of stuff.'"

Chicago's water culture lapping and breaking against the land culture. Or the Ivory Basement, intellect at bay with tough conditions, the thoughtful view from below. You didn't have to be Jewish to be a graduate student in the fifties at Chicago but it helped because of our history of intellect and suffering, and the sense of humor of a people chosen by God to maintain both. Chicago itself was a particularly apt location for the Ivory Basement. Bellow had drawn most of his fiction from it. So had his friend Isaac Rosenfeld. They were born and raised in it. Others passed through Chicago and were confirmed, to a greater or less extent, by it. This was going on, I felt, with the Compass Players, and with many others of us. Incongruity was our way of life, irony the local accent. How could it be otherwise in a community of high liberal ideas that featured Abner Mikva and Saul Alinsky, two of the leading social reformers in America, and Julian Levi, the Baron Haussmann of Hyde Park, who was doing whatever it took to reclaim the area as a mostly white, safe, upper-middle-class community. It was a neighborhood where the smell of the stockyards wafted across the Neo-Gothic campus and whose black population produced the squeaky clean Black Muslims and the funky violent Blackstone Rangers; a campus where the students were cool and the faculty seething with contending orthodoxies, whose graduate student missionaries brought the Great Books to the Calumet region. Such a vivid home of contending extremes: it was all the more natural to try to hold opposing ideas together, to mock one community value with another, to develop an aggressive intellectual style and a wit that hadn't forgotten where it came from.

After our little adventure, Fred Winkle and I became friends for a time. One night he came over to tell us that he was moving to Cicero to live with Junie and her two children, who "had a lot of potential." He also said that he had been named a co-respondent in a divorce suit brought by Joey Romano. Go figure.

7

On the first day of a course on Henry James in the fall of 1957, I found myself sitting next to two newcomers; a small intense guy in an army field jacket who laughed a lot, and a dark debonair fellow in a jacket and tie who kept him laughing but who looked like he had strayed into class from the business school. The first introduced himself as Art Geffen, the second as Phil Roth. With the antenna of New York/New Jersey Jews, we quickly tuned in to each other. They had both been M.A. students the year before I got there and were coming back from two years in the army. As a hardened second-year Ph.D. student I regarded them as a combat veteran might regard two new staffers. They were talking about Leslie Fiedler, who had recently published his notorious outing essay, "Come Back to the Raft, Huck Honey." What did I think of it?

"Fiedler is an intellectual kike," I announced.

The shocking ugliness of the phrase still makes me wince. It was obviously intended to shock, to get these newcomers' attention, But it also indicates something else—that the mask of the committed graduate student that I had begun to wear in order to get through the Ph.D. program was beginning to fit my face, as George Orwell remarked of himself as a colonial police officer in Burma. It was a mask I would continue to adjust, wink through, and sometimes pull off to stay in touch with the dissident me; all in all, an on-again, off-again act I would play for the next three years, that would grow more intense, would require some heavy dues and, in Fiedler's case, some painful restitution.

What effect it had on Art and Phil, beyond startling them, I don't know. But the conversation marked the kickoff of a three-sided friendship in which we played one another friendly and tough—ally and critic. Art in his field jacket was soon as scruffy as most of us; Phil wore GI khaki gloves inside his leather ones, but otherwise dressed

like the junior faculty member that he also was, having been given a
job in the College that the rest of us Ph.D. students would have killed
for. His patron was Napier Wilt, dean of the humanities division, who
was teaching the James course.

Wilt was not a scholar or a critic. His field was nineteenth-cen-
tury American drama, whose slight significance had left him free to
exercise his formidable congeniality and cunning in advancing his
career. A heavy, florid man, he was a traveler, a bon vivant, discreetly
gay, and every year or two he would bring a graduate student under
his warm, powerful wing, where I now hoped to join Phil. Meanwhile,
we were in his course, which he didn't teach as much as preside over.
His authority came partly from being a Jamesian type himself. If Herbert Barrows was a Lambert Strether, Mr. Wilt was an Adam Verver.
He relaxed us and let us run, he held the reins of judgment lightly but
he held them and, when necessary, used them.

Around the second week of class, one of the students was going
on about the religious allegory that underlay "Daisy Miller." Wilt
asked me what I thought of this interpretation. I said that it was idi-
otic to read James as though he were Hawthorne. Then Phil jumped
in and proceeded to show how eschewing the concrete for the symbolic "turned the story inside out," that Daisy had to be established as
an American girl of a certain class and disposition before she became
of any interest as a sacrificial figure. Like two players early in the season who find they can work together, Phil and I passed the ball back
and forth, running up the score of good sense. Mr. Wilt let us go on
for a bit before he blew his whistle. "I think James would have agreed
with you," he said bluntly but was clearly tickled.

A few weeks later he invited Phil and me, along with Lynn, and
Phil's girlfriend, Sally, a Hyde Park siren with whom Jay had had a
fling, to one of the gourmet dinners that Mr. Wilt and his roommate
were famous for. An evening of gracious living and high spirits—for
Lynn and me it was like being whisked from the beachhead to the
officer's club. Phil and I again teamed up, this time as two bright

young wits from northern New Jersey. For the first time since I'd come to Chicago, I felt that I had found what a grad student most needs— a faculty patron with influence.

Whatever nice ideas I'd had about adventuring in the higher realms of Neo-Aristotleanism, or any other school of thought, were far from my mind now. My life was challenging enough; I was looking only for the path of advancement that led to the exit where a decent teaching job elsewhere would be waiting. I couldn't afford to struggle for five years, if not longer, in one of the interdisciplinary committees such as History of Culture or Social Thought where the high-powered dissertations were written that took forever. I had a wife and two little boys pushing me to get done.

Nonetheless, challenge came looking for me. I also was taking a course in contemporary criticism taught by Norman Maclean. His reputation was that of a first-rate teacher but an ornery one, so I'd steered clear of him. But the time had come and there he was, a compact, horse-faced man who looked more like a contractor in a jacket and tie than an English professor. His teaching style was the opposite of Mr. Wilt's: he held the reins tight and the whip poised. Each week there was a ten-minute quiz on the assigned reading. The first text was Croce's *Aesthetics*. What did Croce mean by an intuition?

One of the tricks I'd developed to get through the program was that of partial mimicry, using the subject's terminology, the professor's tone and pet phrases, to season the way I wrote about the subject, a facile way of seeming on the ball. So I wrote down in Crocean fashion something like "An intuition partakes of the relational aspect of consciousness," embroidered it a bit, and handed it in.

The next class meeting, Maclean started off by reading one of the quizzes. "'An intuition is a perception.' That's good," he said. "She puts up her clothesline so that she can hang her washing on it." He then read the rest, which concluded with the phrase "a rumbling in the innards," which he liked a lot too. Then he said he wanted to read another quiz. "'An intuition partakes of the relational aspect of consciousness...'" He read a few more words, then stopped. "I'm sorry," he said. "I love the English language too much to read this kind of hokum. What I don't understand is why a young person of twenty-five or so wants to write like a broken-down philosophy professor in a third-rate teacher's college."

He didn't name me, but my face must have—humiliation and anger contending in a blindsided mind. I remember Phil staring at me, the haughty veteran graduate student suddenly this small. By the end of class, anger had won out—after all, that "partake" construction had come from Croce or at least his translator, and so as I slunk out I gave Maclean a hard look. To which he responded by crooking his finger. When I arrived at his desk, he took a drag of his postclass cigarette and said, "You're pretty smart in class but if you don't start writing clearly I'm going to flunk you."

Flunk me? In my last year of courses? A fellow now of the English department? But you had only to look at those cold hunter's eyes (they turned out to be a fisherman's) and the thick, corded wrists of a former lumberjack to know that he meant what he said.

Except when I was trying to slip by in academic drag, I thought I wrote clearly. But it turned out that I didn't—not by Maclean's glass window standard and not under the pressure of the weekly quiz. The ordeal was worse than coping with Mr. Blair's topic sentence: that was taking a test, this was being on trial. All the twists and turns of my previous styles—Hemingwayesque; Mann-like ponderous; New-Criticism jargonist; metaphorical gamesman; louche academic; delicate, impassive craftsman; and lately, adaptive pedant—were now so many impersonation acts that had caught up with me, so much silt that had accumulated in the lake of my prose and that my anxiety now kept stirring up, so that my quizzes continued to come back from Maclean with the verdict "murky diction" or "wordy point," or "loose syntax," or the most disconcerting of all, "By clear I don't mean superficial."

In despair, I turned to his own writing. There wasn't much of it; he was notorious in the department for a writing block that had all but silenced him throughout his career. (You can perhaps see its foundation being laid in the early pages of *And A River Runs Through It*, when his father hounds him to keep cutting his compositions by half.) Two long essays in *Critics and Criticism*, a collection of the Chicago Critics, was nearly the sum of Maclean's output: one an erudite and readable account of the evolution of poetic theory in the eighteenth century, so solid and intricate as to seem built as much as written; the other on the madness of King Lear as viewed through the lens of Shakespeare's artistry. This was something else, an eloquent masterpiece of Neo-Aristotelian analysis. The criteria of intelligibility and interest, vividness and probability, are emplaced like targets that Shakespeare's writing will be shown to hit—targets all the more distant and elusive in that they lie on the far side of a mind in chaos and darkness. The conduct of the analysis was ingenious, clarifying, powerful, and, most remarkably, moving. Even the standard scholarly preview came across as such:

> We propose to follow Lear and Shakespeare across the heath to the fields of Dover on what for both was a unique experience, and then to be even more particular, [to consider] the individual scenes leading to this meeting of Lear and Gloucester when in opposite senses neither could see. And, for smaller particulars, we shall consider an incident from one of these scenes, a speech from this incident, and, finally, a single word. In this declension of particulars, our problems will be some of those that were Shakespeare's because he was attending Lear and at the same time was on his way toward a consummation in the art of tragic writing.

This style reminded me of what Barrows had meant by his analogy of the expensive simple black dress and Rosenfeld's effort to "come across as truly on the page as I do in everyday life." "Stop being the Felix Krull of graduate school," I said to myself. "Forget everything else about writing except going straight." Which was pretty much the same message I'd gotten from my early failure as a teacher in East Chicago. From my anxiety, opportunism, and fakery, a certain hard clarity began to emerge like a small island in a turbulent sea.

8

Early on, Roth and I exchanged short stories. Mine was the last one I'd written, three years ago, a dialogue between an old Spanish waiter, who was all vanishing vocation, and a young Puerto Rican one, who was all business, in the locker room of the Oyster Bar. Phil's was about a refugee artist working as a pottery teacher in a summer camp who befriends a gifted misfit. He dismissed my story with a sentence or two as "exhausted Hemingway stuff"; I wished that I could have done the same with his, but I couldn't. It had been selected for the Martha Foley collection of *The Best Short Stories of 1956*, but beyond that it was indisputably striking in its deftness and authority. After I'd had to say so, I asked him, "How come you know so much about being a potter?" "I don't," he said. "I read something about it and made the rest up."

This unexceptional piece of information hit me like the Last Judgment. I, who had spent years in restaurants, could make only a derivative story out of them; Phil, who knew hardly anything about his subject's work, could make it not just credible but the significant center of the story. The difference wasn't a matter of mode or taste: it seemed simply, starkly, that of ability, like the difference between an actor who can play any role, as Marvin Feldheim had said, and one who can't. For once and for all, face it.

Which I did. Not very long or hard, for I had other problems to face at home and at work that immediately mattered. Nor was the realization all that painful. It was like seeing the girl you loved married to someone else but knowing that she would remain a close friend if you could find a way to make it so. It cleared the air inside my head and stationed me more firmly in my new ambition to show Maclean. I managed to write a lucid final exam about Eliot's criticism as that of a lyric poet—someone concerned mainly with a writer's sensibility and style and his own tradition—the last point was my own, the first two I owed to Maclean, along with everything else.

Just as I wasn't a pretentious fiction writer in hiding anymore, so, too, I was no longer a contemptuous graduate student These two negatives, multiplied by each other, had turned into a positive: someone who really was what he was doing and trying to do it well. I'd already developed something of a mission as a teacher in East Chicago; now thanks to Maclean I had developed some of the directness and muscle of an interesting critic. I would never have an original mind, but I might develop an incisive one. Also something my father had told me—his one piece of positive advice—kicked in: if it's worth doing at all, it's worth doing well.

The next quarter Phil dropped out as a Ph.D. student and was writing a long story about a romance with a sporty Jewish princess from Short Hills. We still saw a fair amount of each other, usually at his small, orderly studio, where we were both more comfortable. The one time he came to our flat, he sat there like a social worker on the edge of a couch over which I had nailed an old shag rug to cover the holes. Though we both came from the same hard-pressed Jewish middle class, his clothes, his place in the College, and the money he made from writing cast us in adult prince and pauper roles. At one point, a mutual friend was giving my jalopy one of its frequent pushes and, being inexperienced at it, didn't brake when I stuck out my hand and engaged the clutch. We both had slightly dented bumpers but the next day he insisted that I pay him fifty dollars. I borrowed the money from Phil, who continued to kid me about the debt. When I paid him back, I attached a note that read, "Thanks Old Sport, Edmund," which miffed him.

So there were ups and downs. We were both high-energy go-getters, Phil in his career and I, finally, in mine. We tended to spar with ideas and opinions as much as exchange them: the fiction writer and the critic going four fast rounds over, say, *Augie March*. He saw it as a whole new development in American fiction—the novel that had broken the stranglehold of Hemingway, Faulkner, and Fitzgerald, that brought it down to the common urban ground of today and stood it on its own two feet, refreshed and ready for action. Something like that. Now the good Aristotelian, I saw it as a brilliant parade of fresh characters, incidents, ideas, and language, strung out and deflated, rather than unified and empowered, by its action.

We also had a different view of teaching. He regarded his two sections of the freshman writing course in the College as an onerous and at times nonsensical chore because of its rigid structure and narrow standard of "good academic prose." He and his fellow fiction writer on the staff, Tom Rogers, called the course Block That Punt! He also couldn't take the contentious, ego-driven staff meetings. He told me that the amount of sheer mental energy that went into getting George Orwell into the stuffy syllabus could have run a New York advertising agency for a week. His grousing was vivid and funny, but from the lower vantage point of teaching composition in East Chicago they also seemed, well, cavalier. What to him was mostly a frustrating and distracting job that he would give up as soon as he could was to me a mission and a career—that of rescuing young minds from the mass culture. So his irreverence and my sanctimony would duke it out.

What also kept the relationship tense was that we each represented something like the other's missing ingredient. He was interesting as well as enviable to me because he was so free, and I was interesting and even a touch enviable to him because I was so overcommitted. We didn't talk that much about our personal lives, but I could tell that he took his relationship with Sally a lot more seriously than Jay had. With her shining blond hair and milkmaid features she looked like a Clairol Girl with legs that meant business, but Jay had seen that beneath that fetching surface was trouble and he had split fairly quickly. Phil had not; he seemed attracted by her divorce and custody problems and regarded her mind as a project. So we had that to talk about, two saviors of troubled young women comparing notes. But then his affair blew up and soon he moved on to a very put-together Cliffy, the daughter of a Chicago power broker who needed no looking after at all. That was another freedom—to finally walk away from domestic trouble—that I struggled not to envy.

9

At the end of the humanities course that first year, John Dovitch had come to see me during my office hour. He still looked as though he had just gotten off a motorcycle but his derisive stare had mellowed into something like curiosity. As he put it, "You've gotten smarter since you started teaching here."

"Maybe you have too, John," I said. I told him Mark Twain's comment about how much smarter his father had become between the time he was seventeen and twenty-one.

"I see what you mean," he said. "But it's not what I mean. I just wanted to tell you that you said some interesting things. In class. About some of the books we read."

"Which ones?"

"Oh, most of them. But mainly *Huckleberry Finn* and *Crime and Punishment.* You got me really interested in them."

"Well, I think you brought a lot to them yourself. When we got to those books you were the star of the class. In fact, I was partly teaching them off your remarks, your saying that Raskolnikov kills because he's depressed and needs to think of himself as a big shot. Also that Huck likes to hang out with disgraced people because his father was the town drunk. You helped me to see why Huck can attach himself to Jim because of that."

"No shit. I thought you was just agreeing with me to come down to our level, which is one of your tricks. You learn that kind of stuff easy growing up in Calumet City. Anyway, like I said, you got me interested and I'm thinking of taking another literature course. What do you think I should take?"

I told him that one of my friends from Chicago was teaching the sophomore course and that I thought he'd get more from him than from either of the two permanent faculty.

Since I drove Max Halperin back and forth the next year, I was able to keep track of Dovitch's progress. I was worried that he might find Max too formidable and vice versa. Max was the other type of Hyde Park resident intellectual. Far from being depressed and idled by his dissertation experience, Max belonged to the manically challenged wing. Driving home with him after our marathon teaching day I would find him still on his toes.

"So how did you teach *King Lear*?"

"Badly," I said. "I'd just as soon not talk about it."

"Maybe it was your approach," he said. "Which one are you using?"

"I dunno. I tried to get them to see Lear as a rich old entrepreneur who's blinded by vanity when he starts dividing up the family business. But it didn't go anywhere. So after the break I switched over to Francis Fergusson's purpose, passion, and perception, which didn't either."

Even with my eyes on the road I could sense Max squirming with impatience. "Your mistake was to bypass the essential point that this play is called *King Lear*. If you don't emphasize that right from the start, I don't see how you can properly handle the psychological and theological, not to mention the political, implications."

"I think you first have to get them to relate to the basic situation and the characters. But I'm too tired to talk about it, okay?"

"The situation and the characters are mounting, multivalent aggregates of significance. Your scenario is much too reductive…"

About that point my patience broke. "Max this has got to stop or I won't drive you anymore. I'm exhausted and the last thing I want to talk about is teaching."

"Okay," he said. "But I don't see why you're taking it so personally. I'm just raising objections and firing questions."

So I had to wonder how Dovitch was faring with Max's questions and objections. But he was a serious and communicative teacher and the alternatives for the sophomore courses were the two tenured members of the staff who'd told us at a staff meeting that "here we set the bar at two feet."

"What do you raise it to?" I'd asked with my usual tact and discretion. The question proved to be the kickoff of a struggle that year about standards between the East Chicago stalwarts and the University of Chicago crusaders.

Like many other graduate students of the 1950s who had lost their enemy in the collapse of Joe McCarthy and then their hero in the near collapse of Adlai Stevenson's presidential campaign in 1956, I had found in teaching in East Chicago a whole new cause. Just as the last hurrah of the left in the pages of *Partisan Review* became an opposition to what was called "masscult" and "midcult" and "kitsch," so I came to regard teaching students who were the first of their family to go to college or even to graduate from high school as an opportunity to man the barricades of the higher culture against the onslaught of the mass one and its ominous new medium, "the tube." So did my colleagues from the university and, I imagine, most of my generation of graduate students in the humanities. The political struggle between the left and the center for the minds and hearts of the working class was pretty well over by the beginning of the Eisenhower era but there was still a cultural one to join in the so called "battle of the brows." The campus was the natural field of battle because that's where many of the sons and daughters of the working class were now to be found as well as a new faculty of people like myself who had pulled themselves up in the world by becoming college teachers.

That there was some good in our cause, as well as some posturing, came home to me in my teaching at East Chicago. By the second year

I had attracted a small following of serious students: the wife of a steel worker, a young salesman of ball bearings, a sensitive tool-and-dye maker, among others. The climax of my growing sense of vocation came toward the end of the second year when Dovitch dropped into the chair by my desk to tell me he had won a scholarship to the University of Illinois and another to Southern Illinois. Where did I think he should go? After I'd fallen all over myself congratulating him, I said that Urbana would probably offer him a richer experience and told him about the differences between Michigan and Michigan State, which were probably roughly comparable schools. When I'd finished, he said, "I hear what you're saying, but I still think I'm better off in Carbondale with the other Hunkies. I'd be lost with all those fraternity guys and intellectual hotshots. I mean I don't even have the right table manners."

Table manners. I stopped trying to persuade him and just wanted to hug him. How far we had both come in two years.

～

A few days later I found myself in the office of the director of the College. Chuck Jasperson was a relentlessly affable fellow who doubled as the head of the local Rotary Club, and he seemed to see little difference between his two roles. I thought he'd called me in to give me a pat on the back about Dovitch, but instead he told me that he thought I might be happier teaching somewhere else next year.

He was wearing a strange sport jacket with exposed black threads that gave it a hairy appearance, as though it were made from pelts. Shocked, I stared at it, for it seemed to confirm what he was saying.

I said that I liked teaching there and thought I was doing pretty well.

"You're excellent with the very good students, I don't deny that for a minute. It's the others I've got to be concerned about. They just don't feel comfortable with you. For one thing, they complain that you hardly ever smile."

I let that go by and asked if the problem didn't also have to do with my dustups with the two tenured staff about teaching approach and grade standards.

"You might say that's a contributing factor," he said. We both mulled that over. Then he went on. "But what you have to realize is that our students just aren't as well prepared and confident as the students you get at Chicago. So making them feel at home and keeping up their morale is a big part of the job. Most of them don't go on from here, you know. We're preparing them for the community and economy, not for Bloomington. They need to have their noses wiped rather than be pulled by them, if you get my drift."

I thought that he was being pressured by Vessels and McMahon, who regarded me as the ringleader of the "Chicago eggheads." But it also began to dawn on me that for all his glad-handing ways he was more concerned about the students, as they actually were, than I was. For all of my populist ambition, I taught to the brightest ones, try as I would to find examples that everyone could understand, to approach the unfamiliar by the familiar, the abstract by the concrete. But the bottom line was that I still wasn't relating to most of them; the enlightenment of the working-class student took a lot more patience and congeniality than I had.

Fortunately, thanks to Napier Wilt, I'd already been given a joint lectureship in the College and the Downtown College beginning that summer and would only be teaching three classes, for more money than I was making here. So when Steve Daronatsy, the ball-bearing salesman, offered to get up a petition protesting my being canned, I thanked him but said that I was leaving anyway, that I'd gotten a better job at Chicago.

Instead of the petition he organized an informal farewell party at a tavern in Whiting after my last class. About fifteen of my students from the two years showed up. "That's okay," I said to Steve, "We've got the quality instead of the quantity," and told him and myself about Stendhal's Happy Few.

10

All happy families may not be alike but most second-generation Jewish ones were. Since Phil and I came from neighboring Newark and Elizabeth, respectively, we had even more shared experience to get off on, from the Empire Burlesque Theater on Market Street to the boardwalks of Belmar and Bradley Beach—"the Côte d'Azur," as we wisecracked, of our youth. Much of this patter was an off-the-cuff way of connecting where we had come from to where we were at the university, of marking our journey, as it were, from an eccentric to the concentric culture. We sometimes got together on a Saturday night with Art Geffen and one or two other local wits to crack ourselves up with Jewish jokes and zany experiences. Phil was hilarious, of course, but so was Art. As Roth was later to say, "Alongside him I'm John Wayne."

The three of us had another interest that bonded us. Or rather two: Bellow and Malamud. Around this time, *The Magic Barrel* was published to major acclaim and there was much speculation, including ours, about where these sex-crazed rabbis, penitent slumlords, and black angels named Levine came from and what they might portend; for Malamud had shuffled the deck, as Phil put it, of the Yiddish immigrant culture and laid out an entirely new hand. Meanwhile, "Seize the Day" had also just appeared in—or better, loomed over us, from—the pages of *Partisan Review*, dwarfing all the contemporary urban fiction by Bellow's extraordinary portrait of the Upper West Side in its money-driven, idea-ridden Jewish concreteness. Also the story of the agonized *schlemiel,* Tommy Wilhelm, going up against his obdurate father, the retired doctor, and putting himself in the hands of the demonic Tamkin, created a pathos so powerful as to come close to being tragic, far closer than that of Willy Loman, our previous candidate for the honor of representing Jewish angst and suffering in a nondenominational guise. And the prose!—the imaginative heft and glory of it, the details and images as right and reverberant as Tommy's investment in lard futures.

It was a stirring time for me, immersed as I'd been in mostly the Anglo-American canon in which Conrad's *Under Western Eyes* was about as close as I'd come to a literature that I felt was truly my own, that had something of the intense East European heartfulness. But that year, as if I were at a concert of William Byrd and Purcell and Handel and from somewhere out in the streets, there came the faint but unmistakable sound of a klezmer band that grew louder and more distinct as it continued to approach, so the advent of high-quality American Jewish fiction began to draw near and to get my mental fingers snapping, my mind singing along. The trope is imprecise because Bellow and Malamud weren't writing Yiddishkeit but rather adapting it to modernism. So was Phil. Think of me, then, leaving the Henry James seminar that winter or the storage library of the university where I had begun to track the sources of *The Bostonians* through the pages of the *Boston Evening Transcript* and arriving at Roth's little apartment, where he handed me a beer and read me the following:

> Though I am very fond of desserts, especially fruit, I chose not to have any. I wanted, this hot night, to avoid the conversation that evolved around my choosing fresh fruit over canned fruit, or canned fruit over fresh fruit; whichever I preferred, Aunt Gladys always had an abundance of the other jamming her refrigerator like stolen diamonds. "He wants canned peaches, I have a refrigerator full of grapes I have to get rid of…" Life was a throwing off for poor Aunt Gladys, her greatest joys were taking out the garbage, emptying her pantry, and making threadbare bundles for what she still referred to as the poor Jews in Palestine. I only hope she dies with an empty refrigerator, otherwise she'll ruin eternity for everyone else, what with her Velveeta turning green, and her navel oranges growing fuzzy jackets down below.

❧

Which in one respect was right out of the jokes and anecdotes of our Saturday night sessions. (The fruit routine was in fact a variation of the two-neckties joke, just as another story from that time, "The Defender of the Faith," grew out of an experience in basic training that Art had regaled us with.) But the other respect was much more significant—that in adapting and personalizing this raw footage, as it were, of common Jewish experience, Roth was making something new—the first, really telling report from the third generation.

Of course, a young American Jew like myself didn't have to be told his people were vigorous and kvetchy, socially mobile and ethnocentric, that they connived and yet moralized like they had just invented right and wrong; we simply hadn't produced any writers to speak of who viewed them as a forthright, closely observant insider. A story like "The Conversion of the Jews"—the Hebrew school pupil sorely testing his rabbi and the community by his insistence that if God created heaven and earth and "even light," he could certainly have arranged a virgin birth—exemplified the basic conflict between allegiance and resistance that we had grown up with. In personifying and enacting this conflict with unpredictable outcomes ("Eli the Fanatic" was as much a defense of traditional Jewish values as "The Conversion of the Jews" was a satire on them), Roth was making public (since he was getting published left and right) the mentality of many of us who were trying now to liberate ourselves from twenty centuries, or so it felt, of communal solidarity, moral authoritarianism, and adaptive hypocrisy.

So it felt good reading him, as it does when you find a writer who not only speaks to you but for you. Also he appealed to the literary critic in me, who had grown weary of the buttoned-down writing that seemed to be the norm of our generation—the discreet stories of suburban or campus or corporate culture and its discontents, the odes to one's wife's or lover's toothbrush. The story of Neil Klugman and Brenda Patimkin was as overt as the exposed crease of her tush with which it opens, its meaning as out in the open as the diaphragm that Brenda arranges to have discovered—so it couldn't be art by the modernist standards of indirection and obscurity, by the lack of the room it was supposed to leave for the explicators to get in there. But I knew that art did advance in just this way—a sudden sweeping aside of privileged mannerisms and received values for the sake of a fresh view of experience, often so natural a view and so common an experience that one wondered why writers hadn't been seeing and doing this before.

More specifically, a writer like myself. What most fascinated me about the stories that would soon come out in *Goodbye Columbus* was the firm way they dramatized the inner situation that Phil and Art and I had shared as the three Ritz Brothers of English studies. Coming from homes whose taste- and opinion-makers were naturalized comedians like Eddie Cantor, singers like Al Jolson, and gossips like Walter Winchell, we were entering a field whose varieties of Jewish experience were represented mainly by Shylock and Fagin, Meyer Wolfsheim and Robert Cohn. (Leopold Bloom was the great exception, but in his Irish remoteness he was more like an honorary Jew.) This was not just a problem of texts but also of the field, which until recently had had as low a percentage of Jews as their high degree of assimilation. Though Chicago had more than most in its English department, you couldn't have picked them out from their appearance, accent, or teaching style. One came on like an English country squire, the second like a London gentlemen, and the third like a latter-day Puritan. This wasn't just Chicago; I could see the same conditioning going on in the two most successful Jewish literary academics, Lionel Trilling and Harry Levin. There had been little reason to believe I would escape this fate or that, in time, I would want to, for it was already hooking up with the aspiration that I and the rest of us had brought from home, which was known as "refinement."

Around this time, Wallace Markfield wrote a story, "The Country of the Crazy Horse," which contained the immortal line "I was 12 years old before I realized that 'aggravation' was an English word."

The same could have been said of the word *refinement*; indeed it offered, among its other blessings, the place where aggravation ceased and a calm dignity reigned. Our fathers wanted us to make money and our mothers to become refined.

Roth's style was like a tough-minded mediation of our identity conflict between the ungenteel (unGentile) and the refined, showing the way right between our professors' idiom and our fathers', melding the bluntness, the concreteness, the pungency of the talk in the *schvitz* at the YMHA on Sunday morning ("jamming her refrigerator like stolen diamonds") with the smooth cultivated conversation in the faculty dining room ("Though I am very fond of desserts, especially fruit, I chose not to have any"). Roth was hardly the first to write in the mixed style; it was turning up in some of the stories in *Commentary* and in its section of memoirs called "From the American Scene" and in the younger, ballsier fiction and reviews in *PR* by writers like Alfred Chester and Herbert Gold. But that was New York and we were small-time writers of term papers—except for Phil, who was not only in *Esquire* but also writing very funny pieces in the *New Republic*. One of those in *Esquire* wasn't very funny and I told him so. He shrugged and said, "I laughed all the way to the bank." He didn't seem at all worried, as I thought he should be, about the possibility that he was selling out.

During our humor binges Phil would suddenly slip the moorings of his gifts of precise mimicry, timing, suspense, and imagery and get carried away—or better, swept away—into a wild dark sea of vulgarity and obscenity, as far out and obsessed as Lenny Bruce himself. As everyone knew, Bruce used heroin to blast himself past his inhibitions, while the fastidious Roth didn't even smoke cigarettes. Art and I were seeing in an early form the ongoing transactions between Roth's angel of precision and his demon of excessiveness. I also took in his insistence that he couldn't do without the latter. When his strong but over-the-top story, "Epstein," came out, I was put off by all the ugly physical detail of this aging family man's first and last fling. As I put it, "Why all the *shmutz*?" To which he snapped back, "The *shmutz* is the story."

II

Our household remained precarious—a too-long-delayed trip to the dentist, new brakes, or repair of our thirdhand washing machine would take away a week's salary and send me to balance the checkbook in dread. Even among graduate students our poverty was legendary. Art Geffen and John Postel—a charming, elegant West Indian who enabled me, for the first time, to forget about color—came for one of Lynn's clever spaghetti dinners, and as Art later told me, he and John felt like they were taking the food out of Paul's and Ivan's mouths.

But in the fall of 1958 my situation went up a full notch and soon so did Lynn's. Teaching the freshman writing course on campus was a brisk breeze after East Chicago. The weekly staff meetings were lively, sometimes contentious briefings of the "rubrics" of rhetoric with which the course was structured, as it had been for the past twenty years or so. The syllabus was an array of model English and America prose writers from Bacon to E. B. White that I enjoyed teaching. In addition, once a week I would have my ego and fantasies stroked by a group of stylish young South Shore women who made up most of my literature class in the fine arts program downtown. Some were sharp; a few were beautiful; one was provocative. It was like having a mental harem.

A few months after Ivan was born, Lynn began seeing a psychiatrist at Billings, the university hospital. Her two previous ones hadn't made a noticeable difference, but Dr. O did. Far from being a stone-faced Freudian, he was tough, concrete, directive. Being also relatively young and fair, he quickly became the latest and most powerful version of the fantasy lover/savior, displacing, as she told me now, Jay. I'd more or less assumed as much about Jay and welcomed the change, being less jealous of a transference and relieved and hopeful that the storms in her life and ours, the four of us now, would finally be brought under control.

One of the early questions Dr. O asked her was what she most wanted for herself, and when she said a career in Russian literature, he told her to start studying Russian. It was November, she pointed out; she couldn't just walk into the beginning course; she didn't even know the alphabet. Start studying on your own, he said, and catch up. Which she did. Psychologist, art historian, logical positivist, actress— I'd watched Lynn plunge into one ambition after another and then watched her self-doubt and frustration and procrastination triumph over her intelligence, talent, and passion. But this time was different. As she said, she'd been acting, if not speaking, Russian most of her adult life, and she picked it up like a chicken picking up corn. By January she knew enough to speak it with Mr. Bobrinskoy, the dean of graduate students, when she applied for a tuition loan. Impressed and no doubt charmed, he gave her a scholarship. By the end of the next quarter she was the protégé of her teacher, Fruma Gottschalk. She'd found not only a mentor in Fruma but also the good mother she'd never had. By the end of the spring semester she'd been accepted into the M.A. program; given a grant by the Defense Department; which was heavily funding Russian studies, and become a full-time student.

Since I had finished my course work, I looked after the boys when I wasn't teaching on campus or downtown. In between their spats and during their naps I prepared for my orals, which I could do mostly at home. For all his nighttime wheezing, Paul by day had become a very active little boy, prodded by Ivan, a sturdy self-sufficient one who around the age of two had hit the ground running. By three he began to slip away as soon as a parental back was turned and would be found hanging around the bank two blocks away where someone had given him a nickel and where "they got lots more." My present wife, Virginia, who was married then to a colleague, Arthur Heiserman, recalls meeting the three of us for the first time on a street corner, she and Art with their four well-behaved little girls and I with my two Tasmanian devils, who were racing around the periphery of the group. I tried to keep them from darting into the street and to keep up my end of the conversation, while Virginia worried whether they'd get home alive.

12

During Wilt's James seminar I'd dug up some interesting material on the social background of *The Bostonians,* which grew out of two visits James had made to Cambridge in the early 1880s. I'd also stumbled on a significant connection between the male chauvinist views of Basil Ransom, the charming Southern protagonist of the novel, and those of Henry James Sr., which made for some interesting speculations. Also in creating Verena Tarrant, the sweet young suffragist with a talent for speech-making and a sleazy reformist father, James was possibly redrawing the notorious suffragist and free-love advocate Victoria Woodhull, who came from similarly unlikely roots and was the talk of New York during James's sojourn. Mr. Wilt said a lot of this probably constituted original research and hence gave me a dissertation topic. He urged me to press on further and, when I had enough material, to do a proposal and take it to Walter Blair.

"You've got to be kidding," I said. "He still treats me like I'm a suspicious character. What about asking Zabel if he would be interested."

"I'm perfectly serious," Wilt said. His affability was gone, and the cold, political mind I'd seen glimpses of was in full view. "They're probably not going to keep you in the College," he said. "And I can't help you much elsewhere. Morton Zabel will be about as useful to you as a third tit. I hope you understand what I'm saying. If you do, you'll work on that proposal with Blair."

It wasn't that simple for me. One-book dissertations were a favorite of Blair's and were very formulaic: sources, composition, revision, and reception. I was looking for the exit, but this was precisely the sort of scholarly hackwork I still wanted to avoid. On the other hand, I had come to be interested in my research into the sources: how James's imagination adapted his father's surprisingly inflexible views on the role of women (Henry Sr. was otherwise a cloud nine transcendentalist) and Victoria Woodhull's wanton libertarianism to his milder purposes. In other words, how the Young Master's mind worked. Also, the women's movement in Boston was interesting in its own right as the twilight of the Abolition movement. With most of this research already done and written up, the Blair type dissertation would be eminently doable. And, as Wilt had suggested, it could be very rewarding. Bob Lucid, one of my closer colleagues, had done a Blair dissertation on *Two Years Before the Mast* in six months and was now about to go from the College to Wesleyan.

While I was mulling over what to do, I wrote a longish review of *Goodbye Columbus,* which had recently come out, for the *Chicago Review*. It was the first writing I'd done in four years that didn't have footnotes and a narrow topic, and throwing academic caution to the winds, I put Roth with Bellow and Malamud at the head of the line that was forming at the dawn of a new day in American fiction. Partly I was writing out of enthusiasm for the book and its author, partly out of attention-getting for myself, but increasingly as I went along, out of the awakened desire to put my literary experience in bed, as it were, with my Jewish experience—a match that wouldn't have occurred to me before; it would have seemed like mating Man of War and the Old Gray Mare. Modernism said make it new; Judaism said make it ancient.

But such a view, I was now realizing, was mostly my childhood talking, remembrances of the foxed prayer books and yellowing prayer shawls in the musty Murray Street *shul* and chanting in a language I didn't understand. Putting the three authors together made me think again. And then ponder. For I couldn't put my finger on what they had in common that made them significantly Jewish writers besides the affinity that drew me to them that had to do with emotional vulnerability and moral gravity, the inner sweat and strain I felt in myself. At The Shop, when he was in a good mood, Dad would sing a ditty with a Yiddish lilt he likely got from his mother:

Stanislavsky of the Moscow Art Theayter
You will suffer and suffer and suffer

It seemed a link between Russian and Yiddish culture. I knew next to nothing about Judaism, but that has never stopped a Jew from speculating about what it means to be a Jew—a speculation that seems as much a part of his birthright as being circumcised or telling jokes with a Yiddish accent. I had a whole repertoire of such jokes to tell me about the comic side of Jewish identity, but little beyond an intuition about the value of suffering to link up the fiction of Bellow, Malamud, and Roth with its serious side, and my intuition needed help to guide it.

So, in good graduate student fashion, I went into the stacks and discovered Irving Howe and Eliezer Greenberg's long, splendid introduction to *A Treasury of Yiddish Stories*. Writing of the world of eastern European Jewry, they remarked: "Beauty was a quality rather than a form, content rather than arrangement. The Jews would have been deeply puzzled by the idea that the aesthetic and the moral are distinct realms. For they saw beauty above all in behavior."

In commenting on the distinctiveness of this fiction, they seemed to go to the core of the culture that gave rise to it:

The moral and psychological burdens which this world took upon itself were at least as great as the burdens of hatred that fell upon it from the outside.... Yiddish literature should focus upon one particular experience, the life of dispersion; it should release, as only imaginative writing can, the deepest impulses of that life and thereby provide a means of both consecrating and transcending the shtetl.... There is hardly a Yiddish writer of any significance whose work is not imbued with this fundamental urge to portray Jewish life with the most uncompromising realism and yet to transcend the terms of the portrayal. How could it be otherwise? Simply to survive, simply to face the next

morning, Yiddish literature had to cling to the theme of historical idealism. Beyond hope and despair lies the desperate idea of
hope, and this is what sustained Yiddish writing.

This "dispersion" had not ended when our grandparents and parents left the Pale of Settlement. It had continued for a generation or
two, perhaps in its most intensified mode, in the Diaspora. So had its
focus on conduct, on the "moral and psychological burdens," on the
"idea" of hope, often enough the desperate version. I recognized the
illuminating accuracy of Howe and Greenberg's words immediately
in thinking of Rosenfeld's story, particularly the words that had been
such an anthem to me in the ranks of "the desolate": "Theirs is the
necessity without fulfillment, but it is possible that even to them—
who knows—some joy may come." And not just Rosenfeld's story.
Now I found much the same ethos, like an ache in the back of the
novella "Goodbye Columbus," and front and center in "Eli the
Fanatic." I saw it pulsing away at the end of Bellow's "Seize the Day"
and Malamud's *The Assistant*. In the America of their fiction the
assimilated Jew, Eli Peck and Tommy Wilhelm, or the evolving Jew,
Frank Alpine, maintained the "psychological and moral burden" and
the "idea" that Howe and Greenberg had found at the heart of Yiddish
sensibility. The difference is that the Jew who was the whole person
in the Russian Pale of Settlement had now to be located and revived
in the assimilated American or self-implanted in the convert like
Alpine. Both processes came about through suffering. So, too, the
emphasis on the aesthetic of behavior that in Jewish culture found the
most beauty in *rachmones*—the primal Jewish virtue, joining empathy
to compassion—now became in modern Jewish fiction the painful
opening of the heart.

Making these points and connections, I wrote "Philip Roth and
the Jewish Moralists," which put the three narratives into a context of
Jewish heart; that is, the flow of strong, painful feeling into conduct
that separates a true moral self, which is associated with Jewishness,

from a pretender social self, which is associated with assimilation, money, or crime. Just as the steep path of conscience and storms of feeling formed the common ground of the moral growth of Eli Peck, Frank Alpine, and even pathetic Tommy Wilhelm, so, too, the common ground tone of their authors was the empathy and ethical firmness that they managed to hold together.

Written with more intuition than knowledge, the essay was published to no noticeable effect other than an encouraging word from Norman Maclean about my progress in "handling the language." A few months later, *Goodbye Columbus* won the National Book Award. I rejoiced for Phil's sake and even more for my own since I'd taken some ribbing and a few sneers for boosting him into the company of two writers with major reputations.

~

One June morning in 1959, I found in my faculty mailbox, amid the usual staff memos and fliers from textbook houses, a little blue envelope bearing the august crest of the *Times Literary Supplement*. I assumed it was a trial offer for a subscription, but it wasn't. It was a letter from the editor, Alan Pryce-Jones. I could hardly believe what I was reading. Philip Roth had told him about me. Would I do him the favor of contributing a three-thousand-word essay on the Jewish role in American writing today? If I wished to know more about him I might ask his friend Morton Zabel. He would appreciate knowing my decision soon and would need my contribution by July 15.

My scholarly professors walked tall if they got a letter to the editor into the *TLS*, and I was being *asked* for three thousand words. But by the time I got to my cubicle in Cobb Hall, the thought of writing them had become the worm in this large luscious apple. (1) I knew almost nothing about the Jewish role in American letters. (2) The *TLS* was not only preeminently scholarly but fiercely so. Unsound work pointed out there could sink a career. Writing for it would be like having Norman Maclean looking over one shoulder and Walter Blair, the other. (3) July 15th was only six weeks off, hardly enough time to work up a topic, much less a whole field. (4) I needed this time to get on with my research. The first and main section of the dissertation I was doing with Walter Blair had to be in his hands by October 1, at the latest, if it was to prompt him to recommend me for a job this fall, which was the run-up to the interviews at MLA in December. QED: Tell Alan Pryce-Jones no. Tell him he should ask someone like Irving Howe or Alfred Kazin.

But I felt like I was breaking my own heart. Moreover, if I turned down this opportunity, probably of a lifetime, I'd become the prudent, intellectually timid scholar I despised. Once again, you are what you do. So I thought against the grain of my anxiety. I knew my way around a research library by now, and since I would be teaching only a summer course downtown, I could read a ton in five weeks. Art Geffen hadn't said, "Ted's an ox," for nothing. Besides, the piece was for "a special supplement on the American Imagination," so maybe they weren't looking for scholarship but literary journalism, and literary journalism was what I wanted to write once I got the degree and the better job. So why not start now, or rather keep going, since it was the piece on Roth that had made this happen? Before I could turn back to the negatives, I dropped in on a couple of colleagues in their cubicles to bask in their congratulations about the opportunity and thereby locked myself into seizing it.

I gave myself five weeks to research the subject and one week to write. I combed the files of the *Contemporary Jewish Record, Commentary, Midstream,* the *New Leader,* and *Partisan Review,* and gazed at the literary stars with Jewish names—how many there were once you looked!—and read any of their work that seemed "Jewish," however broadly so. Along the way I came upon a seminal essay by Leslie Fiedler on "the breakthrough" in American Jewish fiction, which gave me a throughline on which I could hang the important poets, dramatists, and critics. The Saturday before I was to begin the week of writing I sorted my two hundred or so four-by-six index cards and thought I saw my way.

Sunday morning I played first base as usual for one of the local taverns. Softball in Chicago, like most things, was played the hard way, with an oversized ball and no glove. Our shortstop had a powerful arm and when one of his throws went into the dirt, I tried to dig it out and broke a finger.

The next day I began writing, but little came and nothing stayed. I had gotten used to writing on a typewriter—doing so with a pen or pencil was too much like writing an exam. But I couldn't type in my normal way with the cast on my finger, and dulled by codeine, I couldn't think very well either. By Wednesday I still had no lead and, though in less pain, I was now in the throes of a major anxiety attack: I didn't know nearly enough to write this piece; its reach was too grandiose; my grasp was too tenuous; I had blown it. The broken finger seemed like a perfect metaphor for the vanity and the comeuppance of the project.

As I was writhing in my cubicle, I spotted a copy of the *Chicago Review* that contained a posthumous essay by Isaac Rosenfeld on the experience of writing. I picked it up, began rereading it, and came to a passage in which he talked about feeling "uncertain, alone, and much of the time afraid" when he began to write something. It was as though he had walked into the room and sat down to counsel me in this terrible time. He said that the most important element of writing was the strength of the attitude with which you approached the subject. About the only thing I was sure of about my subject was my attitude, which had become one of mounting interest in and enthusiasm about the sudden importance of Jews in American letters. Until now, I'd regarded Jewish chauvinism in much the same way I regarded the glass business—as something I'd escaped from. But there was no getting around my discovery, amplified enormously by my research, that the contemporary writers who had come to matter most to me and to recent American letters were often Jewish ones. In five weeks I had uncovered the personal literature that I had been seeking ever since I was fourteen, when my aunt Fan had given me a copy of Andreyev's *The Seven Who Were Hanged* and started me on the literary pursuit of my spirit. And now I'd found a whole such literature that had been right under my nose, or at least under my fingers in the card catalog, that I couldn't wait to talk about to Lynn and Geffen and anyone else who would listen: major novels like *Call It Sleep* and *Homage to Blenholt* that had slipped under the sand, awaiting recovery; the gentle, plangent immigrant poetry of Charles Reznikoff and the fierce post-immigrant lyrics of Louis Zukofsky, neither of whom I'd ever heard of before. In one of Zukofsky's poems, I'd found the words that could serve as the motto of the diverse group of novelists, poets, critics, and dramatists I had assembled:

> I'll read their Donne as mine,
> And leopard in their spots.
> I'll do what says their Coleridge,
> Twist red hot pokers into knots.

I felt that this bold appropriation was true of overtly Jewish writers such as Malamud and Roth or the occasionally explicit ones like Fiedler, Howe and Kazin; Bellow, Rosenfeld and Odets; or the more covert but still discernible ones like Muriel Rukeyser and Delmore Schwartz, Karl Shapiro and Arthur Miller; and even, recently, Lionel Trilling. Moreover, I'd been discovering a whole cohort of my own generation—Grace Paley, Herbert Gold, and Wallace Markfield; Irving Feldman and Harvey Shapiro; Norman Podhoretz, Steven Marcus, and Milton Klonsky et al. who were leoparding in *their* spots, each making a fresh literary start out of his or her passage from home. What I could trust then was my own share of this attitude, which now required a boldness from me, the very boldness that had been the missing ingredient in my fiction and had enabled me to write the Roth piece.

So writing directly out of that, plowing through the uncertainties bred by my rapid, cursory research and the misgivings about all the fanfare I was conducting, I forged on through my index cards and got it done in time. I had no expectations about its being accepted, for I had never read anything remotely like it in the decorous pages of the *TLS*. At least you didn't quit, I kept saying to myself as I typed up the final version, having taken off the splint to type almost normally.

About a month later, the dreaded package arrived from the *TLS*. Instead of my manuscript and one of the versions of the disgusted letter I'd been composing for Alan Pryce-Jones and ingesting like small doses of poison, I found inside two rolls of drab paper, long and narrow. My immediate thought was that it was English toilet paper brutally conveying the rejection. But no, they were actually galleys containing my actual words. I read them on the spot in Faculty Exchange and then took them to my cubicle and read them again. It was all there; though I'd run some six hundred words over, nothing had been cut. Moreover it read well, as though the *TLS* typography had laundered and ironed and crisply folded the bag of sweat-soaked prose I'd handed in.

∾

During my six-week stint, Lynn had had to look after the boys and take on much of the household work—duties that we normally shared—and by the end we were at sword points. "I have a career too," she said one morning toward the end. "I need time at the library. You take the boys to the beach this afternoon." I said that in a week I'd be done and would make it up to her. "No, I need to get away. If you want someone to look after your sons, you'll have to do it yourself or hire someone else."

"They're not just *my* sons. You're not working for hire. You're being a mother."

"Well, who's being their father since you're never here?"

"We've been through all that. Over and over. I'm not going to let you hamstring me anymore."

That did it. "Hamstring you! Who the hell has been giving you the time to do nothing but work on this crazy article. Who has time to play softball and break a finger but not to give me a little relief?"

"I took them with me to the game so that you could sleep in. I look after Paul every night so that you can sleep. I've spent years listening to and dealing with your crises. Well I'm in one now. So give me a hand instead of a kick."

"Give you a hand? I've given you an arm and a leg. I've spent years depriving myself because of your frustrated talent. Now all you can think about is your poor broken finger and your missed opportunity. Well, I've had it up to here with your missed opportunities, which is the only thing you're consistent about."

"No, what I'm consistent about is finishing things which you seldom if ever manage to do no matter how much time you have. You're just jealous I'm about to finish something important, something that could make my career."

It was not the worst fight we'd had but it was a pivotal one. Because of her relationship and work with Dr. O as well as her success in Russian, she was no longer as dependent on me and could let me have it with both barrels. And because she was stronger, I was more able to act in my own behalf instead of trying to justify myself by acting in hers. We continued to fight and to threaten to break up, Lynn taking Ivan and I Paul, but the fighting issues were now those of worktime and careers rather than "that night in the Village" or my "selfish, brutal insistence on the hernia operation." Not that the other issues went away. I provided just enough money and stability and she provided just enough sex for us to go on, but neither of us was resigned to the other's stintedness. If she had Dr. O's backing in the front of her mind, I had a doting young matron and a Second City actress who were taking my course downtown, in the back of mine. We were still like two young trees that had been planted too closely together and whose root systems had gotten badly intertwined, but serious winds of change had begun to blow.

Yet young marriages are nothing if not variable and this summer proved to be the most peaceful one we had had. Life in Hyde Park is eased in summer by the proximity to the lake. When I'd get back from my afternoon in the library or Lynn from hers, we would pack a picnic dinner and head for the beach, where the boys could splash and paddle; later on near dusk we usually went to The Point, the green headland extending out to where the Chicago water turned Lake Michigan blue green, cool, and deep and I could swim to my heart's content. Other U of C families would gather there and the atmosphere was relaxed and lively, hard-pressed young couples giving themselves a little slack.

One such evening we approached an enclave of three couples who were the virtually legendary center of the in-group of campus literary society, junior wing—the Heisermans, the Sterns, and the Lymans. Arthur and Virginia, whom you've briefly met on a street corner where my two sons were madly circling their four daughters, lived in a defunct mansion that the university had given them for a nominal rent in recognition of their large family and small income. Arthur, a suave, enterprising fellow, had just gone from an instructorship on campus to associate dean of the Downtown College; Virginia, a very resourceful as well as beautiful young woman, had turned the musty mansion into what passed for an elite boardinghouse favored by single members of the College English staff and oddball intellectuals, and which was the scene, now and then, of a major party. To which Lynn and I were never invited, being on the fringe of things, but which I'd hear about from my colleague Bob Lucid, who lived there and loved it. A Hemingwayesque drinker and raconteur who prided himself on his built-in shit detector, Lucid also played, *mutatis mutandis* as we used to say back then, Nick Carraway to Arthur's Gatsby, while half the English staff claimed to be in love with his Daisy, Virginia.

The other two couples also had a contingent of little children, the Sterns four and the Lymans five, and each their share of campus stardust. Debonair Tom Lyman, an art historian, was a leading model for *Playboy* and had begun to appear as Mr. Playboy on Hugh Hefner's Saturday night program direct from the mansion. According to Lucid, Tom always appeared with his left hand in his pocket because Hefner did not want his wedding ring to show and Tom refused to remove it.

The *Playboy* Bunny craze had hit full force—but no one could be more immune to it than he was, being a devout Catholic whose passion was for Romanesque church architecture. Molly Lyman, a tall, statuesque blonde, was a no-less-successful model downtown as well as a serious painter. They were known for the dinner parties in their spacious apartment near the lake, which, as Lucid admiringly related, finally got to the table whenever Molly got around to cooking, which might not be until close to midnight.

The Stern family was headed by Dick, a bear of a man who was the fiction writer in residence, though he was only thirty or so like the rest of us. Dick had gone from New York to North Carolina as an undergraduate, which made him seem that much more to me like a Central Park West version of Thomas Wolfe—king-size appetites, talent, ambition, erudition, contacts: Ezra Pound, Thomas Mann, Saul Bellow, Norman Mailer, Flannery O'Connor, and W. H. Auden, among others. Dick was the literary impresario in residence, bringing the writers of the day to campus, letting a bit of fresh air and light into our grim, stuffy department. Gay Stern was not a beauty but contributed her piece of the group aura by a face and bearing that were pure American patrician. As I was later to learn, none of the three couples had escaped the deep problems (nor would they the disasters to come) from marrying too young and having children too soon that marked our generation. But that evening, to see these three apparently charmed families making Tolstoy's point made me want to slink past with mine. But Arthur Heiserman waved and walked over to us. He seemed glad to see me and even gladder to meet Lynn. "I've been thinking about you," he said to me. "We're offering another section of the Fine Arts lit course this fall and would like you to teach it. Your husband is a big hit with the South Shore ladies," he said, turning the charm on her.

Our income had just gone up 25 percent. I would be making more than a hundred dollars a week! Enough for nursery school for both boys! So much for my failure to provide.

"Come meet the Sterns and Lymans," Arthur said. "I imagine you know Dick," he said to me.

"A little," I said. We had met at a party. Oil and water. Or rather, lord and truculent commoner. Dick had been holding forth with a young graduate student whom I knew, telling her that being a good critic came down to knowing the right questions to ask. Joining them, I'd immediately put in my two cents. "The deeper writers don't always abide our questions. A really good critic knows that too." "Young Matthew Arnold here," he said, "If there's no answer, I don't ask the question."

But now everything seemed to have changed. He made his way upright from the blanket as we approached and seemed about to give me a hug. "Your piece on Roth was brilliant," he said. "I can't wait to read the *TLS* piece on us Jews."

"Neither can I," I said, trying to roll with the praise. "It's been delayed by a strike at the *London Times*."

"That must be driving you nuts," he said.

I forgave him everything. Suddenly I'd become his peer.

Arthur introduced us to the Lymans and Gay and then to Virginia, whom I could barely look at, much less speak to. She was sitting with Molly and their many daughters. Virginia's three older ones were unmistakable, each a slightly different version of her; her fourth was gamboling about; and her year-old boy was in a stroller. Manet should have been there—*Young Mother in a Frieze of Girls*. The scene shimmered before my eyes and I had only enough words to say, "We've met."

How did these people do it? Fourteen young children among them and yet they seemed to live so easily, even gracefully. Now that I had a fourth course and their interest, would our life come to be like theirs—invited into their magic circle? As though to raise the possibility higher, Tom Lyman handed Lynn and me a paper cup. "There's a little left," he said, pouring from a bottle with an impressive label, though even just a bottle rather than a jug would have been.

~

The step-up days continued. Mr. Wilt thought I should check out the James collections in the Harvard College and New York Public Library and came up with a traveling grant of four hundred dollars, most of which we were able to vacation with by taking to the road in our ten-year-old Plymouth and staying with friends in Marblehead. The Harvard expedition proved to be mostly a waste of time because most of the James papers were sewed up by Leon Edel (my first experience of the *Realpolitik* of scholarship), but Lynn and the boys had two wonderful weeks by the sea, while I played visiting scholar at the Harvard College Library. Then on to New York, where we stayed with Sandra and Hy in Hempstead while I examined the James papers in the Berg Collection at the New York Public Library.

The first morning, I took the train to Penn Station and decided to walk the twelve blocks to the library. It was the first time I had been back to New York in four years, but as I made my way east through the garment district, not much was doing in my head, not even curiosity. The New York where as a youth I had yearned to live and then had struggled in for most of three years had become remote to me. I was a different person and my life was now solidly elsewhere.

So I was just walking along, finding my way through a clogged street amid the vans making or taking deliveries, the porters coming at me with big carts of dresses and coats, when suddenly a familiar feeling of dull misery came over me and then a state of near panic. As though in a dream, I felt that someone was about to grab me, strip off my suit, stick me in my sleazy tuxedo pants and alpaca jacket and send me back to Warren Street. Whatever I had since become meant nothing. My recent success was a masquerade act; the new achiever in me was an impostor.

This daymare was soon over and I came back to my present self. Though not quite. A residue of new consciousness remained—of how deeply the failure in New York had sunk its claws into my spirit, and

I sensed that, like Asa Leventhal in Saul Bellow's *The Victim*, I would go through the rest of my life as someone who had barely gotten away with it.

<h1 style="text-align:center">13</h1>

The College English staff, like the whole undergraduate faculty, was living in interesting times. Chancellor Kimpton and his administration wanted to normalize its curriculum, which remained adamantly committed to its aging experiment of teaching the natural and social sciences as well as the humanities by their classical texts. It was proving easier for Julian Levi to condemn and level whole blocks of buildings than it was for the new administration to introduce a more up-to-date curriculum in the College. Finding it difficult to dismantle this institution, which had its own hardcore faculty, the new authorities turned to the student body, which they felt was overly populated by shaggy young iconoclasts known by the collective name of Aristotle Schwartz. In the interest of "beauty and brawn as well as brains"—the motto of Alan Simpson, the dashing new dean of the College—football was being revived in a modest way, and the admissions office instituted the "Small-Town Talent Hunt" to open the doors of the College to students who didn't come from the urban hotbeds of intellect like Stuyvesant and Bronx Science in New York or New Trier in Chicago.

And so a number of my students had arrived from places like Highmount, North Carolina, and Provo, Utah, as well as Newport Beach and Grosse Point. And within a month, their beauty and brawn had taken on the louche braininess as well as scruffiness of the big-city talents. The main difference I saw was between the young scientists who tended to be eminently teachable, and the young literary types, who tended to be eminently blasé. The high literary curiosity and standards of undergraduates like myself only a decade ago had almost vanished and an enthusiasm for the fugitive, unbuttoned work of Ginsberg and Kerouac was setting in.

The reign of normalcy was put to the test that year by Irving Rosenthal, the editor of the *Chicago Review*. He had assembled a special issue devoted (and then some) to Beat writing that featured a berserk piece of prose by a virtually unknown writer named William Burroughs. Somehow a reporter for the *Chicago Tribune*, which normally didn't cover literary events on campus, particularly future ones, got wind of the offensive mess that young Rosenthal had cooked up. Faced with a situation that it feared would put the old leer on the bright new face of the university, the administration cracked down as much as it could; funding was withdrawn from the issue, and Rosenthal was told that he could publish the contents, a little at a time, in that and succeeding ones. But Rosenthal refused to give an inch, fell in with a campus maverick named Paul Carroll, raised the money to publish the issue, called it *Big Table I,* and made literary history.

People I knew played prominent roles in the affair and as the free-thinking, free-swinging liberal, I was scornful of their compromise—another bad sign of the times in the community; another giving in to the Kimpton/Simpson public relations priority. But when *Big Table I* came out I found myself agreeing with the university's solution: almost all the writing was so blatantly assaultive and kooky that I had to ask myself why the *Chicago Review* should give up its identity as a quality magazine, in which the best Beat writing certainly belonged, to become a staging area for the movement itself—for the so-called Holy barbarians, who were just storming a different gate of the citadel of intellect from the ones that the advertising agencies, TV networks, some new book clubs, and publishers were massed at.

On the other hand, I knew (how could I not?) that literature, like the other arts, pushed forward by assaulting the aesthetic and moral standards of its time, including and perhaps especially the higher ones. One couldn't deny that fact merely by saying that Ginsberg and Corso were not Baudelaire and Rimbaud or that *On the Road* was a steep falling-off from *Tropic of Cancer* or *Journey to the End of*

Night. Was the Burroughs chapter from *Naked Lunch* any more gross, any more an example of the pornography of madness or violence, than, say, Alfred Jarry's *Ubu Roy*, which now had the status of a surrealist classic? As I had learned from one of my current mentors, Lionel Trilling, you not only read a book but the book read you—it could find you as hideboundedly priggish as you found it self-indulgently thuggish.

So I began to see that the Beat writers were doing something for writing that needed to be done. At least part of the problem I had faced as a young writer was the stifling literary situation itself. It was like a huge gathering. In the center of the room were the major writers of the first half of the century, mainly talking to one another. Surrounding and all but obscuring them were the critics and explicators, straining to overhear or else arguing with one another, taking up most of the remaining space. At the entrance were the writers of my generation pushing and jostling to find a little space and a sightline for themselves. What Ginsberg and Kerouac and Gary Snyder were saying was "Let's get the hell out of here and go somewhere else." As a much needed rallying cry maybe it deserved a whole issue of a mainstream journal like the *Chicago Review*.

Arguing one side and then the other, depending on the opposition, I encountered a basic tension between the standard-bearer and the iconoclast, which was to play itself out that year in Chicago and henceforth in my career.

~

The chairman of the College English staff was a highly regarded youngish Russian scholar. Slim, pale, crafty, Serge had a mind that reminded me of a Swiss army knife—lots of parts, all of them clicking precisely into place, the blades well honed. He often smiled but his blue eyes remained humorless behind his rimless glasses, which he kept highly polished, the better to take in everything. Because of his East European background and looks and because he swam so adeptly in the treacherous politics of the changing College ("Everyone around here lies just to stay in practice," Bob Lucid remarked) there was a touch of the commissar about Serge.

The staff was a large and somewhat divided one, ranging from an old guard—who had committed their careers to the Hutchins College and their minds to the protocols of its yearlong rhetoric course—to the younger ones, some committed, most restless, but all of them with careers that would likely be determined now by their graduate departments. The atmosphere of its weekly meeting was a curious mix of tired fervor and cool gamesmanship, stirred now and then by a demurrer from the small faction of dissidents, of which I was becoming a member.

Like a number of us, Serge had come from afar, that is far from the WASP ethos that was making a last stand in the humanities; but unlike most of us who were from blue-collar or frayed white-collar minority backgrounds, he did not wear his advancement ironically. He was a Harvard product and he liked to make you aware of it.

Which he quickly did when, along about November 1959, I applied for an instructorship in the College. "You'll be competing against Harvard candidates," he said, in a tone that seemed doubtful that I'd even make the final cut.

How to respond? Though by now I had a number of interviews at MLA and probably more in the offing, I wanted this job—not so much for my sake as for Lynn's. Because of her relationship with Dr. O it was tremendously important to her that we remain in Chicago. But I could see already that I wasn't going to get anywhere by being docile, which I no longer was as a member of the staff anyway.

"A Ph.D. from Chicago, Serge, isn't as good as one from Harvard?"

He shrugged noncommittally. "I guess it depends whom you ask." Then he said, "In any case you'd do well to apply elsewhere."

"I know," I said, and played another of my cards. "I already have a number of interviews at MLA."

"Where at?"

"Oh, let me see. Brandeis, Cornell, Michigan, Wisconsin, Berkeley… so far."

"So far?"

"Well, I have another month to go. Walter Blair asked me where I wanted to teach and I gave him a list of fifteen schools. So far I've heard from five."

"Walter Blair is doing that for you?" He seemed momentarily suspicious or incredulous; it was hard to tell in that fast-closing poker face.

"I'm sort of like the prodigal son who has mended his ways."

"What do you mean by that?"

I quickly sketched the recently rising course of my relationship with Blair, after I'd handed in my long chapter on the sources of *The Bostonians*. "I still don't think you're going to be a scholar," Serge said when I'd finished. "You're too impulsive and assertive."

It was more a friendly observation than a judgment. Was he after something or was he just blowing me off? "Well, time will tell," I said.

It was not the thing to say. It apparently reminded him that this was a job interview rather than a coffee break. "No," he said. "You'll do what you want to do. What is it? What are you really interested in? Literary criticism? Writing fiction like your friend Roth? Now he was like the relentless detective, Porfiry Petrovich, in *Crime and Punishment*.

"Actually I'm more interested in literary journalism."

"Literary journalism?" he scoffed. "Who writes literary journalism?"

"Edmund Wilson, for one. V. S. Pritchett for another. Randall Jarrell for a third. Come on, you know what I mean. I'm not talking about Orville Prescott or the *Saturday Review*." It was time to casually play my ace. "Like the sort of thing I did in the *TLS*."

He replied with departmental trump. "I haven't seen it. Send me an offprint."

Afterward, I walked around campus for a while, my head spinning. I'd clearly blown it. But what should I have said—that I was dying to work on Henry James's journals for the next ten years, as

Serge was working on his author's? The meeting with Serge had put my conflict squarely on the line. "You are what you do" didn't help here. What was I going to do about being a heavy-duty family man and fledgling academic versus being the independent person I had struggled most of my life to become. I didn't discount the first two: I knew that becoming a father and graduate student and working hard at them had rescued me from the pretentious sad sack in the slovenly waiter's uniform I had reencountered on West Thirty-sixth Street. But whether I liked it or not, and I mostly did, I had a maverick and exhibitionistic streak that worked in tandem, got me into trouble but also got me heard.

~

The special issue of the *TLS* had finally come out in October. My title, "Rising to the Top," had been toned down, but otherwise it was all there. Except my name, since the policy of the journal was to keep its contributors anonymous. Titled "The American Imagination," the issue occasioned a number of reviews in which "A Vocal Group" was mentioned prominently and favorably, notably in *Encounter*, which was more or less *Partisan Review* abroad; the author was Leslie Fiedler, whom I had scorned so viciously that first day with Roth and Geffen and borrowed so gratefully from to write the essay. Even my bad deeds were being rewarded.

Though not entirely. The sketchiness of my research showed through in the following issue, which ran a letter from Karl Shapiro telling the scholarly world that the author had erred in reporting that Shapiro had converted to Catholicism. Soon I learned that the noted critic Richard Chase was furious that the article had lumped him with Steven Marcus and Norman Podhoretz as protégés of his peer Lionel Trilling. Worst of all, my Jewish credential was all but invalidated by the major gaffe of referring to Sholem Aleichem as Aleichem, which I was told was like calling John the Baptist, Baptist. The *TLS* anonymity became more like a blessing.

The next month was MLA. Thanks to Mr. Blair I ended up with seven interviews and a decision to make. I could go as his student, a young Henry James scholar in the making, and not play the *TLS* card, with its glaring errors. Or I could level with each search committee about wanting to write literary journalism and take my chances with riding on the *TLS* piece. The latter, of course, was riskier but in the long run might prove wiser. Otherwise I could end up in a department that preferred scholars and be out on my ear in four years or less. Surely one or another of the search committees would be interested in what I wanted to write.

Which is how it turned out. When I mentioned literary journalism at the interviews, I mostly got a querulous response or else a very querulous one, as though I'd said I hoped to get my dissertation published and then turn to seducing students. The only interviewer who liked my future plan was Robert Heilman, the chairman at the University of Washington. Curiously enough, he was the one I expected to have the most trouble with because he was a New Critic whose book on *King Lear* had been savagely reviewed by one of the Chicago Critics in its house organ, *Modern Philology*. But he turned out to be a princely man who began the interview by asking me if "they were still running that charnel house at *MP*," and then nodded approvingly when I answered the main question by saying that I wanted to continue doing the kind of writing I'd done in the *TLS*. He was the only one who asked to see the piece and, two months later, the only one to offer me a job.

14

The literary event on campus that winter was a visit by Bernard Malamud, who was on his way back to Oregon State from New York, where he had just received a National Book Award for *The Magic Barrel*. Normally our English department took in stride even the big-time writers who came through. But because the NBA was still new and very prestigious and because Malamud was the latest thing—an important Jewish writer, like the U of C's own Saul Bellow and last year's surprise winner, Phil Roth—the news of Malamud's visit set the literary community moderately aflutter.

For me, of course, and my friend Art Geffen, it was a visit from one of the gods. Though we were writing dissertations on Henry James and J. W. DeForest respectively, we felt like gleaners in an alien land while our very own literature had suddenly come into being and was making its way to the forefront. So I was disappointed and pissed off when I wasn't invited to the reception for Malamud the first evening at the Faculty Club. I was just barely on the faculty but even so.

The next day I was told I hadn't missed anything, that all the fluttering wings had quickly come to rest or resumed their preening because Malamud turned out to be dull. So widely regarded as such that Dick Stern phoned me that evening and asked if I would do him a big favor by taking "Bern" to a movie in the Loop.

I immediately called Art and invited him to share the thrill. Along with his dissertation, he was writing, or at least contemplating, a novel with Malamud-like overtones about a Brooklyn Dodger fan who follows the team on its last swing west. He happily took the night off from his job but his enthusiasm waned a bit as we drove to International House to pick up Malamud. It was snowing and visibility wasn't that great. "Tell me something," Art asked in his aggressive way. "You're going to take Bernard Malamud on the Outer Drive in a snowstorm in this piece of shit?"

"Why not? I do it twice a week to teach and it's often snowing or icy."

"But you're not Bernard Malamud. You only have a slightly promising career to lose. In case you didn't know, the floor of your car is rusted out."

"Only on the passenger side. Also it helps the ventilation of the exhaust fumes from the hole in the muffler."

"Well, it isn't helping."

"That's because I have to drive slowly. When we're on the Outer Drive the fumes will disappear."

"It's also giving me another view of the road I'd rather not have."

We waited in the lobby for Malamud to come down. I'd heard him read a story that afternoon—a surprisingly contemporary and realistic one, "The Maid's Shoes," about an aging, perplexing, increasingly vital Italian housemaid and an aging, devitalized, and increasingly perplexed American academic. Though Malamud didn't read well, it didn't matter; the story was so finely turned and inhabited, it acted itself in your imagination. Like *The Natural* and *The Assistant* it also made you realize that he was a more versatile writer than the fantasist who had become famous for his original variations on immigrant Jewish themes. You had to be in our English department to make such a writer dull, just like it did to its graduate students.

The man who got off the elevator, though, did not look like a boldly accomplished writer was supposed to, in my intense but still virginal imagination of the literary life. He was wearing a dapper overcoat and muffler, and a fedora like our fathers wore. Seen up close, his modest mustache and careful mien made him seem more like a reliable pediatrician.

Art and I were in the clothes that had battled several Chicago winters—my old foul-weather jacket from the navy bore a number of holes down the front, made by the acid from the battery that I'd carry up three flights and keep in the kitchen overnight to give my car a better chance of starting on the mornings I drove in the nursery school car pool. After we got into the car Malamud said in a slightly doubtful voice, "Dick mentioned that one of the younger faculty would be driving me."

"That's me," I said. "I teach in the College. I asked Art to join us because he's also a passionate admirer of your work. Art's a bartender in a tavern owned by two ex-mobsters. As well as a graduate student," I added, thinking that the combination might interest the creator of Frank Alpine and Helen Bober.

"I see," Malamud said noncommittally, just like a physician.

We got into the car and headed slowly along the Midway to the Outer Drive. It was a lovely night if you liked snow. There was little wind and the snow fell softly, like confetti, and with Bernard Malamud next to me, I felt like I was driving in a parade. That the car might worry him hadn't occurred to me. If it had, I would have tried to borrow a better one, but my rusted Plymouth, like our noisy household or its frantic schedule, had become so much a part of the working conditions of my life that I took it for granted. And once it started it was pretty dependable.

"I wonder if you could turn up the heater," Malamud asked.

"It's all the way up," I said. "I'm sorry, the car is a little chilly."

"It's the cold coming in through the floor," Art explained, leaning in from the backseat.

"Also the windshield wiper for my window isn't performing well," Malamud went on. "I can hardly see through it. You also seem to have an exhaust problem."

I assured him that I could see perfectly well through mine and that the exhaust fumes would soon be gone, but it didn't assure him. I had been intent on peering and steering and when I turned to give him a confident smile, I saw the face of a worried man who likely was thinking: "Twenty years of teaching composition to night school and forestry students and just when I've finally made it out, I'm going to be killed by this crazy graduate student and his cockamamie car."

By now we had turned onto the Outer Drive, where the snow was swirling a bit less and the traffic was faster. "Don't worry," I said less nervously than I felt now. "I often drive this highway. We'll be there in no time."

Art began to ask the kind of challenging questions he was known for. Something like "Mr. Malamud, you're on record as saying that all men are Jews. Do you really believe that?"

As though he had suddenly been transported from this high-risk vehicle to a podium, Malamud replied in a somewhat didactic tone, free of the anxiety he had been signaling. What he had said was that all men are like Jews but don't realize it. "All men are subjected to their history."

"But doesn't anti-Semitism create very different histories?" Art persisted. His contentiousness sometimes got on my nerves but tonight I was grateful for it.

"The nationalism responsible for Jewish persecution in the modern age, and ultimately the Holocaust, also destroyed or ruined the lives of millions of Gentiles in the two world wars. Six million Jews died in Europe and not enough is made of that. But six to ten million Chinese were drowned in the flood of the Yangtze River in 1936 and not enough has been made of that either." He spoke as though from remarks he had prepared in advance for his first time in the New York spotlight.

"Do you see any *positive* connections between Jewish and Gentile history?" Art pressed on.

"Oh, yes. The antidote to nationalism is humanism, to which both cultures have significantly contributed. If I am a humanist, it is not necessarily because I'm a Jew. For example, Jews and Italians (my wife is Italian) are closely related in their consciousness of the importance of personality and of the richness of life and of the human past. You have only to look at the Renaissance..."

So it went, back and forth between them. To reassure Malamud, I struggled to keep quiet, my eyes on the road. But at a certain point my mental lust overcame me and I asked: "The character of Helen Bober in *The Assistant* seems to gently satirize the typically Jewish notion that if I could only get six more credits at the New School, my life would change. Did you feel that as you were writing about her?"

"Absolutely not!" he said, almost indignantly. "I would never satirize someone's quest for an education. Without my education I could never have become a writer."

His earnestness was both affecting and off-putting. It conveyed a sense of the unworldly will and integrity that created a Morris

Bober and of the almost naive sententiousness that must have gone over like lead at the Faculty Club. What I hadn't seen yet, what seemed amazingly absent, was any of the imagination and wit that wired his fiction and made his wintry Depression-like ghettos as fantastic as Chagall's shtetls, his moral blacks and whites and bits of color as startling as *The Rabbi of Vitebsk*, the first print Lynn and I had bought.

But then Art asked about the "Arthurian parallels" he had found in *The Natural*.

For the first time Malamud smiled. He even chuckled. "I threw in everything," he said.

I heard this with my own glee. "Take that, you English professors!" I thought. Perhaps he would unwind now and give us more of the real stuff. But by then we had reached the Loop and he was concerned about getting through the traffic and parking in good time before the start of the movie.

~

After we had seen Alec Guiness in *The Horse's Mouth*, Art and I invited Malamud for a drink, but he said that he had to catch an early plane. He had been very worried about the snow delaying his flight, and you could tell from his relief when we came out of the theater and saw it had stopped, that for all of the long-awaited recognition and gratification from this trip, he couldn't wait to get back to Corvallis, which he liked more than I would have expected. He told us that he could just as well have seen *The Horse's Mouth* at the new film society there. He talked about the film society and the concert and theater offerings as though the campus of Oregon State were a veritable Lincoln Center.

Perhaps because he could see out the windows, Malamud was more relaxed, or at least less tense, on the ride back. So was I. I asked him what he thought of Phil Roth. He thought Roth was very gifted and very lucky to have his gift recognized so quickly. "I hope his early fame doesn't screw him up as it sometimes does." He mentioned Thomas Heggen and Ross Lockridge. They were both celebrated young novelists of a decade ago who had committed suicide. However, "screwup" was more like it.

Art said that I'd written an essay on Phil and him and Bellow in the *Chicago Review*. Now that the ball was finally rolling, I gave it another push. "I've also written an essay on American-Jewish writing in the *TLS*."

"Yes," he said. "Dick Stern told me that. I'd forgotten. I look forward to reading your articles. Several people favorably mentioned the *TLS* one in New York. They were curious about who had written it."

Which was big news to me. *New York... favorably... curious.* The words in pairs danced in my mind. Was It beginning to happen?

Malamud turned out to be keenly interested in the reputation of different novelists and questioned us as though Art and I were the keepers of it in Chicago. "Is James T. Farrell still widely read here?" he asked.

I glanced back at Art and we shrugged. How out of it could you be? It was like asking if Gabby Hartnet, one of the great prewar catchers, still played for the Cubs. I said that Nelson Algren had pretty much eclipsed Farrell as the novelist of Chicago. Also, of course, Bellow. We got to talking about the two writers and the striking differences between them, the one so urbane, the other so provincial. I asked if he attributed that to Bellow's Jewishness.

"Not necessarily. We have had our own provincial writers," he said. "And still do. I resist the canard of Jewish cosmopolitanism. A tendency toward ethicality in Bellow seems more pertinent."

"Ethicality"?—from the author of *The Natural, The Magic Barrel?* Of course I knew what he meant. I said that Gully Jimson, the anarchic painter and ex-con in the film we had seen was a charming, full-bore example of the nihilistic Gentile artist.

"Jimson is a Gentile all right but I don't think he's a nihilist at all. I don't think an artist can be. Art values life. Art places the highest value on freedom. Not license but genuine freedom that has to be won against the necessity that imprisons each of us. The necessity of our limitations, the necessity of the form we work in. And the daring required to do so. Gully represents that. That's why he's stranded cheerfully at the end in a boat heading out to sea. A perfect image of the artist."

There was a silence in the car. The real Malamud had finally come through.

His words kept turning in my mind as I drove the rest of the way. They threw a new, nonsectarian light on his stories and both of his novels. But mostly they began to speak to me about myself. You didn't have to be an artist to struggle against your limitations in order to win some real freedom for yourself. The important thing is daring. That's what I'd been doing in the two pieces I'd published. going out on a limb, fighting my anxiety until the writing carried me away.

When we stopped in front of International House, Art and I told him what a privilege it had been. "I'll always remember your remarks about Gully Jimson," I said, extending my hand. He gave me his and a long eye-to-eye look. "You need a better car," he said. "This one isn't safe for someone with a wife and two children." His tone was what got me. It wasn't a critical one for putting him through a rough evening but rather came from the same concerned place as his remarks about Jimson. This kind of daring was foolhardy. Cautious in your life, daring in your work. He was a reliable pediatrician all right. A doctor for what ailed young writers like me.

15

At the end of the winter quarter I was proctoring the final exam with Tom Rogers, a fellow dissident who would go on to write several novels, two of them (*The Pursuit of Happiness* and *The Confessions of a Child of the Century*) finalists for National Book Awards. The winter quarter was devoted to Argument, which was taught by much the same analytic "rubrics" as Exposition: A double dose of rules and regulations before the housebroken student writers were let off the leash to practice Style in the spring.

The assigned topic of the exam was whether or not Charles Van Doren should be fired from Columbia for participating in the quiz show fraud that had recently been exposed. To while away the time, Tom proposed that we each write an argument under an assumed name, and the one that seemed the more subversive of the course's standards he'd try to smuggle into the staff grading meeting the next day where three or four borderline essays (A or B? B or C? etc.) would be discussed.

I chose the name Armand Green for a madcap Aristotle Schwartz type who broke the rules of argument we'd taught as well as some of those of syntax, diction, spelling, and punctuation but who could write—indeed was the very bête noire, the "creative writer," the course was designed against. (As his name suggested, there was also a touch in him of Turton, the mad composition student in Lionel Trilling's story "Of This Time, of That Place," who was said to be modeled on Trilling's former student, Allen Ginsberg. There was even more of Morrie Fishkin from the Children's Ward.

As the first of his subversive writing acts, Armand argued both sides of the question. He led off by denouncing the Columbia faculty and administration, who would make Van Doren a scapegoat for all the others who "allowed the academic gown to be trampled in the lucretive dust of veniality," citing among his flailing examples Jacques Barzun and Lionel Trilling, who served as two of the three judges of the Mid-Century Book Club. "Nevertheless," as he concluded, "teachers must teach and professors profess and students must study under them if the life of the mind is to continue and long endure. It can only do so by maintaining some semblance of standards against the inroads and erosion of the mass media, particularly from tv, which the behavior of Charles Van Doren has made him an unfortuneate but permenent example of."

Tom decided that Armand Green was closer than his candidate to what we were looking for. At the rump meeting that evening to select the problem essays, he slipped Armand's blue book into the pile and quietly seconded the interest and outrage it provoked. The next day the packet of mimeographed problem essays was distributed, and there among them was "Nevertheless!" by Armand Green. That afternoon when the staff met, the energy level in the room was up a number of amps.

"Let's do the simpler ones first," Mark Ashin, the course examiner, said with a meaningful look.

"If nothing else," I whispered to Tom, "we may have finally created an interesting grading discussion."

"Very interesting, I expect," he said in his measured way. "But stay cool." Some of Tom's ancestors had been officers and even a general in the Revolutionary War and others prominent in the Civil War, so he had a lot of patrician cool. He looked like a six-foot-five-inch version of Tom Sawyer but had the gifts of an American Evelyn Waugh. (His most brilliant character was to be Samuel Heather, the son of the bishop of Cincinnati, who became one of the group of American soldiers in Korea who defected to Red China—Tom to a T.)

The grades given to Armand at the meeting ranged from A- to D-, though heavily weighted at the lower end. A conflict broke out almost immediately between the old guard and the few other young dissidents. But Armand's most compelling champion turned out to be Bob Streeter, the former dean of the College, who had dropped in to teach this quarter on his way back to the English department. "We've finally produced a writer whom we haven't ruined," he said only half-ironically, "and you want to flunk him." The majority position was that we had let a student get by for two quarters who had "deliberately learned nothing"; who "spat in the face of the course"; whose argument was "bombastic on both sides"; whose "aggression rode roughshod over all distinctions"; whose grammatical, vocabulary, and spelling errors alone deserved a failing grade; who was full of opinions about the profession but couldn't even get *PMLA* right; and on and on. At first, Armand's defenders were mostly amused, while his opponents were incensed, but as the discussion went on, it became more and more heated. Now and then I glanced at Tom quietly enjoying another of his Kents. I tried to maintain the same interested but neutral silence. So did a number of the junior faculty, who weren't sure which way to jump.

The course examiners took their work very seriously, because in a holdover from the radically laissez-faire Hutchins days, the final exam was the only requirement of a course. Mark Ashin, the examiner, let himself into the staff office that evening to see who Armand Green's teacher was, something the chairman and other of the old guard also wanted to know. Mark went through all the class rosters without finding an Armand Green. Suspecting now a student prank, he let himself into the registrar's office and found that no such student was registered in the College. Around eleven that night he called Tom, having remembered that he had put the exam up for discussion. "Did you write it?" Tom said he hadn't. "Did Ted?" As Tom told me the next day, "He was so distraught by now I had to tell him the truth. He told me they would have figured it out anyway because we were conspicuously absent from the argument. That was our one mistake."

"Yeah, I was about to say that I didn't think Armand was arguing both sides of the question but employing the rhetorical strategy of dramatic reversal."

"Well, you're leaving anyway," Tom said.

That evening I told Lynn about the outcome of our prank. She hadn't been especially amused by my account of the grading session and now she was extra sullen. "So you've pretty well screwed yourself out of any chance of a job here."

"What chance? We've known for a month that they were hiring someone else. That's why I jumped at the job at Washington."

"Something still could have come up. Maybe their choice got a better offer elsewhere. Maybe someone will resign like Phil did."

"Then they'll hire someone else. Probably one of the other Harvard candidates."

"Well it sure as hell won't be you after the stunt you pulled. How irresponsible can you get?"

"Oh, cut it out. How aggrieved can you get?"

"Plenty. No sooner do I get over one of your irresponsibilities than you hand me another."

"Get over? You, get over something? The outstanding grievance collector this side of Erie, Pee-Ay?"

"You're someone to talk. Look at this dump. Look at our miserable, unstable lives. See any similarities to what your father provided? You want me to list them?"

And so we were at it again.

16

Toward the end of the spring term, the *Chicago Review* invited Leslie Fiedler to give the annual talk it sponsored. A month or two before, Fiedler had published a review of Walter Blair's book on *Huckleberry Finn* in the *Times Book Review*. Titled "Confessions of a Literary Source Hunter, "it lengthily dismissed Mr. Blair's painstaking scholarship of twenty years as being beside any interesting points to be made about Mark Twain. So it wasn't easy to find someone on campus to introduce Fiedler. Working his way down the list, the editor of the *Chicago Review* came to me; Fiedler was arriving in three days; would I please take on the job. I said that I'd have to think it over.

I put down the phone in a state of rocketing ambivalence. Given what I owed Fiedler for his organizing idea and tips and then his praise for the *TLS* piece, I could hardly say no. Also, the act would help to remove the stain on my conscience for the ugly name I'd called him. But then there was Walter Blair, to whom I now owed all those interviews as well as the job at Washington, not to mention the crucial fact that he was my principal dissertation adviser. Hegel had said somewhere that tragedy was the conflict of two goods, which hadn't checked out for me, but now I was beginning to see his point. Indeed I was now a kind of graduate student Antigone, caught between the Jewish literary family and the academic state. To whom did I owe my allegiance?

To pose the question that way was already to lean in the Jewish direction, my heart prevailing over my head. But what it came down to, finally, was intimidation or, more to the point in this case, self-intimidation. I didn't want to begin my career by caving in to fear. I didn't want to become, in Robert Frost's acid term, "departmental," which I saw happening to some of my younger colleagues on the English staff.

It was one thing, though, to agree to introduce Fiedler and another to write an introduction that would praise him without offending Blair. I labored for days and kept coming up with the same waffling nonsense. "Some would say Leslie Fiedler has traveled the road of excess; others would say, following Blake, that it has led to the palace of wisdom." By Saturday afternoon, hours before the reading, I still had nothing. Throwing the rest of my caution to the winds, I quickly wrote a kind of *homage à Leslie Fiedler* as the critic who had recently shown me a new way to view a subject, as he had done for others throughout his career: like D. H. Lawrence, he had managed to turn a good deal of the overworked field of American literature back into a fertile wilderness. As the introduction went on, the ironic note in the metaphor got buried under the mounting examples of the fresh readings in *Love and Death in the American Novel* and elsewhere.

My one remaining hope was that the event would mostly attract the literary renegades on campus and that the English department, in a show of loyalty or dismissiveness, would boycott it. But as I led Fiedler onstage and then walked to the lectern, there in the middle of the second row was most of the English department looking at me as though they were the eleven other Disciples.

The rest of the evening I continued to pay. My introduction might just as well have been a reading of Fiedler's CV for all the apparent effect it had on him. He brushed by me as though I'd been up there to adjust the mike, and proceeded to give, or rather perform, his second or maybe third most notorious single essay, "No! In Thunder." Pacing up and down on the podium as though he were not so much developing his topic as stalking it, Fiedler began with some explosive remarks on style as ultimately a mode of moral courage (Flaubert, Lawrence, Joyce) and cowardice (Dickens, Zola, James Jones) to zero in on his idea that to fulfill its essential moral obligation, serious fiction must be negative, that "the image of man in art, however magnificently portrayed—indeed precisely when it is most magnificently portrayed—is the image of a failure." Which brought him to Melville's statement about Hawthorne (but really about Melville himself): "He says No! in thunder; but the Devil himself cannot make him say yes.'" Then all hell broke loose as Fiedler proceeded to characterize the "Hard No" of writers he admired as essentially that of biting the hand that fed them—"Dante turns on Florence, Molière on the moderate man, de Sade on reason, Shaw on the socialists, Tolstoy on the reformers, Joyce on Ireland, Faulkner on the South, Graham Greene on the Catholics, Pasternak on the Russians, and Abraham Cahan or Nathaniel West on the Jews. What people, what party, what church, needs an enemy when it has a great writer in its ranks?" Whereupon the warrior of the Hard No proceeded to demolish his other examples of the Easy Yes.

A stocky man with powerful shoulders, his features fixed in a glare, his hair wild, his goatee goatish, his body language as vigorous as his verbal, he looked like he was ready to take on the house as he amplified my remark by coming upon a city and leaving behind a wilderness, in this case of rampant assertions.

After his talk, he took questions and dealt with them in the same savage way. There weren't many and none that addressed the obvious omission of the Hard Yes, the struggle to affirm, which I thought was just as basic to literature. At the party afterward I tried to say that to him but Fiedler, still with his lecture face on, answered with a shrug and turned away, though only to stand there alone, just as I did.

17

Toward the beginning of summer and its easier living, we began to make plans for the move to Seattle. The prospect had become even more appealing when Lynn won a National Defense Fellowship to study Russian there, in a department that featured Victor Ehrlich, one of the leading Russian literature scholars. I was excited by the advantages and prospects—less teaching; a more doable income, plus Lynn's stipend, subsidized faculty housing; and a soft, if moist, climate with splendid variations, so that, as I was told by Bob Lucid, who came from there, we could ski in the morning and swim in the afternoon. After five Chicago winters and five years of scrambling penury, the change was less an uprooting than a reward. But the more I kept talking that way to Lynn, the more it felt like dancing with someone who was glancing elsewhere in the room. Of course I knew whom she was looking at.

Then one afternoon in early June, she came home right after her session with Dr. O, instead of going to the library to work on her M.A. thesis on Gogol as she had determined to do because she was falling behind with it. Her cheeks streaked with mascara, she hurried past the three of us, who were eating lunch, saying she needed to be alone.

I waited awhile and then went into the bedroom. She was lying on the bed—dry-eyed now, her face stony.

"Tough session…?" I asked, sitting down on the bed.

She shifted away from me. "I need to be alone," she said. "I'm in mourning."

"Could you at least tell me who died?"

"The person I was becoming," she said, her voice rising. "You couldn't care less. You pretend you do, which is even worse. So get out. Get out!"

"It's just a bad mood," I explained to the boys, though I knew it wasn't. Something serious and perplexing had happened. I took the three of us to the tot lot and turned them loose—for what we called their "wild Indian time." After Lynn's last remark I needed some centering, and I got it by watching Paul and Ivan climb the jungle gym, swing from the monkey bars, try to run up the business end of the slide. Released from the tension at home, they sprang into activity. Their cavorting seemed the only normal aspect of our situation. I remembered as a boy using the school playground as my haven of normalcy from the raging storms of blame and misery at home. How different from that marriage this one was supposed to be. How different we were as people from my parents, yet the heavy anxiety weighing on me was so similar to what I'd felt as a boy when my father threatened to walk out for good. Could I spare these two boys from growing up with such a weight? Would I have to leave Lynn to do so? But that would mean leaving one of them behind. Impossible.

When we came back, Lynn was sleeping, her thumb in her mouth. She had started doing that again in the past couple of weeks. So I should have known that "the black wing" was approaching again. Instead, I'd just been thinking of leaving her!

I made dinner, ate it with the boys, and then bathed and put them to bed without Lynn once leaving the room.

"Mommy's still sick again," Ivan announced.

"No, she's just got her war paint on," Paul said.

"What's her war paint?" I asked.

"The black stuff. When it comes out of her eyes, you better watch out. She's in her warpath."

I explained that the black stuff was because she was sad, that something had happened today that made her cry. "People don't go on the warpath when they're sad."

Paul, who at five now knew a thing or two about emotions, slowly shook his head. "First she gets sad then she gets angry. Like when she came home."

"She gets fed up," Ivan put in. "She's gonna call the lake and tell them about us so we can't go swimming anymore."

When I came out of the boys' bedroom, Lynn was sitting at the kitchen table, smoking and twitching.

"I saved some spaghetti à la meatballs," I said. "I'll heat it up."

No response. She was in her own space again. At the stove, I heated up the rest of the dinner, hoping the smell would get her eating, bring her back. The twitching also hadn't happened in a year, eighteen months, not since she'd taken up Russian.

Finally she started talking. What had happened was that she had told Dr. O that she desperately needed to remain in Chicago for another year to work with him and that he should back her by telling me that. I could go on teaching in the College or else get another job in the area. He had refused to do so. He told her that as my wife she had to go where I could best earn our living. She said in that case she would stay behind for a year, finish her M.A. thesis, and finish her work with him. He said if she did that he would refuse to see her.

We got through that night and the next on the rest of her sedatives. The following morning she was in a different state, as though she had worked through both her anger and sorrow and arrived at a calm but remote place; though she responded to what I or the boys said, it was as though she were doing so with a corner of her mind while the rest of it was attending to a voice within. An occasional dreamy smile appeared, as though what she was hearing now wasn't all that bad. I was teaching that morning and Lynn had a class, and I asked her to meet me for lunch on campus. I didn't know what was going on inside her now but whatever it was, it made her seem especially vulnerable.

After I dropped the boys and the other kids in the car pool off at the school, I continued on downtown, troubled by the Armand Green question. Was it possible that the incident had cost me the job in the College that would have enabled us to stay in Chicago? That had happened in March, well after the slot had been filled. But that didn't stop me from feeling guilty—for that self-indulgent horseplay but also for wishing Dr. O out of our life. Much more would be required from me now to help her remain on the course that he had guided her to. To make a start, I decided to buy her a watch. A friend who worked for Science Research Associates had given me a lucrative freelance job of creating analogy and reading interpretation questions for its testing service, and before this additional income, just like the rest, disappeared like water into sand, I used it to buy her a sturdy Bulova to replace the piece of junk she was wearing.

"It's a watch for a nurse," she said in her soft, still preoccupied voice when we met in the cafeteria. "Maybe you should be the one to wear it. You're always trying to nurse me through things." There was no sarcasm in the words, but rather a touch of long-term gratitude, as though she wanted to set our record straight.

With her normally intense expression gentled, almost lulled, by the state she was in, she looked as purely lovely as I had ever seen her. Coming back to the table with our coffee, I noticed a good-looking, younger faculty guy at the next table giving her the eye and leaning toward her, evidently attracted by an erotic aura that she appeared to be unaware of. I felt a pang of jealousy, a pride of possessiveness, and an even stronger concern about her vulnerability. When I glimpsed that he was still staring invitingly after I'd sat down, I moved my chair and body between them. The momentary event unfolded with the lucid intensity of a dream.

After lunch I walked Lynn to the library. "You're still a bit drifty," I said. "We could just go home and then maybe take a walk to the Point." I was talking to her, I realized, as though she were in mourning.

"Drifty?" she said, then nodded. "That's about right."

"I'm still a bit worried," I said, waiting for her to say I shouldn't be. But she didn't. She just turned and walked into the library.

I went on to my cubicle and tried to organize the next-to-last chapter of my dissertation. When the phone rang, I thought it might be Lynn, unable to work, taking me up on my offer to go for a long walk. But it was Dr. O, who told me that he had just had Lynn admitted to the psychiatric ward at Billings. She had taken the elevator to the top floor of the library, where she said a powerful force had drawn her to an open window. Fortunately someone had been passing by and grabbed her as she was leaning out of it. She had then come to his office. He would be keeping her under observation, probably for several weeks.

❧

I was finally allowed to see her two days later. Once again, she amazed me. I came there expecting to find her angrily caged or dully sedated, but the young woman who came toward me looked as though she had just returned from two weeks in Paris. Lynn at her most vivacious.

She threw her arms around me and gave me a long, deep kiss. It drew whistles from a couple of onlookers. "You won't believe this place," she said. "I've already made friends with a genius from the math department and with a woman who worked in one of Brecht's companies. There's also an adorable kid from the College who I'm big-sistering. And the nurses and attendants couldn't be nicer or smarter. A great place. It looks like I'm in for at least six weeks.

"How come? You look like you're ready to come home this afternoon and tear into your thesis again."

"That's another plus. Endless peace and quiet. Next time you come, collect my books and notes from my carrel and bring them with you. Also that old Royal of yours. As for the six weeks, you'll have to ask old O. I couldn't get more than that out of him."

It was a delicious visit but I couldn't stay long, since I'd had to bring Paul and Ivan with me. I'd left them in the lobby with coloring books and on their best behavior but that never lasted very long.

"You're going to be able to manage okay?" Lynn asked as I handed over the suitcase of her things.

"Oh, sure," I said. With the relief and high of the moment, I felt capable of anything.

But I was on an emotional roller coaster and the next plunge downward came a day or two later when little red checks appeared on Paul's skin. Chicken pox. No nursery school for a week, probably two, since Ivan was sure to come down with it too. Though my classes on campus were over, I still had to teach downtown. I still had to get to the library to keep my dissertation going. How was I going to do all that and look after two quarantined children?

A social worker from Billings called and asked me to come in. I told her of my situation and she said, all the more reason. I got our babysitter, Mrs. Morgan, to come over and went to the appointment. Ida Gerson, the social worker, proved to be a personable young woman about my age. The more I told her about our situation, the more sympathetic and concerned she became, and though I had come there in the posture of the caring, capable mate, braced by that of a man who wanted to impress an attractive woman, I couldn't cope with being cared about and suddenly burst into tears. Once started, I couldn't stop. It was as though every sorrow and frustration and worry and feeling of inadequacy of the past five years rose up and poured forth in a rushing stream of grief.

Eventually—after a minute? five minutes?—I had no tears or thoughts left, and I took my hands away from my face and began to apologize. "You'll feel better soon," Ida Gerson said, as though a breakdown like mine happened once or twice a day in the chair I was using. "We're going to get you some help."

Later that afternoon she called to say that a Jewish social agency in Chicago was giving me a stipend of eighty dollars a week to pay for Mrs. Morgan to look after the children and manage the household. She had already spoken to Mrs. Morgan, who would be there in an hour so that I could do the shopping.

~

The psychiatric ward at Billings continued to be as much a godsend to Lynn as Mrs. Morgan was to me and to the boys. There she had a benign support system and the full attention of the two men in her life as well as of her ward friend, the mathematician. Meanwhile, Mrs. Morgan was putting our household in order, doing the shopping and cooking, and making Paul and Ivan happier and better behaved than they'd ever been. She was one of those stalwart, capable, Middle West radicals who embodied the spirit of the IWW rather than the CP— a kind of dream mother for me. Lynn and I became friends again, she talked positively of going to Seattle; we even had a blissful tryst one Sunday afternoon, when Tom and Jacquie Rogers lent us their apartment. What had been a bruising marriage became more like a careful courtship.

With this veritable new lease on life and eight free hours five days a week, I drafted all but the final chapter of my dissertation and wrote a long review for *Commentary*. And then, to make my cup runneth over, Dick Stern suggested me to the University of Chicago Press as the editor of a collection of writings by Isaac Rosenfeld and that, too, came to pass.

18

Shortly after dawn one morning in early August, a week after Lynn had come home and three weeks before we were to move to Seattle, I boarded the bargain flight to New York from Midway Airport. I was pretty much a walking bargain myself, wearing my warm-weather teaching suit, a greenish khaki Sears, Roebuck special, and an abrupt haircut that Lynn had given me the night before. My luggage was an oversized attaché case, which I'd purchased from a pawnshop in the Loop two years before, carried away by my ascendancy to the job in the College. Inordinately bulky for its usual contents of student compositions, the course syllabus, and my lunch, it was now jammed with a change of clothes, toilet articles, and a copy of *The Bostonians*, as well as two decks of research cards whose data about the novel's reception I planned to transfer during the flight to a draft of the final chapter of the dissertation I was trying madly to finish. Last, but most important, was a letter of introduction from Curly Bowen, my editor at the U of C Press for the Isaac Rosenfeld collection.

He had told me that though they'd had a contract with Rosenfeld's widow for the past year, she had so far failed to provide the published and unpublished writings and journals from which the selection was to be made. Since I'd be editing the book in Seattle, he thought I should go to New York before we moved and try to see, and if possible, carry away, the material. He said that Vasiliki Sarant, the widow, wasn't difficult so much as disorganized.

Once aloft, I took out the letter rather than the index cards and yellow pad. After two years of making the moves of a born-again James scholar, I now found myself in a real-life version of "The Aspern Papers," the story of a young man who has been sent to Rome to inveigle his way into the good faith of the daughter of a famous Romantic poet. What had been the intense fantasy of a novice writer four years ago, that of getting close to my number one role model, had now taken on reality with a twist, just as it often does in James's fiction.

There was even more to elate and bemuse me. Along with meeting Vasiliki Sarant, I would be having lunch with Norman Podhoretz. In the first eight months of his tenure, he had turned *Commentary* sharply left and made it an exciting, youthful magazine for the bright new decade that the candidacy of John F. Kennedy appeared to be auguring. *Commentary* writers were proposing bold new ideas about the Cold War (Staughton Lynd), education (Paul Goodman), the other, still impoverished America (Michael Harrington).

After making my review the lead one, Podhoretz had asked for an essay on Harry Golden, "the Jewish Will Rogers," as he called him. I'd written back to say that I'd be too busy the next few months relocating in Washington to do it but that the Gentile romance with Golden was at least as interesting as he was and that he should get Dwight Macdonald to do the same kind of job with Golden's reviewers that he had done in his famous attack survey, "By Couzzens Possessed." Podhoretz wrote back that he liked the idea and would wait for me to do it. He also said he would like to meet me. So when I learned I'd be coming to New York, I let him know.

I wondered how I would relate to him. Along with George Steiner, Podhoretz was the only critic of my generation so far to have won a reputation, and like Steiner, he was clearly a young man in a hurry. Also like Steiner he had latched onto an important heritage and regarded himself as a principal heir—Steiner of the shattered tradition of modern European humanism, Podhoretz of the *Partisan Review's* tradition of public intellectualism. Neither lacked for hutzpah. Steiner's first book was titled *Tolstoy or Dostoevsky*; Podhoretz, who had been writing for the *New Yorker*, liked to knock figures like Faulkner and Camus off their pedestals. But there the similarities ended. Steiner was portentous and oracular; Podhoretz was matter-of-fact and blunt. Steiner, another U of C product, liked to float big ideas; Podhoretz, a Columbia one, to take positions. In Isaiah Berlin's typology, Steiner was a fox, Podhoretz a hedgehog. I was a fox, too, but I got more out of reading Podhoretz. I looked forward to conversing with him, as I once would have to playing against a high scorer. I'd probably get skunked, but I'd learn something and maybe surprise myself. With Steiner, I'd merely be his next audience.

Lulled by the hiatus of flight and stroked by anticipation, I settled into a reverie. Instead of writing the novel, or even story, which, once published, would begin to change everything, I now seemed to be living it. Instead of the fledgling academic in a cheap suit with a dissertation to finish, I was now someone who had written his way to the doorstep of the big-time literary world. So it was hard for me to settle down with my index cards and legal pad and easy to stare at the letter and muse on how much things were changing and what they portended. A delicious languor came over me. No Lynn's mood to adjust to; no concern about whether Paul was well enough or rested enough to go to nursery school; no breakfast to make, no car to start, no class to prepare, themes to grade, research to do, chapter to write, bills to pay, checks to cover. Lassitude enfolded me like the embrace of an alluring woman I had long resisted, the last thought I had until the stewardess awoke me to say that I had to fasten my seat belt, we were landing.

⁓

Vasiliki Sarant was the publicity director of a small New York publisher. When I'd phoned her there, she hadn't been enthusiastic about the prospect of meeting me and discussing the material she had. Also for some reason she didn't want me to come directly to her office but to phone her when I reached the neighborhood. All of which seemed both very New York and Jamesian—busyness meets indefiniteness—but I was disappointed not to visit her office. A New York publishing house had much the same mystique for me that a Wall Street brokerage house would have for a penny-stock investor, and I wanted to see one up close and running.

The short, plump, high-energy woman, as exotic looking as her name, who came quickly across the lobby of the office building, grabbed my arm, and steered me out to the street, did not act like a James character but more like one in a story by the new Village writer, Grace Paley. Nonetheless, she had gotten herself into a situation that the Old Master would have relished. Sitting me down in a coffee shop, she said that the reason she had been stalling the U of C Press was that she had since signed a contract with Meridian Books to reprint Isaac's first novel, *Passage from Home*, and that she'd had to give Meridian the same rights to the rest of his writing that she'd already given to Chicago. "I knew how much Isaac wanted the novel back in print and the guy at Meridian, Arthur Cohen, insisted that I give him an option for the rest of the stuff. So..." she concluded with a help-less gesture.

I was wondering where all this left me when she told me. "Would you go to see Arthur Cohen and explain the situation and maybe you can straighten it out. You have a nice way about you. Do you know Cohen? He told me that he used to be at the University of Chicago too."

No, I didn't know him but, as it happened, the editor of Meridian Books, Aaron Asher, had written to me, saying that he'd heard from Phil Roth that I'd written the *TLS* article and that he'd be interested in discussing a possible book on the subject. He, too, was from Chicago. He didn't remember that we'd met when Jay Aronson was taking over his apartment, but why should he? I was just another grad-uate student then. Now I was suddenly so far out of my depth I hardly knew who I was. I who had never even been inside a publishing house was now being asked to wheel and deal in one. And on behalf of my idol's widow no less.

Vasiliki was looking at me as though I were the first good news she'd had in weeks. "Go see Aaron then," she said. "I'm sure you and he can work out some arrangement. There's plenty of Isaac's stuff to publish."

I phoned Aaron, made a date for later in the afternoon, and then walked from somewhere in the West Twenties to East Fifty-sixth Street and Third Avenue to quiet down before my lunch date with Podhoretz. It was virtually a year to the day since I'd walked from Penn Station to the Forty-second Street library and had my revelation of how shallowly buried the failed me still was. But I felt at the moment that the past year had buried him a little deeper, and though I was self-conscious about my baggy and too green suit and my too cropped haircut, I also felt in a curious way empowered by them. If I looked like a hick, I was a hick of parts who, as in some Frank Capra movie, was about to go up against the city slickers.

❦

The office of *Commentary* was in an impressive blue-paneled contemporary building, the headquarters of its sponsor, the American Jewish Committee. I'd anticipated something more nobly deprived, on the order of the squat, blackened loft building off Union Square that housed *Partisan Review*. But from the walnut and leather lobby to the spruce elevator to the young blonde in jeans with the cheekbones of a model who met me in the small reception area of the magazine's office and introduced herself as "Jed McGarvey, Norman's secretary," I could see that the new *Commentary* was not just the rambunctious kid brother of *PR*, it was also the favored grandson of a very well-to-do and well-established Jewish family.

"You don't look like we thought you would," Jed was saying in an uncanny take on my silent words.

"Better or worse?" I managed to reply.

"Different," she said. "More virile than most of our writers." And gave me another appraising look.

Well, welcome to a different New York than I'd known. "Norman's looking forward to seeing you," she went on. "He'll be off the phone any hour now." She went back to her desk, the first one in a line beside a row of five or six individual offices, their handsome, walnut doors discreetly closed.

Soon enough, Norman came rapidly out of his office, a man on the move, his hand already outstretched, a welcoming, one-of-the-guys' smile, followed by a measuring blue-eyed gaze. Heavyset, already balding at thirty, wearing a pale lemon short-sleeve shirt over a summer tan, he had a fresh, vigorous air, as though he had just emerged from a cold shower rather than a phone call.

He led me into an important-looking office, put his elbows on his desk, and continued the simultaneous little smile and slit-eyed scrutiny. "A lot of people in New York have been trying to figure out who you were," he said. "I even had C. P. Snow try to find out your name from the *TLS* but they wouldn't give it to him."

So it was really true. "How did you find out?"

He said that he had come across my piece in the *Chicago Review* and could see that it was by the same person. He asked what had brought me to New York. I told him about the Rosenfeld project and asked if he had known him. "Of course," he said. "Everyone knew Isaac. I used to give him books to review when I was an associate editor here."

Perhaps my expression indicated that the last hadn't gone down well. In any event, he went on the attack: "You're wrong about Rosenfeld, and most of the others you take to be so moral and compassionate. They're a pretty cold bunch."

I'd read enough of him to know that he was an aggressive contrarian, almost always attacking the prevailing view of a writer or subject. But he also was pulling rank, he being in the know, I a dewy-eyed enthusiast. I could either come back at him now or spend the next hour or so nodding agreeably. "I wouldn't know about them personally," I said. "Except for Roth and maybe Malamud, who I happened to meet in Chicago this winter. What I go on is the heart in *Seize the Day* or *The Assistant* or *Passage from Home* or *Goodbye Columbus*. Tolstoy was a real prick of a husband but he also created Anna Karenina."

He seemed less interested in his point than my response. Another long look, but this time a nod. "Don't listen to the teller, listen to the tale," he said.

The quote from D. H. Lawrence changed the mood. It opened some common ground and relaxed us, two former English majors of about the same age. He asked me about my dissertation and I asked him how he had avoided the graduate school track. He hadn't. He talked about being a Kellet Fellow at Cambridge and of studying with F. R. Leavis. "If you're looking for a moralist…" he said.

"I know," I said. "You don't have to be Jewish."

"Speaking of being Jewish, the ending of your piece is dead wrong." Suddenly, the hard blue-eyed stare again.

"You mean about the Puerto Rican breakthrough forty years from now?"

This time he explained himself. He said that the immigrant Jews brought a unique tradition of literacy, of learning for its own sake, of social acquisitiveness and inquisitiveness, so that it was only a matter of time until their children and grandchildren began to take over the professions, including the literary one. The same couldn't be said of the other minority cultures, certainly not the Puerto Rican.

I said that I wasn't so much making a prediction as describing the American pattern of minority writing that had produced fresh and different voices from a whole lot of different regions and peoples. "It's going on now with the Jews and won't stop with us. It was something I thought the English should know about America."

"I can see that point," he said. "But you went too far with the Puerto Ricans. It's a sentimental liberal idea."

"Time will tell," I said. "But if I'm wrong, I'd rather it be on the side of inclusion."

"I'd rather be right," he said.

～

We went to a nice French restaurant around the corner. "My lunch-room," he said.

I told him I'd worked in a lot of restaurants in New York but never a French one. "How come?" he asked.

"You really have to know what you're doing," I said. "I wouldn't have lasted a day."

Which led to the Paris Agency on Warren Street and then the *Paris Review*, which he regarded as a weak alternative to what he was trying to do for our generation with the new *Commentary*. What did I think?

Propelled by a Gibson on the rocks, to which I was unaccustomed at lunch, or any other time, I said that it was "new wine in an old bottle—the twenties revisited. It's just about writing, not about any of the issues that are pressing for expression." I knew that he was all about uncovering such issues, having said as much in one of the editorials in which he'd laid down what he regarded as his mandate.

He turned on the scrutiny again and said, "I could tell from the *TLS* piece that you didn't know what you were talking about but had guessed right about 90 percent of the time. So I figured you'd make a good editor. Are you interested in working for me?"

I got sober very fast. It was as though he'd suddenly arrived at our crowded little flat with four rooms of designer furniture. So much to sort out, including his remark and the attitude behind it, the offer coming more from his astuteness than from my qualifications. Which was why it didn't startle me. It was more like a new direction to the dance he'd been leading than a new step. In any case, I found myself responding as calmly as if I'd expected it. "What do you have in mind?"

"You'd be an associate editor," he said. "At more money than you'd be making in Seattle. How much are they paying you there? Five? Six?"

"In between," I said, "But they throw in good cheap housing and there are other benefits. Plus summer teaching. I'd have to consider all that. How much does your job pay?"

"Seventy-five hundred."

I pretended to think for a moment, then said, "I'd need eighty-five." Where was my coolness coming from? If an hour ago, someone had said, "What would you give to work at *Commentary*?" I'd have held out my right arm and said, "Start cutting." But now I wasn't the green outsider who'd gotten lucky; I was my father's son looking at what Dad called a business proposition. For once, the outer life of anger and telegrams, as E. M. Forster put it, was paying off.

Norman said he'd see what he could do. By now the ramifications of the offer were sinking in. "I've got a lot to think about," I said. "A wife who has a fellowship waiting for her at Washington and two small boys who would flourish there."

We talked about that for a while. I told him the bare minimum, but he seemed to pick up on what was becoming a quandary and his manner turned sympathetic. It brought out another side of him that surprised me. I wouldn't have thought he'd be interested for a minute in family stuff, but he was; indeed he appeared to be as involved with his three daughters as I was with my sons.

So I found myself leveling with him. I told him that my appointment at Washington was also my only offer and that I'd be pulling out of it at the last minute. Also, I had a dissertation that I was no more than a month away from finishing and a five-year investment in an academic career I would be trading in for a job that I'd never done before.

He didn't say that I had nothing to worry about with the job, that he was sure I could do it. His manner said he'd given me a test and I'd passed it but there were no guarantees. (Later I'd learn that the chair I would be sitting in was covered with the blood of my short-lived predecessor.) What he said was, "You could finish your dissertation in New York, and if it didn't work out with me, you could go back to teaching. A year or two at *Commentary* would be a pretty good credential, particularly if you keep writing for the magazine. Which I want you to do in either case." With that he gave me a genuinely appreciative look.

That look, the previous concern, and the refusal to soft-soap me were to go a long way in making up my mind during the next week. He was a difficult man to read as a prospective boss. He seemed, on the one hand, to be a manly guy, a mensch; on the other, a careerist who was likely ruthless. He was superior but also receptive, categorical but also flexible. In some ways he seemed a sophisticated version of my father—the man on the go, the aggressiveness, the know-it-all mindset, the hard shell of egotism just under the rough charm. But in

262 ✣ ted solotaroff

other, humane ways he was not like him at all. So where was that comparison coming from?

To ask the question was to answer it, for the similarity was coming
from me, from the same sense of myself they both gave me—that of
being disadvantageously privileged, of coming from a cushier and
less formidable background, one remote from their urban school of
hard knocks. I had been formed by my elitist education, they by their
rise in the world. I was third-generation acculturated, they second-
generation authentic. Suburbia was in my bones, the immigrant
ghetto in theirs.

Except for the last, this didn't make much sense, since my father
and his tough glass business were so much my background, and I'd
had to scrape by since leaving college much more than Podhoretz had.
True, they were both more Jewish than I was, but since when had that
become an advantage in America? On the contrary—at least until
now. No, what seemed to be going on was that I was taking this image
of myself from them, that they both had stronger personalities that
could impose it. So I needed Podhoretz's approval and candor, neither of which I'd had for a moment from Dad, if I was to climb back
in that ring again.

≈

Podhoretz agreed to give me a week to think over the offer. I walked
on air to the subway and sped downtown to Meridian Books, a young
intellectual on a roll, Meridian being another major harbinger of the
sixties, of the new generation of us. Arthur Cohen, its publisher, was
one of the young fathers of the "paperback revolution," which turned
on the bright idea of reprinting landmark books in quality editions.
Along with publishing such books as Joseph Campbell's *The Hero
with a Thousand Faces,* Eric Bentley's *The Playwright as Thinker,* and
Will Herberg's edition of the writings of Martin Buber, Meridian had
also just made a very big splash with *The Noble Savage,* edited by Saul
Bellow and other well-known writers, which had immediately become

the most lively and significant literary magazine of the day. In its first issue had appeared the phenomenal opening section of Ralph Ellison's much awaited new novel. Also, Phil Roth had chosen Meridian over the powerful New American Library to do the paperback edition of his book. I was as thrilled to go there as I was uncertain about what I was to do there.

Also it was a publishing house. I approached it half expecting to see the next issue of *Noble Savage* rolling off the press. But there was no magic in the air, only a small suite of offices. Aaron Asher, a very sharp and agreeable guy, and I exchanged our U of C ties, then moved on. I asked how they'd gotten Saul Bellow to be the editor of *The Noble Savage*.

"I got him," Aaron said, "and he got us. I'd heard from Herbert Gold that Saul was interested in starting a literary magazine. Arthur was good enough to let me explore it. So I called Saul and said we were interested and that's how it got started."

Aaron almost made light of it, which left me all the more impressed. To pick up the phone and call Saul Bellow still seemed to me almost a supernatural act. Even having met Malamud and knowing Phil didn't bring Bellow any closer in my worshipful ken. But here was Aaron with more or less my background, who was in close contact with him, who screened the manuscripts to send to him, and who was telling me that Bellow's "arias," the short pieces at the front of the magazine, came in as ordinary typing, just like anyone else's. There was a touch of residual awe in Aaron's voice when he told me that, which helped me to get my bearings again. Curly Bowen, my editor, had told me that Bellow was very interested in the Rosenfeld project, so maybe I'd be speaking to him soon myself. I told Aaron about the *Commentary* offer; this, too, helped me to feel more real about being there.

Which was well, since we had hardly gotten into the problem of Vasiliki's two contracts when Arthur Cohen strode into Aaron's office with some question or other. Arthur was about our age and very much a U of C product; his very tone of voice, both ultrarefined and com-

manding, carried the authority of the Great Ideas. He also looked like
the million dollars that Phil Roth had told me was behind Meridian.
His shirt was a resplendent navy blue with a white collar and cuffs set
off by cufflinks and a dotted silk tie. Phil had also told me that Arthur
was an observant Jew and even a modern, German-style theologian.
But after Aaron filled him in, he suddenly was all business. "What's
the difficulty?" he said. "Solotaroff will edit the book for us."

The spell was broken. "Wait a minute," I said. "I'm not here to
offer my editorial services. I'm representing the U of C Press."

Arthur gave me an amused look, which put me back in my suit
and haircut. "How are you representing it? You mean they're paying
for your airline ticket. So I'll pay for your ticket."

"It's not that simple," I said. The literary Big-Time? "The Aspern
Papers"? This was more like the glass business. I was both appalled
and at home. "I'll take the situation back to Curly Bowen," I said to
Arthur. "Then you and he can hash it out. Perhaps you can do a collection of Rosenfeld's stories and his unpublished novel and the Press
can do his essays and reviews."

"Let me ask you something," said Arthur. "Who do you think can
do more for Isaac Rosenfeld's estate and stature—Meridian Books or
a university press? Shouldn't that be your primary concern? The moral
question is moot, since we both have contracts for the same material
that were negotiated in good faith." He had become quite earnest now,
the rather flashy, imperious young publisher giving way to the person
who had impressed Phil Roth by his seriousness and piety. Would Phil
have chosen the U of C Press? On the other hand, it was the Press
that had chosen me, which was why I was here and not back in Cobb
Hall typing my dissertation.

～

My last date that day was for dinner with my mother. She had been
living in Manhattan for the past three years, having sold the house in
Teaneck and used this first independence since she had married my

father to set herself up in a new life. She was studying piano at the well-regarded Turtle Bay School, teaching piano to children, and was living on East End Avenue, no less, in one of the city's toniest neighborhoods. True, she had two young women living with her to help pay the rent and was still just scraping by, but I could see the transformation as soon as she opened the door. Mom in a stylish black dress, her hair cut fashionably short, pearls and nail polish and fine stockings. I recognized a few pieces from the furniture of my youth but the long L-shaped living room was as smoothly and tastefully put together as she was. I couldn't get over either.

As I was sitting down beside her on our old couch, recovered in a plum fabric, I noticed a copy of *Joseph and His Brothers* on the end table. "You reading this?" I asked.

"A little each evening," she said. "It's not exactly a page turner. Often it sets me to thinking. You know, me and my reveries."

"It's meant to," I said. "What do you think about?"

"Jacob reminds me of Poppa and the boys farming in Cream Ridge. Harry was a lot like Reuben too. And Gil, of course, was the Joseph. Also, I remember how much pleasure the book gave you when you were so sick in Chicago. It brings you closer in my mind."

Life is fair as well as unfair and this was one of the evenings in which its just and shining countenance was turned to us: two people who were realizing their most cherished hopes for themselves and for each other. Almost twenty years ago, in the summer of 1941, Mom had left my father for two weeks, which we spent with her two sisters, the Weiss family's high achievers, just off Riverside Drive. Even as a twelve-year-old who wanted back his playground league in Elizabeth, I'd noticed the difference in Mom made by the security and stimulation of being with Aunt Belle and Aunt Fan and their "refined milieu," as she put it. As time went on and our home life got even worse, I'd joined my aunts in urging Mom to end it and take us to live on the Upper West Side, which might well have happened if Aunt Fan hadn't suddenly died. But now Mom had finally made it to Manhattan on her own and been transformed thereby into the freer and revitalized person I'd yearned to see, all of her squelched potential coming into play.

She was clearly as overjoyed by my news and what it betokened. She had told me when I was four or five, "None of this would make sense if it weren't for you," and so I'd grown up as the conquering hero who, according to Freud, is made by winning the Oedipal battle. But in my case, and I'm sure in many others, that was only half the story, because the loser didn't leave the field but returned once or twice a week to wreak his vengeance and havoc on both of us, ensuring that my humiliation and anxiety would be a match for my confidence and resourcefulness. Add a generous amount of filial and marital guilt as a fixative and you have the strange mixture of strength and weakness, success and failure, who has walked these pages, the prospective editor and critic who, as Chekhov put it, has had to squeeze the slave out of himself, drop by drop.

But to my mother I had remained "exceptional," and as we talked about the offers from *Commentary* and then Meridian, I could see in her happy, wet eyes and hear in her sighs, her dream for me coming true. Powerfully affected myself, I reached over and touched her eyes. "Do you remember when I used to do this?" I asked.

"You would do it to make me stop crying when you were little."

"Do you remember what I would say?"

"You'd say, 'Mommy, make the sun come out on your face.'"

"And then after a moment or two you'd make yourself smile. The way you just looked reminded me of it."

So then we then fell into each other's arms and held on, the consummation of all those years of mutual frustrated belief in the other literally shook us. "And you and Lynn and my grandsons will be in New York, too," she said. "What more could I ask?"

Her words called me back to my situation. "Maybe we shouldn't count our chickens too much," I said. "I'm not at all sure I can take the *Commentary* job." I began to list the obstacles, beginning with Lynn's fellowship at Washington. "Though its been awarded to her by the federal government rather than the university, bureaucratic decisions once made tend to be set in stone."

"Lynn's never stood in your way," Mom said. "She has often told me that."

"There's a different Lynn in town now," I said and told her about her remarkable new career, though not about the hospitalization.

"There's always a hitch, isn't there?" Mom sighed. "You can't imagine what I had to go through to rent this apartment. But where there's a will, there's a way, as Ben Solotaroff used to say. Maybe Lynn can transfer to Columbia."

"It's the middle of August, Mom. Classes begin in a month."

The more we spoke, the more formidable the problems became. Having sung so insistently the praises of the good life for Lynn and the boys in Seattle, how was I now to change the song to favor the much more problematical one of raising boys in New York? Having asked Lynn to move her Russian studies to the University of Washington, where she would have a fellowship and likely a small, friendly department, how was I now to ask her to forget about all that and try Columbia where graduate school was like having a tough, lonely job with virtually no sense of community? And how much jerking around could she take before she was back on the ward at Billings?

Such were the questions that weighed on my mind as we took the crosstown bus to Carnegie Hall, where Mom had gotten us tickets to hear Myra Hess play an all-Beethoven program, where I forgot everything except the moment. Sitting beside her, feeling her feeling for the music, I realized how much I owed her, how much the three of us did. Sandy was now working on a Ph.D. at Stony Brook; Bob was starting an M.A. at Chicago. All of us in literature. It was no accident that we had this mother with a high school education who read Thomas Mann and Isak Dinesen and André Gide, who had filled our home with Chopin and Beethoven. Who, despite the discouragement and abuse, had held our household together and kept her head high enough to show us our way.

19

Once back in Chicago, I called the Defense Department fellowship program and was told that Lynn could transfer her fellowship to Columbia once she was accepted into a Ph.D. program. Then I called the Slavic languages department at Columbia. The professor I spoke to there didn't see any problem about her being admitted to the Ph.D. program with a National Defense Fellowship in her credentials.

I didn't tell him that Lynn didn't yet have her M.A. Though she had made some progress with her thesis while she was in Billings, she had done little in the two weeks since she had been discharged. The sunny mood she had brought home with her hadn't lasted much beyond her joy in seeing the boys again. Though I'd scrubbed the flat for her homecoming, she'd quickly settled on it as the objective correlative of the return to her lot. "It is pretty dingy," I'd agreed, seeing with her eyes, fresh from the tasteful ward; the Goodwill furniture was four years further along in decrepitude and the walls were mostly covered with Paul and Ivan's crayon art.

"This isn't dingy," she said. "This is squalor."

"Love and squalor, Esme," I said, putting my arms around her.

Which she'd shrugged off, quickly bringing me, too, back to the way things were.

Where we had more or less remained with our occasional break for joking or sex and a nice Sunday before I left for New York with Marie and Bill Gordon. Also a graduate student in Russian, the scholarly and very witty Marie had become a close second to Dr. O in Lynn's support network. In thin, intense, and brilliant Marie, Lynn had found her soul sister. Marie's marriage was a rocky one, so along with their love of the Russian language and culture, they had that in common too, though Marie and I liked each other and seemed to share a certain tacit understanding of Lynn.

Lynn's mood hadn't much changed in my absence, and certainly wasn't gladdened by the *Commentary* offer. No sooner did I put down my attaché case and the two well-designed tommy guns I'd bought in New York for the boys as a benign outlet for the sibling rivalry, then Lynn was on the case. "I got the *New York Times* yesterday," she said. "Do you have any idea what the rents are in Manhattan? You can't find anything big enough for less than two fifty."

"That's three thousand a year," I said. "I've asked for eight-five; that's a much better percentage than we have here or may even have in Seattle."

"I don't want anything even remotely like what we have here. Ever."

"Agreed," I said. "Let's talk about the real issues."

And so we did, almost constantly, for the next week or so. Lynn didn't budge. Though Seattle had originally been like a rainy exile for her, she had come during her weeks in Billings to accept it and even look forward to it. The main reason was the Russian department's renowned Victor Ehrlich, whom Lynn and Marie regarded as the top man in the field. I didn't have much to say that had an effect on her or even on me. Her situation was precarious; mine was not. The boys would be happier and easier in Seattle than cooped up in Manhattan. I wouldn't have to bug out on the one teaching job I'd been offered or take on one I'd never done before. I was beginning to swallow a gallon of bitter disappointment when fate seemed to intervene.

It came in the form of a letter from Robert Heilman one morning as we were sloughing through the alternatives for perhaps the last time. Heilman wrote that though he had promised me at least one literature course, he had to ask me the great favor of teaching instead two sections of Factual Writing for Forestry Students. Though couched in his gracious prose, it hit me like the opening bar of Beethoven's Fifth, destiny pounding at the door.

"That's it," I said, handing Lynn the letter. "I just can't give up the chance of a lifetime in order to teach two sections of Factual Writing for Forestry Students. We're going to New York." I was surprised by my own conviction but that didn't make it feel any less firm.

I could see her mobilizing herself. She shooed the boys into the backyard, came back, and said with no less conviction. "You're going to New York with Paul. I'm going to Seattle with Ivan. I can't think of a better reason for separating."

There was no point opposing that. By now it was merely a formula for ending our quarrels, a way of having the last word. It was no more likely to happen than our going to Seattle together now. But then I thought, what could happen is that Lynn would go to Seattle with Ivan and call me after a couple of weeks to come and take him off her hands. I began to think of what life might be like in Manhattan or a nearby suburb like Riverdale with someone like Mrs. Morgan running the household. For the moment at least, something basic had changed in the algebra of the relationship—it didn't factor out, as it always eventually had, to Ted + Lynn = 1. But the guilt was still there, and after a delicious few minutes it began rising, a tide that soon began to carry away the thought of freedom. From life at Mom's knee to the glass business to the navy to early marriage, that had been my story: disorder and early bondage. Could one change one's story? Or was the field of choice such that however different a development might seem to be, it soon was either reshaped or rejected by the story to maintain its line? I was too much of an Aristotelian by now to doubt it.

We still had the stipend from the Jewish Board of Guardians, so I dropped the boys off at Mrs. Morgan's and went on to my cubicle to type a little more of my dissertation. Walking on campus I met Art Heiserman who had heard of my news. Art was the smoothest of our cohort of graduate students, which was why he was already an associate dean. He had a caring manner that quickly drew out of me the circumstances of my indecision. "You seem to have a practical decision and a spiritual one," he said.

"Which is which?"

"The practical one is giving up the job at Washington. You should decide that one on your behalf, not the university's. It's an institution and institutions will always find a way to deal with their needs."

"That cuts through a lot," I said gratefully. "Particularly coming from you."

"About the decision affecting you and Lynn, I think it is a spiritual one. Would you like to walk over to Rockefeller Chapel and sit there for a while?"

I'd heard that Art and his wife were Catholic converts, and his handsome face had taken on the soft cast of a priest's. "I don't think so," I said. "I'm not a religious person."

"Everyone has a soul, Ted. I think that something is being asked of yours. That's why I suggested the chapel."

"What do you think is being asked of mine?"

"I can't tell you that. I wouldn't dare to."

"I don't usually think in those terms. Perhaps you're right."

There wasn't much else to say after he had made his point. We went our separate ways and I continued to ponder what he'd said. Thanks to the Neo-Thomist tradition at Chicago and the religious tilt to literature in the 1950s that ran from the later Auden to the later Salinger, there was a good deal of austere spirituality in the campus Zeitgeist, and though I hadn't given a thought to converting or even to going to *shul* on Yom Kippur, I could tune in to where Art was coming from. As I did so, I found myself on Lynn's frequency: her haunting herself as a nun, her fast attachment to Donatello's Mary Magdalene and Bach's Saint Matthew oratorio, her effort to write about the religious motifs in *Dead Souls*. This didn't mean, of course, that she would sacrifice her new vision of herself in Seattle and go with me to New York. Such a decision wasn't in her spiritual makeup. Why then did it seem to be in mine? Because it was. Because my soul was cut along the lines of looking after people rather than making deep contacts with the otherworldly. Because its mechanism was psychological rather than spiritual. It had enabled me to write my essay on suffering as a Russian/Jewish path to redemption. Factual Writing for Forestry Students could be my version of Tommy Wilhelm's money anguish or Frank Alpine's servitude or Eli Peck's self-ostracism. I would go through its fire and be proven by it. I could write for *Commentary* and maybe even *Partisan Review*, serve as Rosenfeld's editor for whomever, and still hold down the fort in Seattle.

By the time I got home that afternoon I had almost talked myself into doing just that. I expected to find Lynn still combative or depressed, which I would use my change of mind and spirit to end or at least see what effect it had. Maybe she'd be so moved by my self-sacrifice…? I found instead that she was brimming with elation. "We're going to New York," she said. Paul and Ivan were also grinning and began jumping up and down, as though they had been told that we'd go to Yankee Stadium as soon as we got there.

"What's going on now in this madcap household?" I asked.

"I talked it through with Marie and she said we'd be crazy to give up the chance to be in New York and to move in the intellectual circles there. She also said there was a terrific guy in the Columbia Russian department named Rufus Mathewson. I'm really sorry I've put you through all this shit. It's that loose screw of mine."

"Luckily Marie has the screwdriver," I said. "Perhaps I can borrow it from her." We sat down and opened the jug of G&D, which we never did before dinner, and I told her about how close we had come to ending up in Seattle. Then I called Podhoretz, who was surprised by my decision.

20

A day or two before we flew to New York, I went to my cubicle to pack up my dissertation material and whatever else I wanted to keep. I slowly made my way through letters, memos, teaching notes, and personal journals that haphazardly documented the last two years and, if all went well, my last ones as a teacher, the vocation in which I'd finally found myself, the ladder that had saved me.

One of the files contained a half dozen or so letters from Phil Roth. I read through them, following the peregrinations of his new topflight writer's life (Paris, New York, Amagansett, Rome, New York again, and now Iowa City, for which he had turned down Stanford).

Early on in the correspondence was the rough patch that had erupted over the *TLS* piece, which I'd sent him while I was waiting to hear about it. His response had been critical of my survey approach and said I should have taken a more introspective one: what it felt like now for a Jewish writer to be regarded and to regard oneself as, of all things, an insider. Despite my own misgivings, or because of them, I'd snapped back that I would hardly know what to say about being an insider. I said that he was being dismissive and condescending of what I did write and maybe what really bothered him was that I hadn't paid enough attention to his work. Which I hadn't, being overly conscious of his sponsorship at the *TLS*. This was followed by another round or two of hurt sparring which he ended by saying, "This is all getting picky and beneath everybody's dignity." In a subsequent letter he'd written:

I have some after the fact thoughts on your TLS piece. Want to hear them? One: you were obviously the star of that issue, and the chances are that you did say the only fresh thing in the whole two pounds of paper. I think what caused trouble for us, however, was that we had shot the shit about that enough for it not to seem brand new to us, and both of us were impatient; you I remember said you were dissatisfied that in spots you could do no more than list authors and books. And of course I found that unfortunate too. But the truth winds up being that that was just what you really should have done. At least I think that's the truth. That this phenomenon was one we knew didn't in any way mean that others knew it. In fact it seems as though they didn't. So the function you served, old chap, was to point out to a large audience of literate people a big change has occurred in the production of American literature. Boston had its day, then specifically Cambridge, and then in the twenties the Midwest, but now the producers are urbanites, and the verbal urbanites, the Jews. (Why do you think the Italian-Americans didn't do it? They have or maybe had so many of the same problems, with Catholicism thrown in.) Anyway, shy as I was some months back about being grouped in with a bunch of Jewish writers, I suddenly find myself willing to believe that this is something.

Rereading the letter now, I was struck by the evenness of temper, the willingness to overcome his own disappointment as well as my previous surliness. Phil really did wish me well. Why did affection and praise still seem so much more illusory than disregard and criticism? Why did I feel so immediately defined by someone's dislike or even indifference and remain basically unaffected by regard? Was that true of everyone or just me, whose father's hostility had been more decisive than his mother's love? Chicago had saved me, strengthened me, but I was still the same person. Probably William James was right, that by thirty, one's character has set like plaster.

I was still saving and discarding, remembering and musing, when the outer door opened and a young man walked in. He was wearing a suit and tie, which was unusual for this time of year, particularly for a student. He looked vaguely familiar, but many students did and I was too caught up in my own mood to want to be even polite. "You looking for someone?" I asked, getting up to get rid of him.

"Yeah, I'm looking for you," he said, with the uncertain smile of an interloper. "I guess you're busy." It was John Dovitch.

I was stunned, virtually speechless; my heart in my mouth, I blurted out something.

"I've been looking all over for you," he said. "Someone in the English department office told me you might be here. There's something I want to tell you but it can wait a bit. How you doing?"

"No, you first tell me how you're doing. John Duvitch in a suit and rep tie." Falling into East Chicago patter to put him at his ease, I said, "Looking boss. Looking sharp."

"Well, University of Chicago and all that. I didn't want them to throw me off the campus before I saw you."

"Most of the students here dress worse than the kids from the Region," I said. "But I like you in the suit."

"You think clothes make the man?" he said, with a bit of the old glint in his eye.

"No, but they can help." I told him about the first time I'd faced a class in East Chicago and how partly because of the suit, I knew my life had changed.

"Funny you should say that. It ties in with what I came here to tell you. I wanted you to know I'm going to graduate school to get a master's. I'm going to be an English teacher. Not a professor of course. Just in a high school."

What could I say? I caught my breath, blinked at the tears. Then the words came. "It means a lot to me that you came here to tell me that. More than you can know."

Then we stepped down the emotion. He asked about the cartons I'd been filling and I told him about the job in New York. He hadn't heard of *Commentary* but he knew about *Partisan Review* and was reading the first issue of *Noble Savage*. "I got a lot to catch up on," he said. "You know us English majors. Stuck in the nineteenth century. I was hoping you'd recommend some current books you really like."

I gave him some authors and titles. A few of them, *The Naked and the Dead, From Here to Eternity, Invisible Man*, he'd already read. Once or twice I asked if that would do and he urged me to go on. "I've got the bug," he said. "I read all the time."

I could see that. He was like someone raised on rice and beans who had immigrated to a country of beef and pork. He gave the cliché *avid reader* its original force—a craving. I told him that.

"You used to say a cliché was an image that was so stale, no one bothered to taste it. Also, a platitude was a truth that had lost its blood supply. I remember stuff like that you taught us. I'll pass it on to my students when I get some. I'm gonna steal like mad from you." Again, the old audacious Dovitch glint.

"That's okay," I said. "I got the platitude thing from one of my teachers here. Mostly that's what good teaching is. Passing it on."

"That's good," he said. He took out his little notebook again and wrote it down.

"I just got it from you, John," I said. "You've taught me a lot too."

After I had walked him to the door and we hugged good-bye, I thought about that last exchange and the meeting itself. Being so proud of John, I felt proud of myself too, the feeling I so rarely had. It seemed the crux of our seeing each other again, the truth beneath the sentiment, the thought that lay too deep for tears. I could even see for the first time what Wordsworth had meant by the line, the blood put back in the platitude. The image was Maclean's.

How things sometimes came together. Wordsworth was Maclean's favorite poet. From Wordsworth to Maclean to me to Dovitch to some student of his. The democratic circuitry of literary culture. Now I was leaving teaching to become an editor, which I hardly knew anything about except that it must be a bit like teaching. Podhoretz had said that if I were a good composition teacher, I'd probably be a good manuscript editor. But it seemed to go beyond that, to the realm of making things clearer and more interesting, which I'd begun to learn to do from the hard time that Dovitch and Maclean had given me.

It was strange to find Maclean and Dovitch in the same train of thought. But there they were—the standard bearer and the bearer of new cultural energy, the nucleus and the outer ring of a serious reading public in America that was once again expanding. And I began to see that if I was to have a vocation and not just a job or a career as an editor and critic, it would come from keeping Maclean and Dovitch together in my mind.

PART FOUR

Mind-Forg'd Manacles

In every parting there comes a moment
when the beloved is already no longer with us.
—Flaubert, *Sentimental Education*

I

In the fall of 1961, about a year after we came to New York, Lynn began seeing a charismatic psychiatrist named Winston McGregor.

We were renting a small brick colonial on a tight little street in Riverdale, the houses attached to one another and most of their residents attached too, as members of the aspiring Irish middle class— lots of pub owners, police and fire captains, post office managers and court clerks—who regarded us as noxious, noisy Jews. After a few months they loudly said as much in the conversations they held about us in the adjacent backyards, their voices raised enough so that we would be sure to know how unwelcome we were, though we already knew that from the way their kids had been bullying Paul and Ivan and from the words I'd had with one of the fathers.

Along with this tension and unpleasantness, there was Lynn's unhappiness at Columbia, where she said her most interesting course so far was in Old Church Slavonic. Meanwhile, the life I was leading, thanks to *Commentary*, was as enthralling as hers was not. The only dull aspect of it was the weekend dinners and parties at the apartment of one or another of the fabled New York intellectuals, which I, along with Lynn, began to be invited or taken to as one of "Norman's young men." Podhoretz called them the Family, and for the most part they behaved like an elderly one whose members were tired even of arguing with one another; mostly they gossiped about others who were not there, grumbled about the latest leftist delinquency of the former favorite son and his "new *Commentary*," and instructed and rivaled each other in gracious living. Coming away from Hannah Arendt's prestigious annual New Year's Eve party in which the Podhoretzes and ourselves were among the few couples there under fifty, Lynn remarked, "So this wake is what I gave up Seattle for?" And then, to more or less complete her demoralization and bring back her suicidal state of mind full force, she became pregnant. The young psychiatrist she had been seeing arranged a medically recommended abortion. Soon after, he left New York and referred Lynn to McGregor, saying that he was somewhat unorthodox but could be just the right man.

McGregor immediately proved him right on both counts. At the first session, when Lynn started talking about her suicidal thoughts, he cut her short by saying that he didn't deal with that problem. If she wanted to do away with herself, he recommended that she do so in a way that left as little mess and fuss as possible. Walking into the sea seemed to him a good way. What else did she want to talk to him about?

She came home in a state close to equanimity. She said it was as though McGregor had taken the bullet out of the pistol she'd been holding to her head. "It left me looking a bit silly to myself to hold the pose." In turn, it left me feeling both relieved and determined not to let myself be intimidated by that gun again. Not that she had said that unless I did this or didn't do that she was going to kill herself. No, her "demon," as she called her suicidal urge, was too clever and effective for that; the threat came in dreams that she would tell me or in her spacey I've-got-a-secret behavior of that day in Chicago when she had come close. It took McGregor's bluff rejection of the demon itself to reveal to both of us that it was no longer an immediate threat but a form of control of both of us, from which I now felt freed.

So I was grateful to him right off the bat. Which was well, since he wanted to see Lynn three times a week and did not offer student discounts. Indeed, his dealing with fees was much like his dealing with suicide. It was not a matter he discussed—nor did he bill. His fee was fifty dollars a session, which meant that a month of seeing him was probably not much less than the rent for his spacious office in the upper Fifth Avenue building, and was, like the rent, payable in advance. That's how he put it: you rented his time as you did his air-purified and dehumidified space, his couch, his box of Kleenex; how Lynn used what she had paid for was up to her. And to me, who began moonlighting like mad, writing two or even three pieces a month, to pay him.

He continued to be worth it. Not only did Lynn's mood improve and her discontent with her academic and our social life abate, but we now had a whole new subject, brimming with interest and speculation, to discuss: McGregor. His eclectic ideas; his forthright methods, which appeared to involve the soul as much as the psyche; his recommended reading. The first book was *Before Mass*, by Father Roman Guardini, an eloquent guide that he gave Lynn to help her prepare for the analytic hour and that even helped me a little with writing. His presence in our life became a sequel to the first year in Ann Arbor, when we both got jobs on the Ward, and a much more interesting, positive, and manifold topic to talk about than that of being married to each other.

Though Lynn was feeling more positive, her demon didn't quit. Instead, as though adapting to its new and more formidable opponent, it replaced the suicide issue in time with new hallucinations that came every week or so and led to more screams in the night. Our harassed landlord was glad to cancel our lease. We moved to Park West Village, a new middle-income project directly across Central Park from McGregor's office. We didn't choose it for that reason but it came to seem as though we had, as more and more of Lynn's mind and our marriage came under his sphere of influence.

Just as McGregor's point of view had defused Lynn's threat to herself, so he now began to modify her fantasy life and the terror and panic that came with it. He led her to view her hallucinations not as the near edge of insanity but instead as a gift for visionary experience that early ages and other cultures would have esteemed and cultivated rather than treated and sedated. He gave her Saint Teresa of Avila's *Life* and her *Interior Castle* to read as a kind of role model of a character and mind distinctively similar to hers—deeply mystical and visionary but also witty, dissimulating, shrewdly practical, widely gifted. He also told her that she was misemploying herself in graduate school, that she should be spending this period of her life in reading, contemplation, and writing meditations and poetry. Guided and inspired by McGregor and Saint Teresa, Lynn settled into her new perspective and identity, gave up her courses and fellowship at Columbia, and entered a period of relative serenity and security.

Engrossed as I was in working at *Commentary*, editing the collection of essays and reviews of Isaac Rosenfeld, and writing about all manner of authors and subjects, I had my hands full and my head often elsewhere. Which was well, because when it turned to McGregor and Lynn now it was wracked by ambivalence. She was more independent and easier to live with. Under his ministrations, her "daimon," as she now called it, could even be gentle and reassuring. I went back to Chicago for several days to gather material for a piece about the university for *Esquire*. When I arrived home late one night. Lynn was lying in bed in one of her entranced states, aware of me but indifferent, as though I had just returned from a trip to the bathroom. I put down my suitcase and started to sit at the end of the bed to tell her about Chicago.

"Be careful of the dog," she said softly.

"What dog?" (We had given up Nada three years ago when she was about to get us evicted from our third flat in four months.)

"The beautiful black Lab who is lying at the foot. He came to look after me and the boys while you were away. He's sweet and tough."

McGregor had a fondness for Labs, and *sweet and tough* was his phrase for what he liked his patients to become. So I figured I knew who had lent the dog to Lynn's imagination. It was around then that I began to feel less grateful to McGregor than diminished by him.

That same winter of 1962, our domestic tranquility suddenly broke wide open when I showed Lynn the manuscript of a piece I had just written for *Commentary* about latent anti-Semitism, based on our experience in Riverdale. Ten minutes later she came back and threw it at my feet. "It's vile!" she announced. "I want you to keep this kind of *dreck* to yourself and not drag me into it." I had indicated that there was some provocation on our side, that we were not the quietest or most conventional family on the block. I didn't put it much more pointedly than that, but Lynn reacted as though I had listed every fight, every morning tantrum she had thrown in getting Paul and Ivan off to school, every scream in the night. She accused me of being worse than Hannah Arendt, in "letting those Irish fascists off the hook and then hanging the Jews themselves on it." She refused to appear in anything I wrote "no matter what it is about."

There was no sense getting into the Hannah Arendt accusation, which was how her hyperbolic rage worked. I said, "Fair enough. I'll publish it under a pseudonym."

She said that anyone who knew us would know who had written it because we had talked about the several incidents to friends.

"That makes about ten people who will gather that we have loud, abusive fights, which they have probably have guessed anyway, not to mention our new neighbors." I had intentionally chosen a corner apartment on the ground floor to minimize the sound effects of the household. "You're being irrational as well as vicious."

"No, I'm asserting my right to privacy. If you insist on publishing that *dreck*, I want you out of here tomorrow."

Which got me furious because the only reason I'd written the piece was to help pay for the two rents—here and at central headquarters across the park. I told her that my life and hers would be better if she just moved in with McGregor. Then I went into Paul and Ivan's room, where they were watching TV, inured to the *Sturm* if not the *Drang* of their home life. "Come on, you guys," I said, "It's time for some offense/defense." That's what I often did at such times—grab a football or a ball and bat and take the three of us into the sane sphere of physical exertion and skill and competition with rules and boundaries and an ethic of fair play.

When the Riverdale piece came out under the name of Boris Weiss, Lynn took a copy to McGregor to restoke her grievance. She then told me that he'd said that she had overreacted to the piece, which was "innocuous," and that what had really struck him was my "weaknesses" as a writer. He had gone over the first two pages with her, pointing out its flaws of organization and style.

I could hardly believe what I was hearing. "You're saying that McGregor used most of the hour to criticize my prose? That that's what he regards as appropriate professional behavior? What else is he providing for that fucking rent of his?"

"He also wants to see you. He says that I can't make the progress he foresees for me unless you're in treatment too. He said that my outrage was really directed against your passivity, which is one of our problems. He knows of someone who would be right for you to see. He understands a lot about you."

"Just from my prose style, no doubt." But I was too upset for sarcasm. If he denied my manhood and writing ability, what was left? I was backed against the ropes and getting pummeled while she coolly looked on. "Lynn, what is happening to us?" It was less a question than an appeal. "This guy is taking over our lives. He's turning you into Saint Teresa and me into shit."

Her new sweet and tough demeanor, accent on the *tough*, cracked at the sight of the tears in my eyes. She got up from the other side of the dining table, where we did most of our talking these days. She took my head and held it against her breasts and said over it, "I know this is hard for you. Change is very painful but we've got to go through it if we're ever going to grow. We're just stunting each other this way. Have been for years." Then she said, "And after I get the boys pacified, I want to show you how unlike shit I think you are."

One of the changes was that she had taken over some of the storytelling at night. There was Moshe the kosher crocodile who guarded a moat in Riverdale and lately a New York version of *Winnie the Pooh*: Pooh was an enforcer for Piglet, the brains behind the notorious Robins mob, whose hideout was across the street in Central Park; Owl was a masterful night burglar, Eyeore an expert counterfeiter, Tigger a holdup artist who often forgot his gun and had to be a mugger. Piglet was Paul's invention, Owl was Ivan's. Lynn's antic voice coming from the bedroom punctuated by the boys' comments and laughter evoked the hilarity and imagination that the household ran on as much as it did on tension and exasperation. We were all characters—Paul a highstrung wisecracker, Ivan a precocious maverick. The other morning when I'd woken him for school, he told me that he'd had a bad dream but wouldn't tell me what it was. Being who I was, I tried to cajole him into doing so. Being who he was, he said, "Your dreams are your own business." Lately he had taken to hanging around the apartment of Miss Swift, his personable second-grade teacher, until she came home and would invite him in for milk and cookies.

The peals of gaiety coming from the bedroom were balm to my aggrieved state of mind. Sure we were a bit nutty, what family of expressive people wasn't? As for McGregor, passivity hadn't gotten me to where I was now in New York. Perhaps I'd ask him to let me take a crack at his prose. I'd go to his office and have that out with him; also to find out how I was standing in Lynn's way, even as I struggled to meet the deadlines that enabled her to see him. But beyond all that, I had to see him because there was too much of what was coming from the bedroom riding on him.

So it was that I found myself a week later sitting across from a crisp, dapper, small, firmly built, and completely self-possessed middle-aged Canadian who gave the impression that he'd look the same on a horse as he did behind the desk: Norman Maclean in tweed. The room was spacious, the furnishings leathery, an in-use eclectic library ranged along the walls, a near shelf featuring the phenomenologists— Saussure, Husserl, Merleau-Ponty—several serious landscapes, well-treated air arising from a filtering system in a slight mist as though going forth to moisten and purify the rest. The office of a thinker who took good care of himself.

He gave me a noncommittal scrutiny as I sat down in the chair he motioned to and settled back in his. We were curious about each other but that was as far as the parity went. He had what Mark Twain called "the calm confidence of a Christian with four aces," and I had the uncertainty of someone who is both angry and grateful. When he asked me to tell him something about myself, I told him that I didn't see how tearing down my prose style was part of his treatment of Lynn.

"That's understandable," he said. "But it's not what I asked you. I don't talk about my treatment of a patient except to my peers and not many of them." He let a moment go by for emphasis, then said, "Why are you so pissed off? Is your style above criticism?"

"Of course not. But I prefer that it not be behind my back."

"That's an impossible demand for anyone whose writing appears in public." Again, the emphatic pause. "You waste a lot of time getting started, don't you—writing the first paragraph or two twenty times before you can get into it."

It was true. I had to say so.

"It shows in your finished prose. There's a certain self-evasiveness going on in the essay I read. It prevents you from going right to the point and sticking to it. What causes it bears looking into, don't you think?"

"My self-evasiveness?"

"No, your guilt that causes it. You write like someone with a lot of unexamined guilt."

Five minutes into the discussion and I was already somewhere else, my grievance dropping away like the city one is flying out of. For the next forty-five minutes or so I was aloft in a new space, the psychoanalytic space, where the normal law of emotional gravity is suspended and one floats freely from one problem to the next. I found myself talking easily and readily even about matters I had heretofore kept to myself and was now getting off my chest—another reason for this feeling of buoyancy. At the end McGregor handed me a slip of paper with a name and a phone number. "He's a man in whom I have a great deal of trust." I thanked him. "You're made of more sensitive stuff than I thought," he said in the same dry way. I thanked him for that too. My resistance was gone along with my resentment. When I got outside and stood there in the street, I realized that my way of regarding my life had shifted. The overtaxed helper was being offered help. That I hadn't asked for it and that an hour ago I would have dug my heels in resisting it signified nothing now. The only doubt in my mind was how I would pay for it.

Peter Wykstrom was like nothing I had expected. A fair, beefy man with a strong but open face, he looked and sounded more like a youngish country doctor than a New York analyst. He told me right off the bat that he was a minister who had completed analytic training. "Would that be a problem for you, since I take it you're Jewish?"

"What faith?"

"Well, I was raised as a Mennonite."

"That's pretty conservative, isn't it?"

"Very," he said, smiling. "I'm still trying to overcome it."

I liked him immediately, though wondered if he could keep up with me. It turned out that he had studied with Tillich and Niebuhr at Union Theological Seminary and that his ministry had been mostly in a drug clinic in Harlem. I found this out over time, just as I found out that I wasn't there to be intelligent. That happened sooner, in about the fifth session, in which I told him about a dream of being back in Ann Arbor and about to fail a course it was too late now to catch up in. I went on for a while, interpreting its situation, making connections, drawing implications. "Pretty significant stuff," I said by way of conclusion. "What do you think?"

"Listening to you I've gotten more and more sad, and I felt pretty good when we started."

Lying there, I burst into tears, and the work began.

2

We spent the last two weeks of that summer in a cabin at North Truro. Two friends of ours from Ann Arbor, Marcia and Jeff Stone, had rented a house there; their child, Amy, was in the same age range as Paul and Ivan and so we spent a lot of time together. Sometimes what a couple most needs is another couple—one that can take up the slack of familiarity and freshen the stale air of togetherness. In the companionable vibes of the Stones, we felt more like our individual selves and also acted more like a team. Jeff, a physicist, was subtle and witty, and Marcia, a writing teacher, was deep; in Ann Arbor she and I might have eventually dated had we not been otherwise involved and so there was a certain poignancy of the might-have-been as well. That came home to me keenly one evening when we all went to a carnival in Provincetown. At one point I lost track of Ivan, and after some anxious looking, came upon him and Marcia walking hand in hand, both lost in the moment.

Meanwhile, Lynn and I became more relaxed with each other, as though the August moratorium in the analytic year were also part of the vacation. Then one morning toward the end of the two weeks, I picked up at General Delivery a thick envelope addressed to Lynn. It bore the name W. McGregor and a return address somewhere in Canada. I was mostly puzzled by it and handing it over, I said, "Maybe it's your schedule of sessions for the fall." Later on that day she handed it to me. "He says you can read it too," she said.

It started out with his saying that since she knew so little about him, he thought it would be a good idea to tell her in some detail how he was spending his vacation at his place in Canada. Something like that. I read that much and handed it back to her. "I'm not interested in his impressions of nature," I said. "I think it's an intervention in our vacation and marriage and I don't want any part of it."

"I'm surprised myself," Lynn said. "But it's very like him. He makes his own rules."

Once the shock began to wear off, I didn't know what to make of the letter myself. He had given me Wykstrom, which had taken the outrage, mostly, out of his using my writing the way he had. But beyond that, he had sent me into analysis in which, more even than in my Marxist phase, the old house was coming down so that the new road could go through. After seven months now of working with Wykstrom, I had been brought to see that the angel-devil dichotomy I had created about my parents and had so deeply believed in for so long was not the way I felt about them in my actual depths, where the love and hate toward them was far from divided or clear. I had seen my beliefs turn into "defenses," my memories into "screens," my ideas into "rationalizations." I had seen my very consciousness defer to my dreams. So, hardly knowing anymore what to think of myself, I was distrustful of my judgments of others, particularly the snap ones.

And this seemed doubly so when it came to McGregor. Though I completely trusted Wykstrom, I'd figured out that he had been supervised, and perhaps still was, by the authority down the hall, and so I was still under McGregor's supervision too, a subject of his realm. That's what it felt like, virtually religious. For what was the core of analysis—all that sacrifice, all that time, all that confession and submission and silence and hope of improvement—if not a process of faith in and attachment to a remote figure and his power of forgiveness and rectitude?

So, on the one hand, McGregor was this arrogant shit who felt free to write semi–love letters to my wife; he couldn't even take August off, like all the others did, from getting into her head. On the other hand, he was He, the analyst's formidable authority raised to the next power. For Lynn certainly, and for the me who entered his domain twice a week.

The only way to untie the knot was with Wykstrom, so I began with my tirade the first day back. But his response was noncommittal. I pressed on. "Are you sure you don't have a conflict of loyalty here that you're hiding under that neutrality? Are analysts supposed to write letters to their pretty married patients so that they won't die of curiosity about them while they're on vacation?"

"That's a question you'll have to ask McGregor. As for your first question, the answer is, I'm pretty sure I don't have a conflict of loyalty."

Well, when it came to integrity I'd already decided that he was the rock of Gibraltar, so we went on to my talking about my jealousy, which was in conflict with the sense of gratitude I'd had for McGregor's taking Lynn off my hands. Soon we were talking about my fear of losing her and then my fear of being alone, though most of my fantasy life was just the reverse.

∽

The two months that followed were stormy ones at home. The climactic fight came over a check to McGregor that bounced because I had made a mistake in totaling the check stubs for the previous month. Lynn shouted that it was a cheap act of revenge on her as well as McGregor, and I shouted that it was an honest mistake bred by the incessant financial pressure I was under, that instead of blaming me for not being able to pay her rapacious analyst, maybe she should stop fucking off and calling it spirituality and get a job. Which is what she did. She got a good one as the assistant to the managing editor of *Foreign Affairs*, but this only shifted the issue of contention from money to time. Meanwhile, what had been skulking in the shadows of the marriage for so long now came directly into the light, dragged there by McGregor and Wykstrom. Lynn knew that I was interested in the ex-girlfriend of one of my summer tennis partners and she made it clear that one of the editors at the journal was very interested in her. What were we going to do about it—besides tormenting each other and ourselves?

Both Wykstrom and McGregor thought we had come to a point of no return, that we both should arrange an affair to make up for the experience we had deprived ourselves of by marrying so young. "A little outside sex can go a long way toward satisfying your curiosity and scaling back your illusions," was the way Wykstrom put it. McGregor thought that an office affair was one of the better ways to arrange such matters. But what made sense on the couch, what had seemed so simple and natural and exciting in my fantasies, turned into a double burden of anxiety and jealousy by the time I got home—anxiety about my performance, jealousy about Lynn's and her prospective lover's. And since the one thing that was on our minds was the last thing we could talk about anymore, I felt out of touch with her for the first since we had been married. However much we'd fought over the thirteen years, however much we'd strained at the chains and wished them broken, there had been a tacit awareness of kindredness that had begun with the Russian vamping and continued through our uncanny similarities of interests and tastes and judgments of people to keep us communicative, the state we always came back to after our fights and crises. But it didn't appear to be there anymore, and so I was more bereft than surprised the evening before Thanksgiving when Lynn joined me after the boys were going to sleep and said, "McGregor thinks we need to separate and so do I." Bereft because I knew that this time it would actually happen.

3

Some marriages end like a business partnership that hasn't worked out. Others, like mine and Lynn's, end like a bank failure in which your life savings were deposited. We behaved like mourners—formal with each other, which we had never been, and delicately tactful, which we had seldom been at the same time, except when we were making up. I felt almost continually heartsick, which only increased as the remaining days dwindled down and the sense of impending loss and failure intensified. Several times I dreamed that we had found a way to stay together. I could hardly bear what I faced when I woke up.

We told Paul and Ivan, and each other, that this separation was probably only temporary and planned it as though it were. I would be away at the new place five nights a week and then Lynn would use it while I stayed with the boys on weekends. Fortunately, one of my friends, the poet and art dealer Stanley Moss, practically gave us the second residence—a two-room flat on West Fifty-seventh Street that he used as an office and storeroom. I could fix up the latter into a studio living space. To keep the apartment as intact as possible I took only the books I needed or most wanted to have with me, a set of the bricks and boards we still used as bookcases, a dresser I'd inherited from my favorite aunt, and the small desk and file in our bedroom. The Saturday afternoon that I was sorting through my papers, Lynn came into the bedroom. We hadn't made love since before the decision to separate, had shared the bed but hardly touched. In a way, it was a relief not to and not get turned down. But as she sat on the bed watching me, her gamey look appeared, her tongue came forth with an invitation. "For old time's sake?" she said.

I checked on the boys, who were raptly watching a basketball game on TV, locked the door, and turned to find her already nude, already in our favorite climax position. "Didn't you ever hear of foreplay?" I asked lightly.

"That's my line," she said. "Steve's Cabins."

"I know. But let me show you how much I've learned over the years." Which I did. And she did. Then I did something I'd never done before. As she crouched over me, I raised her hips and licked her at the precise point with only the tip of my tongue. It produced an exquisite ecstasy, the sexual equivalent of high C, the sense of touch at the peak of its range. "Oh my God," she kept saying above me, in her own heaven.

Afterward, we lay in each other's arms. The misery that I had been living with had gone away but now it returned with redoubled force. "Lynn, I don't want to separate," I said. "Do we really have to?"

After a moment she said, "Ted, we have to. One of the reasons that was so good was that we've begun to feel a little freedom."

"Freedom? I never felt more connected to you than when you were above me."

"McGregor says..."

"Fuck McGregor!" My wet mind suddenly burst into flames as I went from sorrow to rage in the instant. "I don't ever want to even hear his name again."

"Well, blame him if it makes you feel any better."

"It does. It's the only thing that does."

〜

I didn't want the boys to see me packing up, so I waited until the last night, after they were asleep. But I was still at it when Paul awoke wheezing as he still sometimes did and came upon me tying up stacks of books. We went into the bathroom, where I gave him his Theodur and turned on the bath to make steam. Usually we talked sports, which helped to calm him, but tonight he said, "Do you really have to go live on Fifty-seventh Street?"

I couldn't tell him I was still asking myself the same question. "I'm not going far," I said, repeating the party line. "Only about forty blocks and I'll be here on weekends. Also, every Wednesday I'll be taking you and Ivan to the Four Brothers for dinner."

"And what happens when I wake up at night?"

Another question I'd been asking myself and an even harder one to answer. The six years of this routine had bonded us so. "Well, sometimes you're beginning to mostly handle it yourself, when I leave you in here with a comic. And if you can't handle it, you just get your mom, who'll sit with you."

"Oh sure, Mom will calm me down," he wheezed. "I'll probably end up trying to calm her down."

"Now that things will be calmer around here, you probably won't have as much asthma."

He gave me his dubious look. "I'm allergic to dust and pollen, Dad, not you. Then he said, "You'll still have fights about money. Are you going to make more money living on Fifty-seventh Street?

"I'm hoping so. I think I'll be able to concentrate better."

He fell silent. I sat there trying to think of something constructive or consoling to say that we hadn't told him and his brother ten times already. All that came was my own hope. "I'll probably be moving back here before you know it."

Which only made him look more dubious, and the question of why, then, was I leaving hung in the steamy air between us.

4

I moved out the next morning, a Friday, then went on to work, and came back in the evening to a space that pretty much resembled my state of mind: cluttered, dingy, and in disarray. The storeroom part seemed to have been used as a kind of dumpster for the office part and I spent the first evening throwing out cartons of junk mail, soiled stationery, and used carbon paper, as well as broken shipping crates for paintings, a desk chair whose seat had come loose, and other items of office wrack and ruin to be taken to the garbage room in the basement. There were cartons of old correspondence, ledgers, checkbook stubs, etc. that I sorted through and moved back into the office room, so that nothing of possible interest would be lost. By midnight I had cleared enough space for my sticks of furniture and the for the studio couch Stanley had left for me; I fell exhausted onto it and slept like the dead.

When I awoke the next morning, everything seemed unreal, except the heartache. Though hungry for the first time in a good while, I couldn't make myself get up, wash, and go out to eat; though still exhausted and desperate for escape, I couldn't go back to sleep. The more or less cleared room in the baleful December light revealed how much more grimy as well as dismal the space was, how much cleaning and sprucing up it would take to make it bearable, much less enjoyable. What a difference from the pleasantness of 372 Central Park West, colored by the Saturday morning hijinks of Paul and Ivan, the cartoons going full blast, the weekend task of shopping together at Fairway, throwing the football with the boys, a Saturday night out at a movie or a dinner party, the Sunday afternoon Giants or Jets football game. How precious all that taken-for-granted life was now

"Be a mensch," I told myself, my way of pulling myself out of despair. Usually it worked after one or two injections into the mood or thought, but this morning it didn't. Instead, in time, there came my father's words to me, "You will know the meaning of the word *suffer*" and its variants. And that was what finally got me up and doing. For deeper and stronger even than the example of Hy, my brother-in-law, and other mensches I had known or known about, there was the primary dialectic of my life that Wykstrom had helped me to understand, in which I both lived out and resisted my father's image of me.

For the next two days I worked steadily to clean and brighten the space. I washed the walls and woodwork until they looked like they had been recently painted and the windows until they gleamed. I spent Saturday afternoon shopping for household items. In the evening I cleaned the kitchenette and bathroom as though a navy inspection team were coming through. On Sunday I scrubbed and waxed the floors, put the furniture in place, arranged my books, set up my desk and files, and unpacked and put away my clothes. I let the work and the flow of trivia and idiocy that accompanies relatively mindless tasks take my mind off why I was there.

Mostly I succeeded. When the loneliness returned, it took new and strange forms. As I lay in bed on Saturday night, I experienced a fear that I hadn't had since childhood, on the rare occasions when my parents were out for the evening—that of being alone with my little sister and brother in the house and defenseless against the robber who at any moment was about to emerge from the basement and climb the stairs. The studio couch I'd opened and made up was near the door and suddenly I was seized by the terror that someone was just outside it preparing to pick the lock, ease open the door, and hurl himself at me, who would be as powerless as the twelve-year-old I'd regressed to. There was nothing to do but get up, check the double lock, and hear nothing. But when I got back into bed the fear of being overwhelmed returned. I finally managed to allay it by pushing the bed to the far end of the room, where I'd have more of a fighting chance.

Toward morning I awoke and lay there in the grip of a different feeling of aloneness, one of creaturely deprivation, a loss of the closeness of the lair and mate. Those are the terms that came to me, as though the mental chill I was experiencing was from a kind of animal loneliness. Except for a few evenings on the road when my mind was taken up with the opportunity for infidelity that never quite materialized, I had slept in the same bed with Lynn for thirteen years, even when it was at opposite ends. A statement, possibly from James Joyce, ran through my mind about marriage coming down to a warm body in a warm bed. Now the only person I could hug was myself, and I had no comfort to give.

By Sunday evening I was finally finished. The last thing I did in what was now a spic-and-span studio apartment was to hang the two minimalist landscapes of earth, sky, and water that Stanley had given me when he'd showed me the space. Once on the wall, they came alive and gave the room the beginnings of a character that was less Spartan and more tasteful. For the first time since I had gotten there, I felt a positive tug of identification with the room—not the place I had been sent to but the space I would now inhabit and do my work in and bring women to and make my own.

Somewhat buoyed, I took a shower in the gleaming bathroom, put on clean clothes, and went out to find somewhere nice to eat. It was by now around nine o'clock of a Sunday evening. As I went outside and stood for a moment on West Fifty-seventh Street, taking in the deserted Carnegie Hall neighborhood that was now mine, a sudden sense of liberation struck my mind with the force of a certainty. I was someone who had been in prison for the past thirteen years and was now released. Not like someone, but that someone. The realization couldn't have been more felt and decisive if the door to my building had been that of a jail shutting behind me. The marriage to Lynn was over. I would never go back into it. I would do all that I could to help her and to father the boys but I would never go back to her. All the loss I had been feeling so intensely had been superseded by this powerful feeling of freedom, this integral new fact of my life.

5

So it proved to be. The freedom was short-lived, since I remarried eighteen months later. After that marriage failed, I entered a long relationship that also ended in a divorce. Finally, I got the point and lived alone for a number of years until I met up with Virginia Heiserman, who had been recently widowed. We have been happily married for twenty-two years.

Lynn soon had a brief, disastrous affair with McGregor and for years contemplated suing him. We stayed in touch but mostly through fighting about money. After a long period of fruitlessly editing the letters of Tolstoy, she got a job as an editor and writing teacher at Columbia University's Russian Institute and published two well-received translations of A. R. Luria's *The Mind of a Mnemonist* and Tolstoy's *The Death of Ivan Ilyich*. Despite the new psychotropic drugs, her later years were increasingly troubled by what was diagnosed as severe bipolar disorder. In the last year or so of her life, Paul, Ivan, and I helped to maintain her as she fought gallantly against lung cancer, which appeared to alleviate her mental distress. She and I drew close again. Among her effects at the nursing home where she died were all the notes I had sent her during this time with a check, a book, some cassettes. Finding them, I felt that I had joined, at the end, the line of men whose intense presence in her life had kept her going.

After the cremation Lynn's ashes were sent to my home on Long Island. I waited for an especially bright early summer afternoon and then cast them into the sea, fifty miles or so farther along the coast from where I had first seen her coming out of the water.

Ted Solotaroff's first memoir, *Truth Comes in Blows* (1998) won the PEN Martha Albrand Award. An associate editor of *Commentary* and the editor of *Bookweek*, he founded the influential literary journal *New American Review*, later *American Review*, and was a senior editor at HarperCollins, where he edited many of the prominent writers of his generation. He is the editor of *Alfred Kazin's America: Critical and Personal Writings* (2003). His criticism is collected in *The Red-hot Vacuum* and *A Few Good Voices in My Head*. Solotaroff lives in East Quogue, New York; and Paris.